MATRICES

WILLIAM VANN PARKER

HEAD PROFESSOR OF MATHEMATICS
AUBURN UNIVERSITY

and

JAMES CLIFTON EAVES

HEAD OF THE DEPARTMENT OF MATHEMATICS
UNIVERSITY OF KENTUCKY

THE RONALD PRESS COMPANY · NEW YORK

Library of Congress Catalog Card Number: 60–7608
PRINTED IN THE UNITED STATES OF AMERICA

To Our Wives

CAROLYN EDWARDS PARKER

and

MAONA SHINKLE EAVES

PREFACE

The purpose of this book is to present a logical development of the theory of matrices. It is written for introductory college courses on the subject and can be used not only with students of mathematics but also with students in other fields in which a knowledge of matrices is often needed—engineering, statistics, economics, psychology, operations analysis, social studies, agricultural production economics, and others.

The approach to the theory of matrices presented here is an outgrowth of a number of seminars offered by the authors. During these seminars we sought to develop an understandable presentation, plausible and usable definitions, clear proofs, and—above all—a logical sequence of topics. The material in its present form has been used at several universities during the past eight years and has been found to be pedagogically sound.

The classical approach through the use of determinants has been purposely avoided. Rather, the theory of determinants is made to depend upon the properties of matrices. Determinants are introduced in Chapter 9, but this chapter is not essential to the continuity of the course, since only minor references to determinants are made in subsequent sections.

The exercises have been designed not only to illustrate the topics under discussion but also to give the student some insight into future topics. Extreme care was used in attempting to keep the exercises of such nature and dimension as to avoid complete entanglement in manipulation. Many of them are simple and require only a few moments of reflection; others will test the ingenuity of the better students.

Some of the other important features of the book should be mentioned:

1. The first chapter serves as a review of the elementary mathematical concepts for the mathematics student. For students in the various other fields, who usually require only the knowledge necessary for applications of matrices, it provides a concise but ample background for understanding the developments in subsequent chapters.
2. The student's first introduction to matrices is through linear forms and systems of equations—basic material with which he is already familiar.
3. A need for the multiplication of two matrices is recognized, and the usual method for multiplication is demonstrated.

4. Partitioning is introduced early and is used in developing the idea of the "sum of two matrices" as one of the operations belonging to a consistent mathematical system.

5. The investigation of both *elementwise* operations and *blockwise* operations on matrices is encouraged—the former to emphasize for beginners the underlying principles and manipulations, and the latter in the interest of more elegant proofs.

6. The concept of rank is introduced after the concept of equivalence so that the rank canonical form identifies a class of matrices. Thus rank has a usable meaning both for the mathematics student and for the student interested primarily in applications.

7. The concept of row transformations and column transformations is used to introduce the notion of the inverse of a matrix. A method for recording these transformations, in keeping with modern computational techniques, is given. This technique is also employed to obtain the rank canonical form.

8. Systems of linear equations are presented with a complete matrix treatment. This is followed by a discussion of the MURT technique, which is readily adaptable to the many computing procedures now in use.

9. An extensive bibliography is included. We believe that any student of matrices should become acquainted with the literature as soon as possible. If he is to become a consulting mathematician, he should be familiar with the variations in notation and with additional matrix properties set forth in mathematical publications.

It should be emphasized that this is intended to be an introductory work. It is neither an exhaustive treatment of matrix theory nor a text on abstract algebra. A knowledge of the topics presented here will enable the student to read comprehensively much of the new current literature on the subject.

We are deeply indebted to many colleagues who have critically read the manuscript in its various stages of development and have used it in their classes. In particular, we wish to acknowledge the encouragement extended by Dr. A. S. Householder, Oak Ridge National Laboratory, who has shown an interest in the work since its inception. And we wish to thank Dr. R. K. Butz, Auburn University, who has been especially helpful in checking the final manuscript.

To the late Dr. E. T. Browne, Professor of Mathematics, University of North Carolina, under whom both of us studied and from whom we received an introduction to matrix theory, we are forever indebted for guidance and inspiration.

W. V. PARKER
J. C. EAVES

January, 1960

CONTENTS

MATRICES

CHAPTER 1

REVIEW OF ELEMENTARY CONCEPTS

1.1 Introduction. In the course of our study of matrices we shall use the concepts of closure, set, and field. The elements used will be complex numbers unless stated otherwise. When the elements are restricted to some special number field it will be so stated. The reader who is familiar with these concepts may proceed directly to Chapter 2. If a brief review of these topics is needed or desired, then the following résumé should be studied.

1.2 Sets, Closure. In the study of algebraic systems it is often necessary to consider, as a whole, an aggregate of many objects which have some common property. Such an aggregate is referred to as a *set* and the objects themselves are called the *elements* of the set.

The first notion one has of a set of numbers is usually obtained from a consideration of the *positive integers*, 1, 2, 3, 4, 5, . . . , which we shall call the set $\mathcal{P}$. The integer 4 is one of the elements of this set, and we indicate this by the notation $4 \in \mathcal{P}$. This is read, "4 belongs to $\mathcal{P}$." It is sometimes read, "4 is in the set $\mathcal{P}$," "4 belonging to $\mathcal{P}$," etc., according to its usage in the sentence. We indicate that the integer a belongs to the set $\mathcal{P}$ by writing $a \in \mathcal{P}$. The notation $\mathcal{P} \ni a$ is also used and is read "$\mathcal{P}$ contains a." Sometimes it is convenient to use the symbol $\notin$ to indicate "does not belong to"; for example, $\sqrt{2} \notin \mathcal{P}$.

If we are given any two elements, a and b, of the set, $\mathcal{P}$, we have $a \in \mathcal{P}, b \in \mathcal{P}$ and we know that $(a + b) \in \mathcal{P}$ and that $ab \in \mathcal{P}$. This illustrates the *closure* property which is one of the fundamental properties used in the study of sets. Thus we say that the set of positive integers is closed with respect to the operations of addition and multiplication.

As we increase the number of operations between the elements of a set, we may find that it is necessary to enlarge the set in order to maintain closure with respect to these operations. For example, $2 \in \mathcal{P}$ and $5 \in \mathcal{P}$ but $(2 - 5) \notin \mathcal{P}$ and $(5 \div 2) \notin \mathcal{P}$. Thus $\mathcal{P}$ is not closed with respect to subtraction or division. There are elements a and b belonging to $\mathcal{P}$, such that $(a - b) \in \mathcal{P}$. However, to say that the set $\mathcal{P}$ is closed with respect to an operation means that the result of performing the operation between the two elements in each and every pair of elements in the set is, in each case, an element of the set. To state this another way, we say that

3

a set is closed with respect to an operation when it is impossible to get an element not in the set by using only the defined operation on the elements.

We now enlarge the set $\mathcal{P}$ by annexing the elements . . . , -4, -3, -2, -1, 0. A little investigation will show that this new set is also closed with respect to addition and multiplication. Furthermore, it is closed with respect to subtraction. We now have the set of all *rational integers* which we shall denote by $\mathcal{S}$. We observe that $\mathcal{S}$ is not closed with respect to division. We may extend $\mathcal{S}$ to obtain a set which remains closed with respect to subtraction and is also closed with respect to division. To do this, let $\mathcal{R}$ be the set of all elements of the form p/q where $p \in \mathcal{S}$, $q \in \mathcal{S}$, and $q \neq 0$. This set, $\mathcal{R}$, is called the set of *rational numbers*. Applying the usual rules of composition, we see that $\mathcal{R}$ is closed with respect to the four operations, addition, multiplication, subtraction, and division (division by zero always being excluded). These operations are known as the *fundamental rational operations*. A *rational operation*, in general, is any operation expressible as the result of a finite sequence of fundamental rational operations. Every element of the set $\mathcal{P}$ is contained in the set $\mathcal{S}$, and every element of the set $\mathcal{S}$ is contained in the set $\mathcal{R}$. Thus we say that the set $\mathcal{P}$ is *contained in* the set $\mathcal{S}$ and that the set $\mathcal{S}$ is contained in the set $\mathcal{R}$. We indicate this by writing $\mathcal{P} \subset \mathcal{S} \subset \mathcal{R}$, or by writing $\mathcal{R} \supset \mathcal{S} \supset \mathcal{P}$.

New numbers have been invented, from time to time, in order to "solve" certain equations. For example, if we have equations involving x and elements of $\mathcal{P}$, they may not have solutions in $\mathcal{P}$. The solution of $x + 5 = 3$ is in $\mathcal{S}$ but not in $\mathcal{P}$. The solution of $3x = 5$ is in $\mathcal{R}$ but not in $\mathcal{S}$. The solution of $x^2 = 2$ is not in $\mathcal{R}$. We shall not go into the method of extending $\mathcal{R}$ so as to get a set including numbers of the type $\sqrt{2}$, $\sqrt[3]{5}$, etc., nor shall we discuss the closure of this set with respect to the rational operations. We shall assume that the reader is familiar with the *set of all real numbers*.

The set of real numbers does not contain solutions of some equations involving elements of $\mathcal{P}$. For example, there is no real number, x, such that $x^2 + 5 = 1$. To the set of real numbers we *adjoin* a number, i, defined by $i^2 = -1$. We define operations between i and the real numbers in such a way that the associative, commutative, and distributive laws hold. If we then adjoin all elements necessary to make this set closed with respect to the rational operations, we have a set, $\mathcal{C}$, known as the set of all *complex numbers*. It is a simple exercise to show that every element of $\mathcal{C}$ is of the form $a + ib$, where a and b belong to the set of real numbers.

Consider the equation,

$$a_0 x^n + a_1 x^{n-1} + \cdots + a_{n-1} x + a_n = 0,$$

where n is a positive integer and each coefficient a_i is a complex number and $a_0 \neq 0$. The *Fundamental Theorem of Algebra* states that every such equation has a solution r such that $r \in \mathcal{C}$. For this reason the set of complex numbers is usually referred to as the *number system of ordinary algebra*.

1.3 Subsets, Fields. If $\mathcal{K}$ is a set of elements, then any set which contains only elements of $\mathcal{K}$ is called a *subset* of $\mathcal{K}$. The subset may contain all or a part of the elements of $\mathcal{K}$. A subset of $\mathcal{K}$ which does not contain all the elements of $\mathcal{K}$ is called a *proper subset* of $\mathcal{K}$.

A *number field* may be defined as a set of numbers, containing at least one number $a \neq 0$, which is closed with respect to the four fundamental rational operations (excluding division by zero). It is easy to show, by using the closure property, that every number field contains the set of rational numbers. We have also seen that the set of rational numbers is a number field. A subset of a field, $\mathcal{F}$, which is itself a field, is called a *subfield* of $\mathcal{F}$. Hence the field of rational numbers is a subfield of every number field. For this reason, the field of rational numbers is often referred to as the smallest number field. The set of all complex numbers is a field, and the term "number field" as used here includes all subfields of this field.

We shall have occasion, in the course of our study, to consider more general fields. We define a set of elements, $\mathcal{F}$, to be a field if it contains at least two distinct elements, is closed with respect to two operations, usually called addition and multiplication, and if the following properties hold for all elements $a, b, c, \ldots$ of the set:

(1.3.1) $\qquad (a + b) = (b + a), \qquad ab = ba;$

(1.3.2) $\qquad (a + b) + c = a + (b + c), \qquad (ab)c = a(bc);$

(1.3.3) $\qquad a(b + c) = ab + ac;$

(1.3.4) $\qquad$ there exists $x \in \mathcal{F}$ such that $a + x = b;$

(1.3.5) $\qquad$ if $a + c \neq c$, there exists $y \in \mathcal{F}$ such that $ay = b.$

In the course of our study we may find it convenient to restrict the elements to other special sets, but, as previously mentioned, the number elements used will be the complex numbers unless specifically stated otherwise.

For the reader who finds it necessary to review the above brief outline of the fundamental concepts and who may also find it advisable to study a few review exercises covering this material the following problems are suggested.

EXERCISES

1. Show that the solution of $x^2 = 2$ does not belong to the set of rational numbers.

2. Is the set of elements, 1, -1, i, $-i$, closed with respect to multiplication and division?

3. Show that the set of integral multiples of 3 is closed with respect to addition, subtraction, and multiplication.

4. Show that the set of numbers $a + ib$, where a and b are rational, is a field.

5. Investigate the set in Exercise 4 when a and b are real; also, when a and b are integers.

6. Show that the set of numbers $a + b\sqrt{2}$, a and b rational, is a field.

7. Show that every field, $\mathcal{F}$, contains a unique element, t, such that $a + t = a$ for every element a of $\mathcal{F}$.

8. Show that every field, $\mathcal{F}$, contains a unique element, e, such that $ea = a$ for every element a of $\mathcal{F}$.

9. Describe the general element of the smallest number field containing $\sqrt{3}$.

10. Describe the general element of the smallest number field containing both $\sqrt{2}$ and $\sqrt{3}$.

11. Rationalize the denominator of $1/(\sqrt{2} + \sqrt[3]{3})$. *Hint:* This is an element of the smallest field containing both $\sqrt{2}$ and $\sqrt[3]{3}$.

12. Prove that every number field contains the set of rational numbers.

CHAPTER 2

THE ALGEBRA OF MATRICES

2.1 Linear Forms, Rectangular Matrices. In elementary mathematics we have encountered such terms as

$$2x^2, \quad 3x^2y, \quad xyz^5, \quad 7xy^2, \quad 9r^2s^2t^3,$$

called *monomials*. We have also used expressions similar to

$$3x^2 + 2x - 5,$$
$$x^3 + 2x^2y - 3xy^2 + 7y^3,$$
$$x^2y^2 + y^4,$$
$$a_1x_1 + a_2x_2 + a_3x_3 + a_4x_4,$$

and

$$a_1x_1^2 + a_2x_1x_2 + a_3x_3x_4,$$

referred to as *rational integral expressions* or *polynomials*. These are all special cases of the general algebraic expression called a *polynomial in k variables over a field*, $\mathcal{F}$, which we now review.

A *polynomial over a field*, $\mathcal{F}$, is the sum of a finite number of terms of the type $ax_1^{p_1}x_2^{p_2} \ldots x_k^{p_k}$, where the x_i are variables, the p_i are nonnegative integers, and a is an element of $\mathcal{F}$. The sum of the integers p_i in any term is the *degree* of the term. If all terms of a polynomial are of the same degree, the polynomial is said to be *homogeneous* and is called a *form*.

Illustration: $2x_1^2 + 3x_1x_2 - 7x_2^2$ is a form of degree two; $3x_1^2 + 2x_1x_2^3$ is a polynomial but is not a form, since the degree of the first term is two and the degree of the second term is four.

It is assumed that the reader is familiar with those properties of polynomials found in the usual text on college algebra.

A linear homogeneous function, such as $2x_1 + 3x_2 - 7x_3$, is called a *linear form*. It is customary to represent such a function by the single letter y or by the symbol $f(x_1, x_2, x_3)$ and to write

$$y = 2x_1 + 3x_2 - 7x_3,$$

or

$$f(x_1, x_2, x_3) = 2x_1 + 3x_2 - 7x_3.$$

The general linear form in three variables would be indicated by

$$y = a_1x_1 + a_2x_2 + a_3x_3.$$

And, if we consider two linear forms in three variables simultaneously, it will be necessary to modify the notation so as to distinguish one form from the other. For example, if x_1 and x_2 are linear forms in y_1, y_2, and y_3, then we may write these as

$$x_1 = a_{11}y_1 + a_{12}y_2 + a_{13}y_3,$$

$$x_2 = a_{21}y_1 + a_{22}y_2 + a_{23}y_3.$$

Here the notation for the coefficient a_{ij} is such as to indicate that it is associated with x_i and y_j. If only the coefficients a_{ij} are of interest, then we may write these without the associated x_i, y_j, and in the order in which they occur, this being

$$\begin{pmatrix} a_{11} & a_{12} & a_{13} \\ a_{21} & a_{22} & a_{23} \end{pmatrix}.$$

This array of a_{ij} is called a *matrix*, and the a_{ij} is such that the subscripts indicate its *row* and *column* position in the array. We shall now consider a set of linear forms and its associated matrix in general.

Consider m variables $x_1, x_2, \ldots, x_m$, which are linear forms in the n variables $y_1, y_2, \ldots, y_n$, defined by

$$x_1 = a_{11}y_1 + a_{12}y_2 + \cdots + a_{1n}y_n,$$

(2.1.1)
$$x_2 = a_{21}y_1 + a_{22}y_2 + \cdots + a_{2n}y_n,$$
$$\cdots\cdots\cdots\cdots\cdots\cdots\cdots\cdots\cdots,$$
$$x_m = a_{m1}y_1 + a_{m2}y_2 + \cdots + a_{mn}y_n.$$

The rectangular array

(2.1.2)
$$\begin{pmatrix} a_{11} & a_{12} & \ldots & a_{1n} \\ a_{21} & a_{22} & \ldots & a_{2n} \\ \cdots & \cdots & \cdots & \cdots \\ a_{m1} & a_{m2} & \ldots & a_{mn} \end{pmatrix},$$

which is obtained by writing the coefficients of the form (2.1.1), in order, in successive rows, is called the *matrix* of this set of forms. This matrix has m rows and n columns and is called an $m \times n$ (read "m by n") matrix. The numbers m and n are sometimes referred to as the dimensions of the matrix. In every case, the number of rows is always mentioned first. The mn numbers a_{ij} are called the *elements* of the matrix. Those elements of the matrix for which $i = j$ are called *diagonal elements*, and the line of these elements from the upper left-hand corner is called the *diagonal*. If $m = n$, the matrix is square and will be referred to as an *n-row square* matrix or as a matrix of *order n.* To say that a matrix is of order n always implies that the matrix is square. Two matrices are said to be *equal* if and only if they have the same number of rows, the same number of columns, and each element in one equal to the corresponding element in the other.

The matrix (2.1.2) may be considered an entity in itself, independent of the forms (2.1.1), and denoted by the single symbol A. In fact, any rectangular array of numbers may be considered a matrix. For example, (x_1, x_2, x_3), denoting a point in three-space, is a matrix having one row and three columns. The commas are used here to assure clarity in distinguishing the individual elements. The coordinates of a point in three-dimensional space are sometimes indicated by writing $(x_1 \; x_2 \; x_3)$, the usual matrix without the use of commas to separate the elements. One should be careful not to confuse this 1×3 matrix with the 1×1 matrix $(x_1 x_2 x_3)$. This is to say that commas are usually not needed to assure proper delineation, but, if there is chance for ambiguity, then commas should be inserted between elements or between subscripts. It would be confusing to represent the element in the twelfth row and the forty-fifth column of $A = (a_{ij})$ by a_{1245}. Custom would require that we depict this element more precisely as $a_{12,45}$.

In order to develop an algebra of matrices it will be necessary to define certain operations between two matrices. For an introductory study of the behavior of two matrices let us return momentarily to the problem of the rotation of axes, Fig. 2.1, usually first encountered in plane analytic geometry. For convenience of notation call the original rectangular reference frame the X_1,X_2-axes rather than use the conventional term x,y-axes. These are to be rotated to the Y_1,Y_2-axes by rotating the reference frame through an angle of α_1 about the origin, and furthermore this new reference

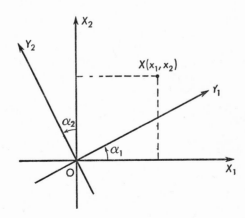

Fig. 2.1.

frame is to be subjected to an additional rotation α_2, about the origin, getting as the new reference frame the Z_1,Z_2-axes.

The transformations necessary for these rotations are given respectively by

$$x_1 = y_1 \cos \alpha_1 - y_2 \sin \alpha_1,$$

$$x_2 = y_1 \sin \alpha_1 + y_2 \cos \alpha_1,$$

and

$$y_1 = z_1 \cos \alpha_2 - z_2 \sin \alpha_2,$$

$$y_2 = z_1 \sin \alpha_2 + z_2 \cos \alpha_2.$$

Direct substitution of the values of y_1, y_2 in order to get x_1, x_2 in terms of z_1 and z_2 gives

$$x_1 = z_1(\cos \alpha_1 \cos \alpha_2 - \sin \alpha_1 \sin \alpha_2) - z_2(\sin \alpha_2 \cos \alpha_1 + \sin \alpha_1 \cos \alpha_2),$$

$$x_2 = z_1(\sin \alpha_1 \cos \alpha_2 + \cos \alpha_1 \sin \alpha_2) + z_2(-\sin \alpha_1 \sin \alpha_2 + \cos \alpha_1 \cos \alpha_2).$$

This simplifies to

$$x_1 = z_1 \cos (\alpha_1 + \alpha_2) - z_2 \sin (\alpha_1 + \alpha_2),$$

$$x_2 = z_1 \sin (\alpha_1 + \alpha_2) + z_2 \cos (\alpha_1 + \alpha_2),$$

which, from the general transformation, is the obvious result of one rotation α_1 followed by a second rotation α_2.

Now let us examine the matrices of the sets of forms. These are, respectively,

$$\begin{pmatrix} \cos \alpha_1 & -\sin \alpha_1 \\ \sin \alpha_1 & \cos \alpha_1 \end{pmatrix}, \quad \begin{pmatrix} \cos \alpha_2 & -\sin \alpha_2 \\ \sin \alpha_2 & \cos \alpha_2 \end{pmatrix},$$

and

$$\begin{pmatrix} \cos \alpha_1 \cos \alpha_2 - \sin \alpha_1 \sin \alpha_2 & -\cos \alpha_1 \sin \alpha_2 - \sin \alpha_1 \cos \alpha_2 \\ \sin \alpha_1 \cos \alpha_2 + \cos \alpha_1 \sin \alpha_2 & -\sin \alpha_1 \sin \alpha_2 + \cos \alpha_1 \cos \alpha_2 \end{pmatrix}.$$

A study of the third matrix will give some idea of how it may be obtained from the other two; however, this may be more easily seen from the general notation used in the following forms.

Suppose that x_1 and x_2 are given as linear forms in y_1 and y_2 and that y_1 and y_2 are given as linear forms in z_1, z_2, and z_3. Thus we have

$$x_1 = a_{11}y_1 + a_{12}y_2,$$

$$x_2 = a_{21}y_1 + a_{22}y_2,$$

and

$$y_1 = b_{11}z_1 + b_{12}z_2 + b_{13}z_3,$$

$$y_2 = b_{21}z_1 + b_{22}z_2 + b_{23}z_3.$$

Direct substitution for the y_1 and y_2 in the first set of forms gives the x_1 and x_2 in terms of z_1, z_2, and z_3 as

$$x_1 = (a_{11}b_{11} + a_{12}b_{21})z_1 + (a_{11}b_{12} + a_{12}b_{22})z_2 + (a_{11}b_{13} + a_{12}b_{23})z_3,$$

$$x_2 = (a_{21}b_{11} + a_{22}b_{21})z_1 + (a_{21}b_{12} + a_{22}b_{22})z_2 + (a_{21}b_{13} + a_{22}b_{23})z_3.$$

The corresponding matrices of these three forms are

$$\begin{pmatrix} a_{11} & a_{12} \\ a_{21} & a_{22} \end{pmatrix}, \qquad \begin{pmatrix} b_{11} & b_{12} & b_{13} \\ b_{21} & b_{22} & b_{23} \end{pmatrix},$$

and

$$\begin{pmatrix} a_{11}b_{11} + a_{12}b_{21} & a_{11}b_{12} + a_{12}b_{22} & a_{11}b_{13} + a_{12}b_{23} \\ a_{21}b_{11} + a_{22}b_{21} & a_{21}b_{12} + a_{22}b_{22} & a_{21}b_{13} + a_{22}b_{23} \end{pmatrix},$$

and here the *row-column* combination of the elements is obvious in obtaining the third matrix above from the first two. This third matrix is said to be obtained from the other two matrices by the process of multiplication. Thus, if we indicate the matrices above by A, B, and C respectively, then we would write $AB = C$. The element in the first row and the first column of C is obtained by multiplying the elements in the first row of A, namely the a_{11}, a_{12} by the corresponding elements in the first column of B, namely b_{11}, b_{21}, getting $a_{11}b_{11}$ and $a_{12}b_{21}$ and forming the sum $a_{11}b_{11} + a_{12}b_{21}$ for the first row, first column element of the product matrix C. The element in the second row and the third column of the product matrix C is obtained by pairing the elements in the second row of A, namely a_{21}, a_{22}, with the elements in the third column of B, namely b_{13}, b_{23}, and forming the sum of the products of the corresponding pairs, getting $a_{21}b_{13} + a_{22}b_{23}$. We now proceed to define the multiplication of two matrices in general.

The forms (2.1.1) may be written in the more compact notation

$$(2.1.3) \qquad x_i = \sum_{j=1}^{n} a_{ij}y_j \qquad (i = 1, 2, \ldots, m).$$

Similarly, we may write the matrix (2.1.2) compactly as

$$(2.1.4) \qquad A = (a_{ij}) \qquad (i = 1, 2, \ldots, m; j = 1, 2, \ldots, n).$$

Suppose that the n variables $y_1, y_2, \ldots, y_n$ are themselves linear forms in p new variables $z_1, z_2, \ldots, z_p$ and that

$$(2.1.5) \qquad y_j = \sum_{k=1}^{p} b_{jk}z_k \qquad (j = 1, 2, \ldots, n).$$

The matrix B, of the forms in (2.1.5), is

$$(2.1.6) \qquad B = (b_{jk}) \qquad (j = 1, 2, \ldots, n; k = 1, 2, \ldots, p).$$

Substitution from (2.1.5), in (2.1.3), yields

$$(2.1.7) \quad x_i = \sum_{j=1}^{n} a_{ij} \sum_{k=1}^{p} b_{jk}z_k = \sum_{k=1}^{p} \left(\sum_{j=1}^{n} a_{ij}b_{jk} \right) z_k = \sum_{k=1}^{p} c_{ik}z_k$$

$$(i = 1, 2, \ldots, m),$$

where

$$(2.1.8) \quad c_{ik} = \sum_{j=1}^{n} a_{ij}b_{jk} \quad (i = 1, 2, \ldots, m; k = 1, 2, \ldots, p).$$

If we denote by C the matrix (c_{ik}), we write $C = AB$ and define C to be the *product* of A by B, in this order, A on the left, B on the right. Recalling that $A = (a_{ij})$ was an $m \times n$ matrix and that $B = (b_{jk})$ was an $n \times p$ matrix, we see from (2.1.8) that $C = (c_{ik})$ is an $m \times p$ matrix. In general, we see by (2.1.8) that the element in the ith row and kth column of C, namely c_{ik}, is the sum of the products of the elements of the ith row of A, namely $a_{i1}, a_{i2}, \ldots, a_{in}$, by the corresponding elements of the kth column of B, namely $b_{1k}, b_{2k}, \ldots, b_{nk}$, which yields $c_{ik} = a_{i1}b_{1k} + a_{i2}b_{2k} + \cdots + a_{in}b_{nk}$, which may be expressed as in (2.1.8) above.

It should be noted that the product AB is defined if and only if the number of columns in A is the same as the number of rows in B. Hence BA may be undefined even though AB is defined. Even when both AB and BA are defined, they are not necessarily equal. The product AA is defined if and only if the matrix A is square. When the product AA is defined, it will be denoted by A^2.

Illustration: Suppose that

$$x_1 = y_1 + 2y_2 - y_3,$$
$$x_2 = \qquad y_2 - 2y_3,$$

and that

$$y_1 = 2z_1 + z_2,$$
$$y_2 = -z_1 - z_2,$$
$$y_3 = z_1.$$

Then, by substitution, we obtain

$$x_1 = -z_1 - z_2,$$
$$x_2 = -3z_1 - z_2.$$

Illustration: Consider the 2×3 matrix A and the 3×2 matrix B, where each has as elements the numerical coefficients in the preceding illustration, given by

$$A = \begin{pmatrix} 1 & 2 & -1 \\ 0 & 1 & -2 \end{pmatrix} \quad \text{and} \quad B = \begin{pmatrix} 2 & 1 \\ -1 & -1 \\ 1 & 0 \end{pmatrix}.$$

If we denote the product AB by C, then the elements c_{ij} of C are

$$c_{11} = (1)(2) + (2)(-1) + (-1)(1) = -1,$$

$$c_{12} = (1)(1) + (2)(-1) + (-1)(0) = -1,$$

$$c_{21} = (0)(2) + (1)(-1) + (-2)(1) = -3,$$

$$c_{22} = (0)(1) + (1)(-1) + (-2)(0) = -1.$$

Then we have

$$AB = C = \begin{pmatrix} -1 & -1 \\ -3 & -1 \end{pmatrix}.$$

We note that the product BA is also defined and that

$$BA = \begin{pmatrix} 2 & 5 & -4 \\ -1 & -3 & 3 \\ 1 & 2 & -1 \end{pmatrix}.$$

Since BA is a 3×3 matrix whereas AB is a 2×2 matrix, it is obvious that these two products are not equal.

2.2   Associative Law for the Multiplication of Matrices.   We shall show that whenever AB and BC are defined then $A(BC)$ and $(AB)C$ are defined and are equal.   Let $A = (a_{ij})$, $B = (b_{jk})$, and $C = (c_{kl})$ $(i = 1, 2, \ldots, m; j = 1, 2, \ldots, n; k = 1, 2, \ldots, p; l = 1, 2, \ldots, q)$.   Then A is $m \times n$, BC is $n \times q$, AB is $m \times p$, and C is $p \times q$.   Hence the products $A(BC)$ and $(AB)C$ are defined and each is $m \times q$.   The element in the ith row and lth column of $(AB)C$ is

$$\sum_{k=1}^{p} \left(\sum_{j=1}^{n} a_{ij}b_{jk} \right) c_{kl} = \sum_{j=1}^{n} \sum_{k=1}^{p} a_{ij}b_{jk}c_{kl}.$$

However,

$$\sum_{j=1}^{n} \sum_{k=1}^{p} a_{ij}b_{jk}c_{kl} = \sum_{j=1}^{n} a_{ij} \left(\sum_{k=1}^{p} b_{jk}c_{kl} \right),$$

and the right member of this equality is the element in the ith row and the lth column of $A(BC)$.   It follows that $A(BC) = (AB)C$, and we may denote this product, without ambiguity, by ABC.

Illustration: Consider the matrices A, B, and C, where

$$A = \begin{pmatrix} 2 & 1 \\ -1 & 0 \end{pmatrix}, \qquad B = \begin{pmatrix} 1 & -1 & 2 \\ 2 & 1 & 3 \end{pmatrix}, \qquad C = \begin{pmatrix} 1 & 1 \\ 2 & -1 \\ 0 & 1 \end{pmatrix}.$$

Then, by multiplication, it is seen that

$$AB = \begin{pmatrix} 4 & -1 & 7 \\ -1 & 1 & -2 \end{pmatrix}, \qquad BC = \begin{pmatrix} -1 & 4 \\ 4 & 4 \end{pmatrix}$$

and that

$$(AB)C = A(BC) = \begin{pmatrix} 2 & 12 \\ 1 & -4 \end{pmatrix}.$$

We note here, also, that $(AB)(BC)$ is not defined.

It may be shown by induction that the product $A_1A_2\cdots A_s$ is uniquely defined if and only if each of the products A_iA_{i+1} ($i = 1, 2, \ldots, s - 1$) is defined. If A is a square matrix and s is a positive integer, A^{s+1} is defined to be the product A^sA. It is easy to show that $A^sA^t = A^tA^s = A^{s+t}$, where s and t are positive integers.

For convenience in writing the *one-column matrix* with elements $x_1, x_2, \ldots, x_m$ in that order, we use the notation

$$X = (x_i) \qquad (i = 1, 2, \ldots, m).$$

If

$$X = (x_i) \qquad (i = 1, 2, \ldots, m),$$

$$Y = (y_j) \qquad (j = 1, 2, \ldots, n),$$

and

$$Z = (z_k) \qquad (k = 1, 2, \ldots, p),$$

we may write the sets of equations in (2.1.3) and (2.1.5) in matrix notation as

$$(2.2.1) \qquad\qquad X = AY,$$

$$(2.2.2) \qquad\qquad Y = BZ.$$

From these we get the set of equations (2.1.7), in matrix notation, to be

$$(2.2.3) \qquad X = A(BZ) = (AB)Z = CZ,$$

where $C = AB$.

Illustration: The set of equations

$$x_1 = y_1 + 2y_2 - y_3,$$

$$x_2 = \quad\quad y_2 - 2y_3,$$

may be written

$$\begin{pmatrix} x_1 \\ x_2 \end{pmatrix} = \begin{pmatrix} 1 & 2 & -1 \\ 0 & 1 & -2 \end{pmatrix} \begin{pmatrix} y_1 \\ y_2 \\ y_3 \end{pmatrix}.$$

If y_1, y_2, and y_3 are linear forms in z_1 and z_2, given by

$$y_1 = 2z_1 + z_2,$$
$$y_2 = -z_1 - z_2,$$
$$y_3 = z_1,$$

we may write

$$\begin{pmatrix} y_1 \\ y_2 \\ y_3 \end{pmatrix} = \begin{pmatrix} 2 & 1 \\ -1 & -1 \\ 1 & 0 \end{pmatrix} \begin{pmatrix} z_1 \\ z_2 \end{pmatrix}.$$

Thus we have, by substitution,

$$\begin{pmatrix} x_1 \\ x_2 \end{pmatrix} = \begin{pmatrix} 1 & 2 & -1 \\ 0 & 1 & -2 \end{pmatrix} \begin{pmatrix} 2 & 1 \\ -1 & -1 \\ 1 & 0 \end{pmatrix} \begin{pmatrix} z_1 \\ z_2 \end{pmatrix} = \begin{pmatrix} -1 & -1 \\ -3 & -1 \end{pmatrix} \begin{pmatrix} z_1 \\ z_2 \end{pmatrix}.$$

EXERCISES

1. Write the matrix of the set of linear forms

$$x_1 = 2y_1 + y_2 - 3y_3,$$
$$x_2 = y_1 + 2y_2 + y_3.$$

2. Given the set of linear forms

$$x_1 = a_{11}y_1 + a_{12}y_2 + a_{13}y_3 + a_{14}y_4,$$
$$x_2 = a_{21}y_1 + a_{22}y_2 + a_{23}y_3 + a_{24}y_4,$$
$$x_3 = a_{31}y_1 + a_{32}y_2 + a_{33}y_3 + a_{34}y_4.$$

(a) Write the matrix of the set of forms.
(b) Write the forms in the compact notation (2.1.3).
(c) Write the matrix of the set of forms in the compact notation (2.1.4).
(d) Write the set of equations in the matrix notation (2.2.1), writing out the matrices elementwise.

3. Given

$$x_i = \sum_{j=1}^{5} a_{ij}y_j \qquad (i = 1, 2, 3).$$

Write this set of forms as in (2.1.1), and write the matrix of this set of forms as in (2.1.2).

4. Given the linear forms

$$x_1 = y_1 + 2y_2,$$

$$x_2 = 2y_1 - y_2,$$

$$x_3 = -y_1 + 3y_2,$$

and the linear forms

$$y_1 = z_1 + 2z_3,$$

$$y_2 = z_1 + z_2.$$

By substitution, obtain x_1, x_2, x_3 as linear forms in z_1, z_2, z_3.

5. Write the forms in Exercise 4 using matrix notation $X = AY$ and $Y = BZ$. Obtain $X = (AB)Z$ by matrix multiplication. Compare the matrix AB with the matrix of the set of forms obtained in Exercise 4.

6. Given the matrices

$$A = \begin{pmatrix} 2 & 3 \\ 2 & 1 \end{pmatrix}, \qquad B = \begin{pmatrix} 2 & 1 & 3 \\ -1 & 1 & 0 \end{pmatrix}, \qquad C = \begin{pmatrix} 1 \\ -1 \\ 1 \end{pmatrix}.$$

Verify that $A(BC) = (AB)C$.

7. Given the matrices

$$A = \begin{pmatrix} 1 & -1 \\ 1 & -2 \end{pmatrix}, \qquad B = \begin{pmatrix} 2 & 1 \\ -1 & 5 \end{pmatrix}, \qquad C = \begin{pmatrix} 2 & 1 \\ 1 & 1 \end{pmatrix}.$$

Compute A^2B, ABA, BA^2, A^2C, ACA, and CA^2. Note that the first three of these products are equal but that no two of the last three are equal.

8. Show that $A_i(A_jA_k) = (A_iA_j)A_k$ implies that $(A_1A_2)(A_3A_4) = A_1(A_2A_3)A_4$.

9. Compute A^2 and A^3 and show that $A^2A^3 = A^3A^2$, where A is the matrix

$$A = \begin{pmatrix} 2 & -1 & 4 \\ 0 & 3 & -2 \\ -4 & 1 & 1 \end{pmatrix}.$$

10. Find the products AB and BA, where

$$A = \begin{pmatrix} a & 0 & 0 \\ 0 & b & 0 \\ 0 & 0 & c \end{pmatrix}, \qquad B = \begin{pmatrix} p & 0 & 0 \\ 0 & q & 0 \\ 0 & 0 & r \end{pmatrix}.$$

11. Find the products AB and BA, where

$$A = \begin{pmatrix} a & 0 & 0 \\ 0 & b & 0 \\ 0 & 0 & c \end{pmatrix}, \qquad B = \begin{pmatrix} 2 & 1 & -1 \\ 3 & -4 & 7 \\ 5 & 2 & 2 \end{pmatrix}.$$

12. Find the products AI and IA, where

$$A = \begin{pmatrix} a_{11} & a_{12} & a_{13} \\ a_{21} & a_{22} & a_{23} \\ a_{31} & a_{32} & a_{33} \end{pmatrix}, \qquad I = \begin{pmatrix} 1 & 0 & 0 \\ 0 & 1 & 0 \\ 0 & 0 & 1 \end{pmatrix}.$$

13. Find the products AB and BA, where

$$A = \begin{pmatrix} 2 & 5 & 1 \\ 0 & 2 & -1 \\ 0 & 0 & -2 \end{pmatrix}, \qquad B = \begin{pmatrix} 1 & 2 & -1 \\ 0 & 1 & 1 \\ 0 & 0 & 3 \end{pmatrix}.$$

14. Find the products AB and BA, where

$$A = \begin{pmatrix} 1 & 1 & -5 \\ 1 & 2 & 4 \\ 1 & -3 & 1 \end{pmatrix}, \qquad B = \begin{pmatrix} 1 & 1 & 1 \\ 1 & 2 & -3 \\ -5 & 4 & 1 \end{pmatrix}.$$

15. If A is a square matrix and s and t are positive integers, prove that $A^s A^t = A^t A^s$.

16. Generalize the associative law to include the product $A_1 A_2 \cdots A_s$, where s is any positive integer greater than three.

17. Given $A = (a_{ij})$, $B = (b_{jk})$, $C = (c_{kl})$, and $D = (d_{lm})$ $(i, j, k, l, m = 1, 2, 3, \ldots, n)$. Compute the elements in the pth row and qth column of each of the products $A(BC)D$ and $(AB)(CD)$ and show that these elements are equal.

18. Same as Exercise 17, except that

$$i = 1, 2, \ldots, n_1; \quad j = 1, 2, \ldots, n_2; \quad k = 1, 2, \ldots, n_3;$$

$$l = 1, 2, \ldots, n_4; \quad m = 1, 2, \ldots, n_5.$$

2.3 Square Matrices. We have noted that the $m \times n$ matrix A is square whenever $m = n$. If A and B are n-row square matrices, both products AB and BA are n-row square matrices but are not necessarily equal.

Certain special types of square matrices occur frequently in the study of matrices, and they have been given special names. We consider, first, the *triangular matrix*, which is defined to be a square matrix having only zero elements on one side of the diagonal. There are two types of triangular matrices, one having the defining zeros to the left and below the diagonal and the other having the defining zeros to the right and above the diagonal. If each of the diagonal elements of a triangular matrix is zero, the matrix is called *strictly* triangular. If the triangular pattern of the matrix is known, we sometimes indicate that A is a triangular matrix by using the notation

$$A = \text{tri.} \{a_{11} \quad a_{22} \quad \cdots \quad a_{nn}\}.$$

If each of the nondiagonal elements of a square matrix is zero, then the matrix is called a *diagonal* matrix. We usually indicate that A is a diagonal matrix by writing

$$A = \text{diag.} \{a_{11} \quad a_{22} \quad \ldots \quad a_{nn}\}.$$

If, in the diagonal matrix, all diagonal elements are equal, the matrix is called a *scalar matrix* or simply a *scalar*.

Illustration: The matrices

$$\begin{pmatrix} 2 & 1 & 7 \\ 0 & 5 & -1 \\ 0 & 0 & -2 \end{pmatrix}, \begin{pmatrix} -3 & 0 & 0 \\ 0 & 1 & 0 \\ 2 & 5 & 4 \end{pmatrix}, \begin{pmatrix} 2 & 0 & 0 \\ 0 & -3 & 0 \\ 0 & 0 & -1 \end{pmatrix}, \text{ and } \begin{pmatrix} 3 & 0 & 0 \\ 0 & 3 & 0 \\ 0 & 0 & 3 \end{pmatrix}$$

are triangular. The last two are diagonal matrices, and the last one is a scalar matrix. The third matrix may also be written diag. $\{2, -3, -1\}$.

A scalar matrix in which each diagonal element is the number one is called an *identity matrix* and is usually designated by I.

If A is any n-row square matrix, the reader may readily verify that

$$IA = AI = A.$$

Illustration: For the 2×2 identity matrix and the matrix

$$\begin{pmatrix} 2 & 3 \\ 5 & 7 \end{pmatrix}$$

it is clear that

$$\begin{pmatrix} 1 & 0 \\ 0 & 1 \end{pmatrix} \begin{pmatrix} 2 & 3 \\ 5 & 7 \end{pmatrix} = \begin{pmatrix} 2 & 3 \\ 5 & 7 \end{pmatrix} \begin{pmatrix} 1 & 0 \\ 0 & 1 \end{pmatrix} = \begin{pmatrix} 2 & 3 \\ 5 & 7 \end{pmatrix}.$$

It is also clear that

$$\begin{pmatrix} 1 & 0 \\ 0 & 0 \end{pmatrix} \begin{pmatrix} 3 & 7 \\ 0 & 0 \end{pmatrix} = \begin{pmatrix} 3 & 7 \\ 0 & 0 \end{pmatrix}$$

and that

$$\begin{pmatrix} 3 & 7 \\ 0 & 0 \end{pmatrix} \begin{pmatrix} 1 & 0 \\ 0 & 0 \end{pmatrix} = \begin{pmatrix} 3 & 0 \\ 0 & 0 \end{pmatrix} \neq \begin{pmatrix} 3 & 7 \\ 0 & 0 \end{pmatrix}.$$

If D, an n-row square matrix, is such that $DA = A$ for every n-row square matrix A, then, since $ID = DI = D$ and $DI = I$, it follows that $D = I$. The reader may easily prove that, if $AE = A$ for every n-row square matrix A, then $E = I$. That is, the matrix I plays the same role in the multiplication of square matrices as does the number one in the multiplication of numbers; and it is the only matrix which has this property. If it is desirable to indicate the order of the identity matrix, the n-row identity matrix will be denoted by I_n. It may be easily shown that, for any $m \times n$ matrix A,

$$I_m A = A I_n = A.$$

Let A be an $m \times n$ matrix and let B and C be diagonal matrices of m rows and n rows, respectively. The elements in the ith row of BA are obtained by multiplying each element of the ith row of A by the ith diagonal element of B. The elements in the jth column of AC are obtained by multiplying each element of the jth column of A by the jth diagonal element of C.

In particular, if B is a scalar matrix and A is a square matrix, the elements of AB and of BA are obtained by multiplying each element of A by the diagonal element of B. In this case $AB = BA$, and we say that A and B are *commutative*. Thus we have

THEOREM 2.3.1 *Every n-row scalar matrix is commutative with every n-row square matrix.*

Illustration: For the scalar matrix

$$\begin{pmatrix} t & 0 \\ 0 & t \end{pmatrix} \quad \text{and the matrix} \quad \begin{pmatrix} a_{11} & a_{12} \\ a_{21} & a_{22} \end{pmatrix},$$

we have

$$\begin{pmatrix} t & 0 \\ 0 & t \end{pmatrix} \begin{pmatrix} a_{11} & a_{12} \\ a_{21} & a_{22} \end{pmatrix} = \begin{pmatrix} ta_{11} & ta_{12} \\ ta_{21} & ta_{22} \end{pmatrix}$$

and

$$\begin{pmatrix} a_{11} & a_{12} \\ a_{21} & a_{22} \end{pmatrix} \begin{pmatrix} t & 0 \\ 0 & t \end{pmatrix} = \begin{pmatrix} ta_{11} & ta_{12} \\ ta_{21} & ta_{22} \end{pmatrix}.$$

Let $A = (a_{ij})$ be an n-row square matrix and let

$$B = \text{diag.} \{ b_1 \quad b_2 \quad \ldots \quad b_n \}.$$

Then $AB = BA$ if and only if $a_{ij}b_j = b_i a_{ij}$ $(i, j = 1, 2, \ldots, n)$. Thus $a_{ij} = 0$ whenever $b_i \neq b_j$. Hence, if no two diagonal elements of B are equal, then A must be a diagonal matrix, and we have

THEOREM 2.3.2 *If B is a diagonal matrix having no two equal diagonal elements, then the only matrices commutative with B are diagonal matrices.*

Suppose that C is a matrix which is commutative with every n-row square matrix. Then, from theorem 2.3.2, C must be a diagonal matrix.

Write $C = \text{diag.} \{c_1, c_2, \ldots, c_n\}$ and $A = (a_{ij})$. Since $CA = AC$, for every square matrix A, it follows that $(c_i - c_j)a_{ij} = 0$ for all choices of the a_{ij} and, hence, $c_i = c_j$ $(i, j = 1, 2, \ldots, n)$. This establishes

THEOREM 2.3.3 *The only matrices which are commutative with every n-row square matrix are n-row scalar matrices.*

The results of theorem 2.3.1 and theorem 2.3.3 immediately above may be combined into the one theorem,

THEOREM 2.3.4 *An $n \times n$ matrix A commutes with every $n \times n$ matrix B if and only if A is scalar.*

EXERCISES

1. Given the matrices

$$A = \begin{pmatrix} 2 & 3 & 5 \\ -5 & 2 & 7 \\ 3 & 0 & -4 \end{pmatrix}, \qquad B = \begin{pmatrix} 3 & 0 & 0 \\ 0 & 2 & 0 \\ 0 & 0 & -1 \end{pmatrix}.$$

Compute AB and BA.

2. Given the matrices

$$A = \begin{pmatrix} 2 & 3 & 1 \\ 0 & 5 & -2 \\ 0 & 0 & -3 \end{pmatrix}, \qquad B = \begin{pmatrix} 3 & 0 & 1 \\ 0 & 2 & 3 \\ 0 & 0 & -5 \end{pmatrix}.$$

Compute AB and BA.

3. Given the matrices

$$A' = \begin{pmatrix} 2 & 0 & 0 \\ 3 & 5 & 0 \\ 1 & -2 & -3 \end{pmatrix}, \qquad B' = \begin{pmatrix} 3 & 0 & 0 \\ 0 & 2 & 0 \\ 1 & 3 & -5 \end{pmatrix}.$$

Compute $A'B'$ and $B'A'$. Note the relationship between A and A'; B and B'; and AB and $B'A'$ in Exercises 2 and 3.

4. Using the matrices in Exercises 2 and 3, compute AA' and $B'B$.

5. Given the matrices

$$A = \begin{pmatrix} 1 & i \\ i & -1 \end{pmatrix}, \qquad D = \begin{pmatrix} 1+i & -1 \\ 1 & 1+i \end{pmatrix}.$$

Compute AD and DA. Note that $DA = A$ and yet D is not the identity matrix. Consider also

$$E = \begin{pmatrix} \dfrac{1+i}{1+2i} & \dfrac{1}{1+2i} \\[2ex] \dfrac{-1}{1+2i} & \dfrac{1+i}{1+2i} \end{pmatrix}$$

and find the products AE, EA, ED, and DE.

6. Given

$$\begin{pmatrix} x & a \\ b & y \end{pmatrix} \begin{pmatrix} 1 & 2 \\ 2 & 4 \end{pmatrix} = \begin{pmatrix} 1 & 2 \\ 2 & 4 \end{pmatrix}.$$

Determine the x and y in terms of a and b.

7. Prove that the product of two $n \times n$ triangular matrices of the same type is an $n \times n$ triangular matrix of this type.

8. Prove that the product of any finite number of $n \times n$ triangular matrices of the same type is an $n \times n$ triangular matrix of this type.

9. Compute all matrices commutative with diag. $\{1, 2, 3\}$.

10. Compute all matrices commutative with diag. $\{1, 1, 2, 2\}$.

2.4　Submatrices. If, from an $m \times n$ matrix, A, a number of rows or a number of columns, or both, are deleted, the remaining array is a matrix which is called a *submatrix* of A. In particular, the elements of A may be considered 1×1 submatrices, or the rows and columns of A may be considered $1 \times n$ and $m \times 1$ submatrices, respectively. Also, the matrix A is sometimes considered to be a submatrix of itself.

Illustration: If, in the 3×3 matrix (a_{ij}), the second row and third column are deleted, the submatrix remaining is

$$\begin{pmatrix} a_{11} & a_{12} \\ a_{31} & a_{32} \end{pmatrix}.$$

By drawing horizontal lines between certain rows and vertical lines between certain columns of an $m \times n$ matrix, A, we divide the matrix into non-overlapping submatrices. Every element will be contained in some submatrix, and no two submatrices will contain the same element. Such division of the matrix A into submatrices is called *partitioning* of A. If A is partitioned by drawing $(p - 1)$ horizontal lines and $(q - 1)$ vertical lines, then it is often convenient to think of A as a $p \times q$ matrix having as elements the submatrices obtained by this partitioning. The set of elements in each rectangular block thus formed constitutes a submatrix.

Illustration: If we partition the 3×5 matrix $A = (a_{ij})$ by a vertical line between the third and fourth columns and a horizontal line between the second and third rows, we get

$$(2.4.1) \qquad A = \left(\begin{array}{ccc|cc} a_{11} & a_{12} & a_{13} & a_{14} & a_{15} \\ a_{21} & a_{22} & a_{23} & a_{24} & a_{25} \\ \hline a_{31} & a_{32} & a_{33} & a_{34} & a_{35} \end{array} \right).$$

This may be written

$$(2.4.2) \qquad A = \begin{pmatrix} A_{11} & A_{12} \\ A_{21} & A_{22} \end{pmatrix},$$

where

$$A_{11} = \begin{pmatrix} a_{11} & a_{12} & a_{13} \\ a_{21} & a_{22} & a_{23} \end{pmatrix}, \quad \text{etc.}$$

Note that to partition a matrix means to divide it into submatrices in a definite way. For example, the matrix in (2.4.1) above is partitioned, whereas the matrix

$$\begin{pmatrix} \begin{pmatrix} 1 & 2 \\ 2 & 0 \\ 2 & 3 \end{pmatrix} & \begin{pmatrix} 1 \\ -2 \\ -1 \end{pmatrix} \end{pmatrix}$$

is divided into submatrices but is not partitioned.

A matrix is referred to as a *block matrix* whenever the submatrices obtained by a partitioning are considered as the elements of the matrix. In the block matrix $A = (A_{ij})$ $(i = 1, 2, \ldots, u; \; j = 1, 2, \ldots, v)$, the submatrices A_{ij} for which $i = j$ are called the *diagonal blocks* of the matrix. The matrix A is called a *square block matrix* if $u = v$. For example, (2.4.1) is a square block matrix. If A is a square block matrix and all elements of the submatrices on one side of the line of diagonal blocks are zero, the matrix is called a *triangular block matrix*. If A is a square block matrix containing nonzero elements in the diagonal blocks only, then A is called a *diagonal block matrix*. This is indicated by writing

$$A = \text{diag. } \{ A_{11} \quad A_{22} \quad \ldots \quad A_{uu} \}.$$

A square matrix is said to be *regularly partitioned* if it is partitioned into a square block matrix so that each diagonal block is square. For example,

$$\begin{pmatrix} a_{11} & a_{12} & a_{13} \\ a_{21} & a_{22} & a_{23} \\ \hline a_{31} & a_{32} & a_{33} \end{pmatrix} \quad \text{and} \quad \begin{pmatrix} a_{11} & a_{12} & a_{13} & a_{14} & a_{15} & a_{16} \\ a_{21} & a_{22} & a_{23} & a_{24} & a_{25} & a_{26} \\ a_{31} & a_{32} & a_{33} & a_{34} & a_{35} & a_{36} \\ \hline a_{41} & a_{42} & a_{43} & a_{44} & a_{45} & a_{46} \\ \hline a_{51} & a_{52} & a_{53} & a_{54} & a_{55} & a_{56} \\ a_{61} & a_{62} & a_{63} & a_{64} & a_{65} & a_{66} \end{pmatrix}$$

are regularly partitioned. It is obvious that only square matrices can be regularly partitioned.

Any submatrix, B, of A, will contain elements from certain rows of A and elements from certain columns of A. The elements common to the remaining rows and columns of A form another submatrix, C, of A. This submatrix C is called the *complementary submatrix* of B in A. Obviously B is also the complementary submatrix of C in A. If B is an $r \times s$ submatrix, then its complementary submatrix is an $(m - r) \times (n - s)$ matrix. In (2.4.1) and (2.4.2) above, each of the submatrices which we have denoted by A_{11} and A_{22} is the complementary submatrix of the other in A.

EXERCISES

In each of the exercises to follow, the matrix A is taken to be the 3×3 matrix

$$\begin{pmatrix} a_{11} & a_{12} & a_{13} \\ a_{21} & a_{22} & a_{23} \\ a_{31} & a_{32} & a_{33} \end{pmatrix}.$$

1. Write the submatrix obtained by deleting the second row and the third column of the matrix A.

2. Consider each element of the first column of A to be a submatrix of A and write its complementary submatrix.

3. Partition A into the type

$$\begin{pmatrix} A_{11} & A_{12} \\ A_{21} & A_{22} \end{pmatrix}$$

in all possible ways and indicate the A_{ij} in each case.

4. Write all possible 3×1 submatrices of A.

5. Partition A in such a way that you may write

$$A = \begin{pmatrix} A_1 \\ A_2 \\ A_3 \end{pmatrix}.$$

6. Partition A in such a way that you may write $A = (B_1 \ \ B_2 \ \ B_3)$.

7. Show that the product $A_i B_j$, where A_i and B_j are the submatrices indicated in Exercises 5 and 6, is the element of the ith row and the jth column of the matrix A^2.

8. Deduce a rule for addition of matrices such that

$$A^2 = (B_1 \ \ B_2 \ \ B_3) \begin{pmatrix} A_1 \\ A_2 \\ A_3 \end{pmatrix} = B_1 A_1 + B_2 A_2 + B_3 A_3$$

will be a true relation.

2.5 Addition of Matrices. Using the definition of matrix multiplication, we observe that

$$(a_{i1} \ \ a_{i2} \ \ \ldots \ \ a_{in}) \begin{pmatrix} b_{1k} \\ b_{2k} \\ \vdots \\ b_{nk} \end{pmatrix} = \sum_{j=1}^{n} a_{ij} b_{jk}.$$

Hence, if $(a_{i1} \ a_{i2} \ \ldots \ a_{in})$ is the ith row of A and is indicated by A_i and if

$$\begin{pmatrix} b_{1k} \\ b_{2k} \\ \vdots \\ b_{nk} \end{pmatrix}$$

is the kth column of B and is indicated by B_k, then the element $A_i B_k$ is the element in the ith row and the kth column of AB, as given in equation (2.1.8). Thus, partitioning A into one-row matrices and partitioning B into one-column matrices, the product AB is given by

$$AB = \begin{pmatrix} A_1 \\ A_2 \\ \vdots \\ A_m \end{pmatrix} (B_1 \ \ B_2 \ \ \ldots \ \ B_p) = (A_i B_k),$$

$$\text{for } i = i, 2, \ldots, m; \ k = 1, 2, \ldots p.$$

We also note that the products A_iB and AB_k are both defined and we have

$$A_iB = A_i(B_1 \quad B_2 \quad \ldots \quad B_p) = (A_iB_1 \quad A_iB_2 \quad \ldots \quad A_iB_p).$$

Consequently, the ith row of AB is A_iB. Similarly, the kth column of AB is AB_k, since

$$AB_k = \begin{pmatrix} A_1 \\ A_2 \\ \vdots \\ A_m \end{pmatrix} B_k = \begin{pmatrix} A_1B_k \\ A_2B_k \\ \vdots \\ A_mB_k \end{pmatrix}.$$

Hence, we may write the product AB in several ways. For example,

$$\begin{pmatrix} A_1B_1 & A_1B_2 & \ldots & A_1B_p \\ A_2B_1 & A_2B_2 & \ldots & A_2B_p \\ \hdotsfor{4} \\ A_mB_1 & A_mB_2 & \ldots & A_mB_p \end{pmatrix}, \quad \begin{pmatrix} A_1B \\ A_2B \\ \vdots \\ A_mB \end{pmatrix},$$

and $(AB_1 \ AB_2 \ \ldots \ AB_p)$ each represents this product.

If we partition AB with elements

$$A_iB_k \ (i = 1, 2, \ldots, m; k = 1, 2, \ldots, p)$$

into a 2×2 block matrix such that the submatrix in the upper left-hand corner has r rows and s columns, we have

$$\begin{pmatrix} A_1B_1 & \ldots & A_1B_s & A_1B_{s+1} & \ldots & A_1B_p \\ \hdotsfor{3} & \hdotsfor{3} \\ A_rB_1 & \ldots & A_rB_s & A_rB_{s+1} & \ldots & A_rB_p \\ \hline A_{r+1}B_1 & \ldots & A_{r+1}B_s & A_{r+1}B_{s+1} & \ldots & A_{r+1}B_p \\ \hdotsfor{3} & \hdotsfor{3} \\ A_mB_1 & \ldots & A_mB_s & A_mB_{s+1} & \ldots & A_mB_p \end{pmatrix} = \begin{pmatrix} R_1S_1 & R_1S_2 \\ R_2S_1 & R_2S_2 \end{pmatrix}$$

where R_1 is the matrix composed of the first r rows of A, R_2 is the matrix composed of the last $(m - r)$ rows of A, S_1 is the matrix composed of the first s columns of B, and S_2 is the matrix composed of the last $(p - s)$ columns of B. Thus we see that

$$(2.5.1) \qquad AB = \begin{pmatrix} R_1 \\ R_2 \end{pmatrix} (S_1 \quad S_2) = \begin{pmatrix} R_1S_1 & R_1S_2 \\ R_2S_1 & R_2S_2 \end{pmatrix}.$$

This is the same rule for multiplication that applies when R_1, R_2, S_1, S_2 are elements which are complex numbers except that, in this case, the order of multiplication is important.

Suppose now that we have two matrices A and C each of which has m rows, and suppose that we have two matrices B and D each of which has n columns. Furthermore, suppose that the products AB and CD are defined. We have seen that the matrix product AB may be written (A_iB_k) and also that CD may be written (C_iD_k), where A_i and C_i are one-row matrices and B_k and D_k are one-column matrices. Thus

$$(A \quad C)\begin{pmatrix} B \\ D \end{pmatrix} = (A_iB_k + C_iD_k), \qquad i = 1, 2, \ldots, m; k = 1, 2, \ldots, n,$$

since

$$(A_i \quad C_i)\begin{pmatrix} B_k \\ D_k \end{pmatrix} = (A_iB_k + C_iD_k).$$

Hence we may write

$$(2.5.2) \qquad (A \quad C)\begin{pmatrix} B \\ D \end{pmatrix} = AB + CD$$

if we define the sum of two $m \times n$ matrices in the following manner.

DEFINITION. *The sum of two $m \times n$ matrices A and C is an $m \times n$ matrix whose element in the ith row and jth column is the sum of the element in the ith row and jth column of A and the element in the ith row and jth column of C, $i = 1, 2, \ldots, m; j = 1, 2, \ldots, n$.*

In order that the relation (2.5.2) holds for all $m \times n$ matrices, the sum of two $m \times n$ matrices must be defined in this manner. This may be seen by taking A and C to be $m \times n$ matrices and B and D each to be the n-row identity matrix. Then we have

$$(2.5.3) \qquad (A \quad C)\begin{pmatrix} I_n \\ I_n \end{pmatrix} = A + C.$$

Illustration:

$$\begin{pmatrix} a_{11} & a_{12} & c_{11} & c_{12} \\ a_{21} & a_{22} & c_{21} & c_{22} \end{pmatrix}\begin{pmatrix} 1 & 0 \\ 0 & 1 \\ 1 & 0 \\ 0 & 1 \end{pmatrix} = \begin{pmatrix} a_{11} + c_{11} & a_{12} + c_{12} \\ a_{21} + c_{21} & a_{22} + c_{22} \end{pmatrix}.$$

Under this definition of sum, $A + B = B + A$. That is, *addition of matrices is commutative.*

Illustration:

$$\begin{pmatrix} 2 & 1 \\ 7 & 5 \end{pmatrix} + \begin{pmatrix} 3 & -2 \\ -1 & 4 \end{pmatrix} = \begin{pmatrix} 3 & -2 \\ -1 & 4 \end{pmatrix} + \begin{pmatrix} 2 & 1 \\ 7 & 5 \end{pmatrix} = \begin{pmatrix} 5 & -1 \\ 6 & 9 \end{pmatrix}.$$

Suppose now that R_1, R_2, S_1, and S_2 are partitioned as follows:

$$(2.5.4) \quad A = \begin{pmatrix} R_1 \\ R_2 \end{pmatrix} = \begin{pmatrix} M_1 & M_2 \\ M_3 & M_4 \end{pmatrix} \quad \text{and} \quad B = (S_1 \quad S_2) = \begin{pmatrix} N_1 & N_2 \\ N_3 & N_4 \end{pmatrix},$$

where M_1 is an $r \times t$ submatrix and N_1 is a $t \times s$ submatrix. Then, using (2.5.1) and (2.5.2), we have

$$AB = \begin{pmatrix} M_1 & M_2 \\ M_3 & M_4 \end{pmatrix}\begin{pmatrix} N_1 & N_2 \\ N_3 & N_4 \end{pmatrix} = \begin{pmatrix} M_1N_1 + M_2N_3 & M_1N_2 + M_2N_4 \\ M_3N_1 + M_4N_3 & M_3N_2 + M_4N_4 \end{pmatrix}.$$

We may continue to partition A and B and obtain the following theorem.

THEOREM 2.5.1   *If the $m \times n$ matrix A be partitioned into submatrices A_{ij} with r_i rows and s_j columns, where*

$$\sum_{i=1}^{u} r_i = m \quad and \quad \sum_{j=1}^{v} s_j = n,$$

and if the $n \times p$ matrix B be partitioned into submatrices B_{jk} with s_j rows and t_k columns, where

$$\sum_{k=1}^{w} t_k = p,$$

then the matrix $C = AB$ may be partitioned into submatrices C_{ik} with r_i rows and t_k columns such that

$$C_{ik} = \sum_{j=1}^{v} A_{ij}B_{jk} \quad (i = 1, 2, \ldots, u; k = 1, 2, \ldots, w).$$

If the matrix A is added to itself for k summands, the resulting matrix is the same matrix as that obtained by multiplying each element of A by the number k. It is natural to denote such a sum by kA. Consequently we make the following definition.

DEFINITION.   *The product, in either order, of the matrix A and any number t is the matrix obtained by multiplying each element of A by t.*

Thus, if $A = (a_{ij})$ and if t is any number, then

$$tA = At = (ta_{ij}) \quad (i = 1, 2, \ldots, m; j = 1, 2, \ldots, n).$$

In particular, the scalar matrix whose diagonal element is t may be written tI. Hence the product of A by the scalar matrix tI is identical with the product of A by the number t.

Illustration: (a) For the matrix

$$A = \begin{pmatrix} 1 & 2 & -1 \\ 5 & 0 & 3 \end{pmatrix} \quad \text{and} \quad t = 3,$$

we have

$$\begin{pmatrix} 1 & 2 & -1 \\ 5 & 0 & 3 \end{pmatrix} + \begin{pmatrix} 1 & 2 & -1 \\ 5 & 0 & 3 \end{pmatrix} + \begin{pmatrix} 1 & 2 & -1 \\ 5 & 0 & 3 \end{pmatrix} =$$

$$3 \begin{pmatrix} 1 & 2 & -1 \\ 5 & 0 & 3 \end{pmatrix} = \begin{pmatrix} 3 & 6 & -3 \\ 15 & 0 & 9 \end{pmatrix}.$$

(b) For A, above, and $t = \frac{2}{3}$, we have

$$\frac{2}{3} \begin{pmatrix} 1 & 2 & -1 \\ 5 & 0 & 3 \end{pmatrix} = \begin{pmatrix} \frac{2}{3} & \frac{4}{3} & -\frac{2}{3} \\ \frac{10}{3} & 0 & 2 \end{pmatrix}.$$

(c) The scalar matrix

$$\begin{pmatrix} \sqrt{2} & 0 \\ 0 & \sqrt{2} \end{pmatrix}$$

may be written $\sqrt{2}I$. And thus, for A above,

$$\begin{pmatrix} \sqrt{2} & 0 \\ 0 & \sqrt{2} \end{pmatrix} A = \sqrt{2}I \begin{pmatrix} 1 & 2 & -1 \\ 5 & 0 & 3 \end{pmatrix} = \begin{pmatrix} \sqrt{2} & 2\sqrt{2} & -\sqrt{2} \\ 5\sqrt{2} & 0 & 3\sqrt{2} \end{pmatrix} = \sqrt{2}A.$$

Since the distributive law holds for numbers, it follows that $t(A + B) = tA + tB$ and that $(t + s)A = tA + sA$.

If A and B are two $m \times n$ matrices, it is possible to determine uniquely an $m \times n$ matrix X such that $A + X = B$ since this merely involves finding numbers x_{ij} such that $a_{ij} + x_{ij} = b_{ij}$. In particular, if $A = B$, then we have $A + X = A$, where X is the matrix in which all the elements are zero. It is natural to call this matrix, X, the $m \times n$ *zero matrix*. We shall use the symbol 0 to denote the number zero and also to denote any matrix whose elements are all zero. There should be no confusion in this dual use of the symbol since the context will indicate which is meant.

If $A + X = 0$ it is easy to see that $x_{ij} = -a_{ij}$ for $i = 1, 2, \ldots, m$; $j = 1, 2, \ldots, n$. It is customary to call X the additive inverse of A in this case and to indicate this matrix X by the symbol $-A$. It is consistent to write $-A = (-1)A$. In this connection we shall interpret $A - B$ to mean $A + (-1)B$. Thus, for any matrix A, we have

$$A - A = 0, \qquad A + 0 = A, \qquad 0 \cdot A = 0, \quad \text{and} \quad A \cdot 0 = 0.$$

In the last two of these equations the 0 appearing in the left member may be the number zero or any zero matrix for which the product is defined. Each 0 appearing as a right member is a zero matrix. It should be pointed out that the product matrix AB may be a zero matrix even though neither A nor B is a zero matrix.

Illustration:

$$\begin{pmatrix} 0 & 1 \\ 0 & 2 \end{pmatrix} \begin{pmatrix} 2 & 3 \\ 0 & 0 \end{pmatrix} = \begin{pmatrix} 0 & 0 \\ 0 & 0 \end{pmatrix} = 0.$$

If $A \neq 0$ and $B \neq 0$ but $AB = 0$, then A and B are called *proper divisors of zero*.

EXERCISES

1. Given

$$A = \begin{pmatrix} 2 & 3 & -5 \\ -10 & 1 & 0 \\ 7 & 2 & 1 \end{pmatrix}, \qquad B = \begin{pmatrix} -3 & 2 & 4 \\ 0 & -4 & 2 \\ 5 & -4 & 3 \end{pmatrix}.$$

Write the matrices $A + B$ and $A - B$.

2. In Exercise 1, partition A by drawing a line between the second and third rows. Partition B by drawing a line between the first and second columns. Write

$$A = \begin{pmatrix} A_1 \\ A_2 \end{pmatrix} \quad \text{and} \quad B = (B_1 \quad B_2)$$

and verify that

$$AB = \begin{pmatrix} A_1 B_1 & A_1 B_2 \\ A_2 B_1 & A_2 B_2 \end{pmatrix}.$$

The product BA is defined and

$$BA = (B_1 \quad B_2) \begin{pmatrix} A_1 \\ A_2 \end{pmatrix}.$$

Why is it not correct to say that $BA = B_1 A_1 + B_2 A_2$?

3. Write the matrix A, of Exercise 1, partitioned as

$$A = \begin{pmatrix} \begin{array}{cc|c} 2 & 3 & -5 \\ -10 & 1 & 0 \\ \hline 7 & 2 & 1 \end{array} \end{pmatrix} = \begin{pmatrix} A_1 & A_2 \\ A_3 & A_4 \end{pmatrix}.$$

Partition B, from Exercise 1, in the form

$$B = \begin{pmatrix} B_1 & B_2 \\ B_3 & B_4 \end{pmatrix}$$

in all possible ways so that the product AB may be obtained by block multiplication. Show that this partitioning of B can be done in one, and in only one, way so that both AB and BA may be obtained by block multiplication.

4. Assume that

$$(A_1 \quad A_2) \begin{pmatrix} B_1 \\ B_2 \end{pmatrix} = A_1 B_1 + A_2 B_2$$

for all matrices A_1, A_2, B_1, and B_2 for which both operations are defined. Prove that

$$(A_1 \quad A_2 \quad \ldots \quad A_k) \begin{pmatrix} B_1 \\ B_2 \\ \cdot \\ \cdot \\ \cdot \\ B_k \end{pmatrix} = \sum_{i=1}^{k} A_i B_i$$

whenever all operations are defined.

5. Define $\frac{1}{2}A$ to be a matrix B such that $B + B = A$. Prove that B is the matrix obtained by multiplying each element of A by the number $\frac{1}{2}$.

6. Prove that the sum of two $n \times n$ triangular matrices of the same type is a triangular matrix of this type.

7. If A is a triangular matrix and k is a positive integer and a_i ($i = 0, 1, \ldots, k$) are numbers, show that

$$a_0 A^k + a_1 A^{k-1} + \cdots + a_{k-1} A + a_k I$$

is a triangular matrix.

8. Given

$$A = \begin{pmatrix} 2 & 1 \\ 3 & 2 \end{pmatrix}, \qquad B = \begin{pmatrix} 3 & 1 \\ -1 & -2 \end{pmatrix}.$$

Compute $(A + B)^2$ and $A^2 + 2AB + B^2$; compute $(A + B)(A - B)$ and $A^2 - B^2$.

9. Perform the computations asked for in Exercise 8, using

$$A = \begin{pmatrix} 0 & 1 \\ 1 & 2 \end{pmatrix}, \qquad B = \begin{pmatrix} 2 & 1 \\ 1 & 4 \end{pmatrix}.$$

10. If

$$A = (a_1 \quad a_2 \quad a_3) \quad \text{and} \quad B = \begin{pmatrix} b_1 \\ b_2 \\ b_3 \end{pmatrix},$$

then does

$$B(a_1 \quad a_2 \quad a_3) = (Ba_1 \quad Ba_2 \quad Ba_3) = (a_1B \quad a_2B \quad a_3B)$$

behave as if B is a scalar and then as if each of the a_1, a_2, a_3 is a scalar?

11. Given the $m \times n$ matrix A, the $n \times p$ matrix B, and the $p \times q$ matrix C, partition A into an $n \times 1$ matrix, B into a $1 \times p$ matrix, and C into a $p \times q$ matrix. Write the element in the ith row and jth column of $(AB)C$ and of $A(BC)$ and show that these elements are equal.

2.6 The "Sum Columns, Rows and Multiply" Product Check.

It will probably become apparent, after a few matrix products have been computed, that some type of check method is desirable. This need will be more evident after one reaches the position where he assumes the responsibility for setting up the problem and then passes the problem on to someone else to record the data, prepare the program, and obtain the final solution. It is difficult to excuse expensive negligence when errors are made in transcription and are not detected and when no checks are attempted.

We shall illustrate the details of the "*sum columns, rows and multiply*" product check, briefly referred to hereinafter by the letters SCRAM. This procedure, although a very useful check, nevertheless possesses limitations. It is not an absolutely perfect procedure for revealing an error. Also, its use compels one to manipulate and reckon with matrices of increased dimensions. Relevant to the technique is the fact that its effectiveness lies in the order of its step-by-step applications since its application to the final product of two or more matrices reveals nothing. The reader will be aware of the effectiveness of this technique after he has analyzed the routine. The SCRAM product check is illustrated here with numerical data, and proof for the general case follows the example.

Suppose that we are required to find the product of the two matrices given by

$$A = \begin{pmatrix} 1 & 0 & 2 \\ 3 & 5 & -1 \\ 7 & 2 & -3 \end{pmatrix}, \quad B = \begin{pmatrix} 1 & 2 & -1 \\ 2 & 1 & -2 \\ -3 & 5 & 4 \end{pmatrix}.$$

If we apply the SCRAM product check to the rows of B above, it is necessary to replace B with the matrix $B^\vee$ (called "B check") by appending a fourth column to B. The new element for the first row and fourth column of $B^\vee$ is obtained by adding the three elements of the first row of B and changing the sign of the sum. The new element for the second row and fourth column of $B^\vee$ is obtained by adding the elements of the second row of B and changing the sign of this sum. Similarly we obtain the last element of $B^\vee$. We now have

$$B^\vee = \left(\begin{array}{ccc|c} 1 & 2 & -1 & -2 \\ 2 & 1 & -2 & -1 \\ -3 & 5 & 4 & -6 \end{array} \right).$$

Using a vertical line in this fashion enables us to distinguish at a glance the original matrix B and the check column. The product AB is now obtained from $AB^\vee$, and we see that

$$AB^\vee = \left(\begin{array}{ccc} 1 & 0 & 2 \\ 3 & 5 & -1 \\ 7 & 2 & -3 \end{array} \right) \left(\begin{array}{ccc|c} 1 & 2 & -1 & -2 \\ 2 & 1 & -2 & -1 \\ -3 & 5 & 4 & -6 \end{array} \right)$$

$$= \left(\begin{array}{ccc|c} -5 & 12 & 7 & -14 \\ 16 & 6 & -17 & -5 \\ 20 & 1 & -23 & 2 \end{array} \right).$$

From this we get, by appending an additional column to the product matrix $AB^\vee$,

$$(AB^\vee)^\vee = \left(\begin{array}{ccc|c|c} -5 & 12 & 7 & -14 & 0 \\ 16 & 6 & -17 & -5 & 0 \\ 20 & 1 & -23 & 2 & 0 \end{array} \right),$$

where, if the work is correct, the new column must possess only zero elements, since each element of the fifth column of $(AB^\vee)^\vee$ is the sum of all elements in the row represented. It is easy to see that the first three columns of $AB^\vee$ and likewise of $(AB^\vee)^\vee$ constitute the 3×3 product matrix AB.

It is helpful to note that the matrix $B^\vee$ may be formed by multiplying B on the right by the matrix

$$\left(\begin{array}{ccc|c} 1 & 0 & 0 & -1 \\ 0 & 1 & 0 & -1 \\ 0 & 0 & 1 & -1 \end{array} \right)$$

which we shall indicate by the symbol $I_3^{\vee}$, and that the matrix $(AB^{\vee})^{\vee}$ may be obtained by multiplying $AB^{\vee}$ on the right by the matrix

$$\begin{pmatrix} 1 & 0 & 0 & 0 & \Big| & -1 \\ 0 & 1 & 0 & 0 & \Big| & -1 \\ 0 & 0 & 1 & 0 & \Big| & -1 \\ 0 & 0 & 0 & 1 & \Big| & -1 \end{pmatrix}$$

indicated by $I_4^{\vee}$, where the vertical partitioning lines are used to emphasize the fact that the first three columns of the first matrix above and the first four columns of the second matrix are, respectively, the 3×3 and 4×4 identity matrices. Thus $ABI_3^{\vee} = AB^{\vee}$, and multiplication in the order stipulated below yields

$$A \left\{ B \begin{pmatrix} 1 & 0 & 0 & \Big| & -1 \\ 0 & 1 & 0 & \Big| & -1 \\ 0 & 0 & 1 & \Big| & -1 \end{pmatrix} \right\} = ABI_3^{\vee} = AB^{\vee}$$

and

$$(AB^{\vee}) \begin{pmatrix} 1 & 0 & 0 & 0 & \Big| & -1 \\ 0 & 1 & 0 & 0 & \Big| & -1 \\ 0 & 0 & 1 & 0 & \Big| & -1 \\ 0 & 0 & 0 & 1 & \Big| & -1 \end{pmatrix} = (AB^{\vee})I_4^{\vee} = (AB^{\vee})^{\vee}.$$

Now let us examine this SCRAM product check in general, where $A = (a_{ij})$, $B = (b_{jk})$, for $i = 1, 2, \ldots, m$; $j = 1, 2, \ldots, n$; $k = 1, 2, \ldots, p$. The meaning of $I_p^{\vee}$ is obvious from the use of $I_3^{\vee}$ and $I_4^{\vee}$ above, and hereafter as usual the subscript p indicating the dimension of $I^{\vee}$ will be omitted unless needed for clarity. Thus $BI^{\vee} = B^{\vee}$, which may be indicated elementwise by

$$B^{\vee} = \begin{pmatrix} b_{11} & b_{12} & \ldots & b_{1p} & \Big| & -\sum_{\lambda=1}^{p} b_{1\lambda} \\ \ldots\ldots\ldots\ldots & & & \ldots\ldots \\ b_{j1} & b_{j2} & \ldots & b_{jp} & \Big| & -\sum_{\lambda=1}^{p} b_{j\lambda} \\ \ldots\ldots\ldots\ldots & & & \ldots\ldots \\ b_{n1} & b_{n2} & \ldots & b_{np} & \Big| & -\sum_{\lambda=1}^{p} b_{n\lambda} \end{pmatrix}.$$

Consequently it follows that

$$AB^{\surd} = \begin{pmatrix} \sum\limits_{\mu=1}^{n} a_{1\mu}b_{\mu1} & \sum\limits_{\mu=1}^{n} a_{1\mu}b_{\mu2} & \cdots & \sum\limits_{\mu=1}^{n} a_{1\mu}b_{\mu p} & \bigg| & -\sum\limits_{\mu=1}^{n} a_{1\mu} \sum\limits_{\lambda=1}^{p} b_{\mu\lambda} \\ \cdots\cdots\cdots\cdots\cdots\cdots\cdots\cdots\cdots & & & & & \cdots\cdots\cdots\cdots\cdots \\ \sum\limits_{\mu=1}^{n} a_{i\mu}b_{\mu1} & \sum\limits_{\mu=1}^{n} a_{i\mu}b_{\mu2} & \cdots & \sum\limits_{\mu=1}^{n} a_{i\mu}b_{\mu p} & \bigg| & -\sum\limits_{\mu=1}^{n} a_{i\mu} \sum\limits_{\lambda=1}^{p} b_{\mu\lambda} \\ \cdots\cdots\cdots\cdots\cdots\cdots\cdots\cdots\cdots & & & & & \cdots\cdots\cdots\cdots\cdots \\ \sum\limits_{\mu=1}^{n} a_{m\mu}b_{\mu1} & \sum\limits_{\mu=1}^{n} a_{m\mu}b_{\mu2} & \cdots & \sum\limits_{\mu=1}^{n} a_{m\mu}b_{\mu p} & \bigg| & -\sum\limits_{\mu=1}^{n} a_{m\mu} \sum\limits_{\lambda=1}^{p} b_{\mu\lambda} \end{pmatrix}$$

and it is easily seen that the sum of the elements of the ith row of $AB^{\surd}$ is given by

$$\sum_{\lambda=1}^{p} \sum_{\mu=1}^{n} a_{i\mu}b_{\mu\lambda} - \sum_{\mu=1}^{n} a_{i\mu} \sum_{\lambda=1}^{p} b_{\mu\lambda} \qquad (i = 1, 2, \ldots, m),$$

which is zero. Thus the last column of $(AB^{\surd})^{\surd}$ contains only zero elements. It is also seen that the first p columns of $AB^{\surd}$ and consequently the first p columns of $(AB^{\surd})^{\surd}$ constitute the product AB. This may more easily be seen if we partition $I_p^{\surd}$ to get $I_p^{\surd} = (I \ C)$ and $I_{p+1}^{\surd}$ to get $I_{p+1}^{\surd} = (I \ K)$, where C and K are one-column matrices having as each element -1. Then $AB^{\surd} = ABI^{\surd} = AB(I \ C) = A(B \ BC) = (AB \ ABC)$, and $(AB^{\surd})^{\surd} = AB^{\surd}I^{\surd} = AB^{\surd}(I \ K) = (AB^{\surd} \ AB^{\surd}K) = (AB \ ABC \ AB^{\surd}K)$.

The reader will observe that, if the SCRAM product check is administered by using check matrices $E_p = (I \ C)$ and $E_{p+1} = (I \ K)$, where C and K are one-column matrices having as each element 1, then, in this case,

$$B^{\surd} = BE = (B \ BC)$$

and

$$AB^{\surd} = (AB \ ABC).$$

Also,

$$(AB^{\surd})^{\surd} = (AB^{\surd})E = (AB^{\surd} \ AB^{\surd}K) = (AB \ ABC \ AB^{\surd}K).$$

From these products it is seen that $ABC = \frac{1}{2}AB^{\surd}K$, and thus the corresponding row elements of the last two columns of $(AB^{\surd})^{\surd}$, namely ABC and $AB^{\surd}K$, will have the ratio $1:2$. This is sometimes a more desirable check than the one obtained by using the $I^{\surd}$ above.

Another convenient check is the one obtained by using the E_p above and using as E_{p+1} the matrix $(I \ Z)$, where $z_i = 1$ for $i = 1, 2, \ldots, p$ and $z_i = 0$ for $i = p + 1$. In this case we have

$$AB^{\surd} = (AB \ ABC)$$

and

$$(AB^{\surd})^{\surd} = (AB \ ABC \ ABC),$$

and the last two columns of the product matrix are identical.

If the matrices A and B are of large order, then it is desirable to insert check columns throughout B. For example, if B is of dimension 18×30, then one may wish to insert a check column after each ten columns. In some cases it may even be desirable to insert check columns after each five or six columns. A cross section of check columns used with the possible cross section of check rows for the matrix A gives a network of check rows and columns which makes it almost impossible to obtain products possessing undetected transcription, transition, or arithmetic errors. A study of the final product will reveal where any error may have been made. It does not take many applications of this technique for the solver to develop skill in the location of inconsistencies.

It is obvious that the SCRAM product check applies even though the last column of $BI^{\vee}$ contains only zero elements. In this case the last column of $(AB^{\vee})^{\vee}$ also contains only zero elements, if the work is correct. It is immediately evident that in this case B may be used instead of $B^{\vee}$, and then $(AB)^{\vee}$ instead of $(AB^{\vee})^{\vee}$. Again, it may be desirable to do a partial check if B is of small order, using a check column inserted somewhere before the last column. If B is of large order, then several such check columns may be desirable and the final check column of $B^{\vee}$ may be used to check subtotals for consistency or may be omitted in the interest of space and time.

It is pertinent to mention that round-off errors distort the elements of the check columns, and one would not always expect to obtain a final column of $\{A(BI^{\vee})\}I^{\vee}$ containing only zero elements, but nearness to zero would be an influencing factor favoring acceptability.

EXERCISES

1. Apply the SCRAM product check in finding the product AB where

$$A = \begin{pmatrix} 1 & 5 \\ 3 & 9 \end{pmatrix}, \quad B = \begin{pmatrix} 2 & 4 \\ 6 & 8 \end{pmatrix},$$

(a) using the row check $BI^{\vee}$ on B; (b) using the column check $I^{\vee}A$ on A; (c) using both $I^{\vee}A$ and $BI^{\vee}$.

2. Repeat Exercise 1 above where

$$A = \begin{pmatrix} 1 & -1 & 3 \\ 5 & 1 & 7 \\ 3 & 5 & -1 \end{pmatrix}, \quad B = \begin{pmatrix} 2 & -2 & 2 \\ 4 & 2 & -4 \\ 6 & 4 & -2 \end{pmatrix}.$$

3. Repeat Exercise 1 above where

$$A = \begin{pmatrix} 1 & 3 & 2 \\ -2 & -1 & 3 \\ 5 & -3 & 2 \end{pmatrix}, \qquad B = \begin{pmatrix} 1 & 2 & -3 \\ 3 & 4 & -7 \\ 1 & -1 & 0 \end{pmatrix}.$$

4. Prove $(AB)^{\sqrt{}} = AB^{\sqrt{}}$ where $B^{\sqrt{}} = BI^{\sqrt{}}$.

5. What is the possibility of a significant row check on both A and B to check AB?

6. Find $I_3^{\sqrt{}}I_4^{\sqrt{}}$ and show that this product applied to the 3×3 matrix AB in the manner $(AB)(I_3^{\sqrt{}}I_4^{\sqrt{}})$ does not provide a check on the product of AB.

7. Use both row checks and column checks to check the product

$$\begin{pmatrix} 1 & 2 \\ 3 & 4 \end{pmatrix}\begin{pmatrix} 2 & -1 \\ 7 & 3 \end{pmatrix}.$$

8. Discuss the effectiveness of the check on the product AB when applied to general 4×4 matrices A and B by inserting subtotal columns after the second and fourth columns and appending a seventh total sum column to B and making comparable adjustments to the rows of A.

9. Find matrices $I^{\sqrt{}}$, for Exercise 8, by which B may be multiplied on the right and A on the left so as to obtain the $I^{\sqrt{}}A$ and $BI^{\sqrt{}}$ from which we would then obtain $I^{\sqrt{}}I^{\sqrt{}}ABI^{\sqrt{}}I^{\sqrt{}}$, the product desired.

2.7 The Distributive Law for Matrices.

We have seen that multiplication of matrices is associative but is not, in general, commutative. It is obvious, from the definition, that addition of matrices is both associative and commutative. We may now ask whether the distributive law holds for matrices.

Let $A = (a_{ij})$, $B = (b_{ij})$, and $C = (c_{jk})$ $(i = 1, 2, \ldots, m;$ $j = 1, 2, \ldots, n;$ $k = 1, 2, \ldots, p)$. The products and sums AC, BC, $(A + B)$, and $(A + B)C$ are defined. The element in the ith row and kth column of $(A + B)C$ is

$$\sum_{j=1}^{n} (a_{ij} + b_{ij})c_{jk}.$$

This sum is equal to

$$\sum_{j=1}^{n} a_{ij}c_{jk} + \sum_{j=1}^{n} b_{ij}c_{jk},$$

which is the element in the ith row and kth column of $AC + BC$. Hence we have $(A + B)C = AC + BC$. Similarly, $C(A + B) = CA + CB$ whenever the matrices A, B, and C are such that all the operations are defined. That is, the *distributive law* holds for matrices. It is easy to show that both the sum and the product of two matrices are defined if and only if the matrices are square and of the same order.

EXERCISES

1. Prove that $A + B$ and AB are both defined for matrices A and B if and only if A and B are square and of the same order.

2. If A and B are matrices such that $AB = BA$, prove that A and B must be square and of the same order.

3. If A, B, and C are matrices such that $AC = CB$, prove that A and B must be square but not necessarily of the same order.

4. Given

$$A = \begin{pmatrix} 2 & 3 \\ -1 & -2 \end{pmatrix}, \quad B = \begin{pmatrix} 1 & 1 \\ 3 & -2 \end{pmatrix}, \quad \text{and} \quad C = \begin{pmatrix} -2 & -1 \\ 3 & 5 \end{pmatrix}.$$

Verify that $(A + B)C = AC + BC$.

5. Let $A = (a_{ij})$, $B = (b_{ij})$, and $C = (c_{ij})$ be square matrices of order three. Write the element in the second row and third column of $(A + B)C$ and of $AC + BC$ and show that they are equal.

2.8 The Transpose of a Matrix. Associated with every $m \times n$ matrix, $A = (a_{ij})$, there is a matrix A^T, called the *transpose* of A, obtained by writing the columns of A as the rows of A^T in the same order. That is, $A^T = (\alpha_{ji})$, where $\alpha_{ji} = a_{ij}$ $(i = 1, 2, \ldots, m; \; j = 1, 2, \ldots, n)$. Let $B^T = (\beta_{kj})$, where $\beta_{kj} = b_{jk}$ $(j = 1, 2, \ldots, n; \; k = 1, 2, \ldots, p)$, be the transpose of $B = (b_{jk})$. The transpose of the matrix AB is defined and is denoted by $(AB)^T$. We may expect some relationship to exist between $(AB)^T$ and A^T and B^T. However, the symbol $A^T B^T$ is not necessarily defined, but $B^T A^T$ is always defined when AB is defined and the element in the ith row and kth column of $B^T A^T$ is

$$\gamma_{ki} = \sum_{j=1}^{n} \beta_{kj} \alpha_{ji} = \sum_{j=1}^{n} a_{ij} b_{jk} = c_{ik},$$

where $C = (c_{ik}) = AB$. Hence $C^T = (AB)^T = B^T A^T$.

Illustration: Consider the two matrices

$$A = \begin{pmatrix} 3 & 1 \\ 5 & -2 \end{pmatrix} \quad \text{and} \quad B = \begin{pmatrix} 1 & -1 \\ 2 & 7 \end{pmatrix}.$$

Then

$$A^T = \begin{pmatrix} 3 & 5 \\ 1 & -2 \end{pmatrix}, \qquad B^T = \begin{pmatrix} 1 & 2 \\ -1 & 7 \end{pmatrix},$$

$$AB = \begin{pmatrix} 5 & 4 \\ 1 & -19 \end{pmatrix}, \qquad (AB)^T = \begin{pmatrix} 5 & 1 \\ 4 & -19 \end{pmatrix},$$

$$B^T A^T = \begin{pmatrix} 5 & 1 \\ 4 & -19 \end{pmatrix} = (AB)^T.$$

We now state

Theorem 2.8.1 *The transpose of the product of two matrices is the product of the transposes of the matrices taken in reverse order.*

This result may be extended to the product of k matrices, giving the general result

$$(A_1 A_2 \cdots A_{k-1} A_k)^T = A_k^T A_{k-1}^T \cdots A_2^T A_1^T.$$

The operation of *transposition* is obviously of *period two*. That is, the transpose of the transpose of A is A itself. If A is any matrix and $B = AA^T$, then $B^T = (A^T)^T A^T = AA^T = B$. Any matrix B having the property that $B^T = B$ is said to be *symmetric*. A symmetric matrix is necessarily square. It is left as an exercise to show that $(A + B)^T = A^T + B^T$.

Illustration: Let

$$A = \begin{pmatrix} 2 & 1 & 3 \\ 5 & -2 & 4 \end{pmatrix}.$$

Then

$$AA^T = \begin{pmatrix} 2 & 1 & 3 \\ 5 & -2 & 4 \end{pmatrix} \begin{pmatrix} 2 & 5 \\ 1 & -2 \\ 3 & 4 \end{pmatrix} = \begin{pmatrix} 14 & 20 \\ 20 & 45 \end{pmatrix}.$$

Also,

$$A^T A = \begin{pmatrix} 2 & 5 \\ 1 & -2 \\ 3 & 4 \end{pmatrix} \begin{pmatrix} 2 & 1 & 3 \\ 5 & -2 & 4 \end{pmatrix} = \begin{pmatrix} 29 & -8 & 26 \\ -8 & 5 & -5 \\ 26 & -5 & 25 \end{pmatrix}.$$

Note that $A^T A = A^T (A^T)^T$.

Let A be a square matrix and write $B = A + A^T$ and $C = A - A^T$. Then $B^T = A^T + (A^T)^T = A^T + A = A + A^T = B$ and $C^T = A^T - (A^T)^T = A^T - A = -(A - A^T) = -C$. A matrix C such that $C^T = -C$ is said to be *skew symmetric* or *skew*. Thus we have

Theorem 2.8.2 *If A is any matrix, then AA^T is symmetric; if A is a square matrix, then $A + A^T$ is symmetric and $A - A^T$ is skew.*

Illustration: Consider the square matrix

$$A = \begin{pmatrix} 1 & 2 \\ 3 & 5 \end{pmatrix}.$$

Then

$$A^T = \begin{pmatrix} 1 & 3 \\ 2 & 5 \end{pmatrix}.$$

Thus

$$AA^T = \begin{pmatrix} 5 & 13 \\ 13 & 34 \end{pmatrix},$$

$$A + A^T = \begin{pmatrix} 2 & 5 \\ 5 & 10 \end{pmatrix},$$

and

$$A - A^T = \begin{pmatrix} 0 & -1 \\ 1 & 0 \end{pmatrix}.$$

Hence we see that AA^T and $A + A^T$ are symmetric and that $A - A^T$ is skew. Also

$$\tfrac{1}{2}(A + A^T) + \tfrac{1}{2}(A - A^T) = \begin{pmatrix} 1 & \tfrac{5}{2} \\ \tfrac{5}{2} & 5 \end{pmatrix} + \begin{pmatrix} 0 & -\tfrac{1}{2} \\ \tfrac{1}{2} & 0 \end{pmatrix} = \begin{pmatrix} 1 & 2 \\ 3 & 5 \end{pmatrix} = A.$$

Since the sum of the symmetric matrix $A + A^T$ and the skew matrix $A - A^T$ is $2A$, the following theorem is suggested.

THEOREM 2.8.3 *Every square matrix can be expressed as the sum of a symmetric matrix and a skew matrix in one and in only one way.*

Let A be any square matrix and let k be any number. It is obvious that kA is symmetric whenever A is symmetric and that kA is skew whenever A is skew. Write $B = \tfrac{1}{2}(A + A^T)$ and $C = \tfrac{1}{2}(A - A^T)$. Then $B = B^T$, $C = -C^T$, and $A = B + C$. Conversely, let $A = M + N$, where $M^T = M$ and $N^T = -N$. Then $A^T = M^T + N^T = M - N$ and $M = \tfrac{1}{2}(A + A^T) = B$ and $N = \tfrac{1}{2}(A - A^T) = C$. This completes the proof of theorem 2.8.3.

If the matrix A is partitioned so that

$$A = \begin{pmatrix} A_{11} & A_{12} \\ A_{21} & A_{22} \end{pmatrix},$$

then it is easy to see that

$$A^T = \begin{pmatrix} A_{11}^T & A_{21}^T \\ A_{12}^T & A_{22}^T \end{pmatrix}.$$

EXERCISES

1. Given $A = (2, 1, 3, 5)$, compute AA^T and A^TA.
2. Given

$$A = \begin{pmatrix} 1 & 3 & 0 \\ 2 & -1 & 1 \\ -5 & 0 & 7 \end{pmatrix},$$

compute AA^T, A^TA, $A + A^T$, and $A - A^T$.

3. Given

$$A = \begin{pmatrix} 1 & -2 & 3 & -1 \\ 2 & 0 & 5 & 3 \end{pmatrix} \quad \text{and} \quad B = \begin{pmatrix} 2 & 7 \\ 3 & 1 \end{pmatrix},$$

compute AA^T and A^TA; also compute A^TB^T and $(BA)^T$.

4. If A is any matrix, prove that A^TA is symmetric.

5. If A and B are $m \times n$ matrices, prove that $(A + B)^T = A^T + B^T$.

6. Make all possible *regular* partitions of A, in Exercise 2, into 2×2 block matrices and write the corresponding block matrices for A^T.

7. Let $A = (a_{ij})$, $B = (b_{ij})$, and $C = (c_{ij})$ be 2×2 matrices. Compute the matrices $(ABC)^T$ and $C^TB^TA^T$.

8. Use theorem 2.8.1 and mathematical induction to prove that

$$(A_1A_2 \cdots A_{k-1}A_k)^T = A_k^T A_{k-1}^T \cdots A_2^T A_1^T.$$

9. Given the partitioned matrix

$$A = \begin{pmatrix} A_{11} & A_{12} & A_{13} & A_{14} \\ A_{21} & A_{22} & A_{23} & A_{24} \\ A_{31} & A_{32} & A_{33} & A_{34} \end{pmatrix}.$$

where the A_{ij} are submatrices of A. Write A^T.

10. For $P = (p_1 \, p_2 \, \ldots \, p_n)$ and $Q^T = (q_1 \, q_2 \, \ldots \, q_n)$ find PQ, P^TQ^T, Q^TP^T, $(PQ)^T$ and show that $(PQ)^T = Q^TP^T$, $QP \neq Q^TP^T$, $P^TQ^T \neq PQ$, and that QP and P^TQ^T are not necessarily the same.

11. If A is an $m \times n$ matrix and B is an $n \times p$ matrix, write $A = (A_i)$ as an $m \times 1$ column block matrix and write $B = (B_j)$ as a $1 \times p$ row block matrix. Express AB as an $m \times 1$ column block matrix having elements A_iB. Express AB as a $1 \times p$ row block matrix having elements AB_j.

12. Use the results of Exercise 11 above and write A^T and B^T in terms of the block matrices A_i and B_j. Show that $A_iB_j = B_j^TA_i^T$. Find the ijth element of $(AB)^T$ and of B^TA^T and thus establish that $(AB)^T = B^TA^T$.

CHAPTER 3

TRANSFORMATIONS

3.1 Linear Transformations. Using the notation of Chapter 2, the equation

$$(3.1.1) \qquad\qquad X = AY,$$

in which $X = (x_i)$, $A = (a_{ij})$, and $Y = (y_i)$ $(i, j = 1, 2, \ldots, n)$, is called a *linear transformation*. It transforms a form of degree k in $x_1, x_2, \ldots, x_n$ into a form of degree k in $y_1, y_2, \ldots, y_n$. The matrix A is called the matrix of the linear transformation. If $Y = BZ$ is another linear transformation which transforms the form in $y_1, y_2, \ldots, y_n$ into a form in $z_1, z_2, \ldots, z_n$, then $X = ABZ$ is a linear transformation which transforms the form in $x_1, x_2, \ldots, x_n$ into the form in $z_1, z_2, \ldots, z_n$. We now have

THEOREM 3.1.1 *A linear transformation with matrix A followed by a linear transformation with matrix B is a linear transformation with matrix AB.*

The equation (3.1.1) may be thought of as a single equation in matrices or as n equations expressing $x_1, x_2, \ldots, x_n$ as linear forms in $y_1, y_2, \ldots, y_n$. We say that (3.1.1) is *solvable* if and only if there exist linear forms

$$y_j = \sum_{k=1}^{n} p_{jk} x_k \qquad (j = 1, 2, \ldots, n),$$

which, when substituted in the n equations of (3.1.1), reduce them to $x_i = x_i$ $(i = 1, 2, \ldots, n)$. In matrix notation, (3.1.1) is solvable if there exists a square matrix P such that when PX is substituted for Y in (3.1.1) the equation becomes $X = IX$.

DEFINITION. *The linear transformation (3.1.1) and its matrix A are said to be nonsingular if (3.1.1) is solvable; otherwise A is singular.*

To say that a matrix is nonsingular implies that the matrix is square. If A is nonsingular and $Y = PX$ is a solution of (3.1.1), then $X = APX = IX$ and, since the matrix of a set of linear forms is unique, $AP = I$. The transformation $Y = PX$ followed by the transformation $X = AY$ gives $Y = PAY = IY$. Thus $PA = I$. Suppose now that Q is a square matrix such that $QA = I$, then $P = IP = QAP = QI = Q$. Similarly, if

41

$AQ = I$, then $Q = P$. Hence, if A is nonsingular, there is a unique square matrix P such that $AP = PA = I$. Conversely, if there exists a matrix P such that $AP = I$, then $X = AY$ is solvable since $Y = PX$ is a solution and consequently A is nonsingular. We shall denote this P by A^I (read "A inverse") and call it the *inverse* of A.

THEOREM 3.1.2 *A square matrix A is nonsingular if and only if there exists a square matrix A^I such that $AA^I = A^IA = I$. The matrix A^I is unique.*

Let A and B be two nonsingular n-row matrices and write

(3.1.2) $$X = AY \quad \text{and} \quad Y = BZ.$$

Since both equations in (3.1.2) are solvable, we have

(3.1.3) $$Y = A^IX \quad \text{and} \quad Z = B^IY.$$

From (3.1.2), $X = ABZ$, and if we substitute $Z = B^IA^IX$ we get $X = ABB^IA^IX = AIA^IX = AA^IX = IX$. Hence $X = ABZ$ is solvable and consequently AB is nonsingular. Furthermore, if $(AB)^I$ denotes the inverse of AB, then $(AB)^I = B^IA^I$. This establishes

THEOREM 3.1.3 *The product of two nonsingular matrices is a nonsingular matrix, and the inverse of this product is the product of the inverses of the nonsingular matrices taken in reverse order.*

Let A be a nonsingular matrix. Then $AA^I = I = I^T = (AA^I)^T = (A^I)^TA^T$, and hence A^T is nonsingular. Furthermore, since the inverse of a nonsingular matrix is unique, $(A^T)^I = (A^I)^T$. There is no ambiguity in writing $(A^I)^T$ as A^{IT} and $(A^T)^I$ as A^{TI}, and we shall use the shorter notation hereafter. We have established

THEOREM 3.1.4 *The transpose of a nonsingular matrix, A, is nonsingular, and the inverse of the transpose of A is the transpose of the inverse of A.*

If all the elements of the ith row of a matrix A are zero, then it follows from the definition of the product of two matrices that all the elements of the ith row of AB are zero; and, if all the elements of the jth column of A are zero, then all the elements of the jth column of BA are zero. Since there is a nonzero element in each row and in each column of I, we have

THEOREM 3.1.5 *There is at least one nonzero element in each row and in each column of a nonsingular matrix.*

COROLLARY. *The zero matrix is singular.*

We now establish a theorem which will be found useful in much of the work to follow.

THEOREM 3.1.6　*If A is a matrix which can be regularly partitioned into a triangular block matrix, then A is nonsingular if and only if each diagonal block of A is nonsingular.*

It is sufficient to establish this theorem for a 2×2 block matrix since every regularly partitioned triangular block matrix, or its transpose, can be put in this form.

In the equation $X = AY$ we partition X into $\begin{pmatrix} X_1 \\ X_2 \end{pmatrix}$, A into $\begin{pmatrix} A_1 & A_3 \\ 0 & A_2 \end{pmatrix}$, and Y into $\begin{pmatrix} Y_1 \\ Y_2 \end{pmatrix}$, where X_i and Y_i have the same number of rows as A_i. Then $X = AY$ may be written

$$(3.1.4) \qquad \begin{pmatrix} X_1 \\ X_2 \end{pmatrix} = \begin{pmatrix} A_1 & A_3 \\ 0 & A_2 \end{pmatrix} \begin{pmatrix} Y_1 \\ Y_2 \end{pmatrix} = \begin{pmatrix} A_1 Y_1 + A_3 Y_2 \\ A_2 Y_2 \end{pmatrix},$$

from which it follows that

$$X_1 = A_1 Y_1 + A_3 Y_2,$$
$$X_2 = A_2 Y_2.$$

If A_2 is nonsingular, then $Y_2 = A_2^I X_2$ and consequently $X_1 = A_1 Y_1 + A_3 A_2^I X_2$, from which $A_1 Y_1 = X_1 - A_3 A_2^I X_2$. If A_1 is also nonsingular, then $Y_1 = A_1^I X_1 - A_1^I A_3 A_2^I X_2$. Thus, if both A_1 and A_2 are nonsingular, we have $Y = PX$ and $PA = I$, where

$$P = \begin{pmatrix} A_1^I & -A_1^I A_3 A_2^I \\ 0 & A_2^I \end{pmatrix}.$$

Hence (3.1.4) is solvable and A is nonsingular.

Conversely, if A is nonsingular there exists a matrix P such that $PA = I$. We partition P regularly in the same way as A and indicate this by

$$P = \begin{pmatrix} P_1 & P_2 \\ P_3 & P_4 \end{pmatrix}.$$

Then it follows that

$$PA = \begin{pmatrix} P_1 A_1 & P_1 A_3 + P_2 A_2 \\ P_3 A_1 & P_3 A_3 + P_4 A_2 \end{pmatrix} = \begin{pmatrix} I & 0 \\ 0 & I \end{pmatrix}.$$

Thus we have

(3.1.5) $$P_1 A_1 = I,$$

(3.1.6) $$P_1 A_3 + P_2 A_2 = 0,$$

(3.1.7) $$P_3 A_1 = 0,$$

(3.1.8) $$P_3 A_3 + P_4 A_2 = I.$$

From (3.1.5) it follows that A_1 is nonsingular and that $P_1 = A_1^I$. Multiplication of both members of (3.1.7) on the right by A_1^I gives $P_3 = 0$. Therefore (3.1.8) becomes $P_4 A_2 = I$. Hence A_2 is nonsingular and $A_2^I = P_4$. Now (3.1.6) becomes $A_1^I A_3 + P_2 A_2 = 0$, from which we get $P_2 = -A_1^I A_3 A_2^I$.

We have thus shown that, if A is nonsingular, then both A_1 and A_2 are nonsingular. Furthermore, we have determined A^I in terms of A_1^I, A_2^I, and A_3. This completes the proof of the theorem.

COROLLARY. *A triangular matrix is nonsingular if and only if its diagonal elements are all different from zero.*

COROLLARY. *The diagonal elements of the inverse of a nonsingular triangular matrix are the reciprocals of the corresponding elements of the triangular matrix.*

EXERCISES

1. Given the transformations

$$x_1 = 2y_1 + y_3, \qquad y_1 = z_1 - z_2 + 2z_3,$$

$$x_2 = y_1 + y_2, \quad \text{and} \quad y_2 = z_2 - z_3,$$

$$x_3 = y_2 - 2y_3, \qquad y_3 = z_3.$$

Substitute for the y_i in the first transformation the corresponding linear forms in the second transformation, thus obtaining the transformation giving x_1, x_2, x_3 as linear forms in z_1, z_2, z_3. Write these transformations as $X = AY$, $Y = BZ$, $X = CZ$ and verify that $C = AB$.

2. Given the transformation

$$x_1 = 2y_1 + y_2 - y_3,$$

$$x_2 = 2y_2 + 3y_3,$$

$$x_3 = 3y_3.$$

Solve for y_1, y_2, y_3 as linear forms in x_1, x_2, x_3. Write the transformations as $X = AY$ and $Y = PX$ and show that $PA = AP = I$.

   3. Given

$$A = \begin{pmatrix} 2 & 3 & -1 \\ 1 & 2 & 1 \\ 3 & 5 & 1 \end{pmatrix} \quad \text{and} \quad P = \begin{pmatrix} -3 & -8 & 5 \\ 2 & 5 & -3 \\ -1 & -1 & 1 \end{pmatrix}.$$

Show that $AP = PA = I$. Write the system of equations

$$2x + 3y - z = 1,$$
$$x + 2y + z = -2,$$
$$3x + 5y + z = 2$$

as an equation in matrices and show how the matrix P may be used to obtain the solution of the system.

   4. If A is a skew matrix and $I + A$ is nonsingular, show that $I - A$ is also nonsingular.

   5. If

$$B = \begin{pmatrix} 1 & -2 \\ 2 & 1 \end{pmatrix},$$

show that

$$B^I = \begin{pmatrix} \tfrac{1}{5} & \tfrac{2}{5} \\ -\tfrac{2}{5} & \tfrac{1}{5} \end{pmatrix}.$$

Also, show that $(B^I B^T)^T$ is the inverse of $B^I B^T$.

   6. If A is a matrix with the properties that $I + A$ is nonsingular and $AA^T = A^T A$, and if C denotes the matrix $(I + A)^I (I + A)^T$, then show that $C^T = C^I$. Note that $B - I$ in Exercise 5 satisfies the conditions imposed on A here.

   7. The matrix

$$A = \begin{pmatrix} 2 & 3 & 5 \\ 0 & 3 & -1 \\ 0 & 0 & -2 \end{pmatrix}$$

is nonsingular. Use the 3×3 matrix given by

$$P = \begin{pmatrix} x_1 & x_2 & x_3 \\ y_1 & y_2 & y_3 \\ z_1 & z_2 & z_3 \end{pmatrix}$$

and determine the elements of P so that $P = A^I$.

8. Let A be any nonsingular 3×3 triangular matrix, and show that A^I is a triangular matrix of the same type.

9. Given the block matrix

$$A = \begin{pmatrix} A_1 & A_4 & A_6 \\ 0 & A_2 & A_5 \\ 0 & 0 & A_3 \end{pmatrix},$$

where A_1, A_2, and A_3 are nonsingular matrices. Write

$$P = \begin{pmatrix} P_1 & P_2 & P_3 \\ P_4 & P_5 & P_6 \\ P_7 & P_8 & P_9 \end{pmatrix}$$

and determine the blocks in P so that $P = A^I$.

10. Show that the inverse of a nonsingular triangular matrix is a triangular matrix of the same type.

11. Let A be a triangular matrix with real elements such that $AA^T = A^TA$. Show that A must be a diagonal matrix.

3.2 Elementary Transformations and Elementary Matrices. If the equation $X = AY$ is solvable, then one method of solving is the process of elimination. Since A is nonsingular, there is a nonzero element, a_{k1}, in the first column of A. The transformation $U = PX$, given by

$$u_i = x_i \qquad (i \neq 1, k),$$

(3.2.1) $\qquad u_1 = x_k,$

$$u_k = x_1,$$

replaces the transformation $X = AY$ by the transformation

(3.2.2) $\qquad\qquad\qquad U = BY,$

where $B = PA = (b_{ij})$. The transformation (3.2.1) is obviously non-singular, and hence B is nonsingular and $b_{11} = a_{k1} \neq 0$. The transformation $V = QU$, given by

$$v_1 = \frac{1}{b_{11}} u_1,$$

(3.2.3)

$$v_i = u_i \qquad (i \neq 1),$$

is nonsingular and replaces (3.2.2) by

(3.2.4) $\qquad\qquad\qquad V = CY,$

where $C = QB = (c_{ij})$. The transformation (3.2.4) is nonsingular and $c_{11} = 1$. The transformation $W = RV$, given by

(3.2.5)
$$w_1 = v_1,$$
$$w_i = v_i - c_{i1}v_1 \qquad (i \neq 1),$$

is nonsingular and replaces (3.2.4) by

(3.2.6)
$$W = DY,$$

where $D = RC = (d_{ij})$ is nonsingular. We see that $d_{11} = 1$ and $d_{i1} = 0$ for $i \neq 1$. Retracing our steps, we have $D = RC = RQB = RQPA$. Now, setting $T_1 = RQP$, we have

(3.2.7)
$$D = T_1 A = \begin{pmatrix} 1 & D_1 \\ 0 & D_2 \end{pmatrix}.$$

Since D is a nonsingular triangular block matrix, the matrix D_2 is non-singular. The same process may now be applied to the last $n - 1$ equations of the system (3.2.6). Continuing, we ultimately obtain one equation in one unknown, and this equation can be solved. Assuming that the last $n - 1$ equations of (3.2.6) are solved for $y_2, y_3, \ldots, y_n$ as linear forms in $w_2, w_3, \ldots, w_n$, these forms may be substituted into the first equation to obtain y_1 as a linear form in $w_1, w_2, \ldots, w_n$. But $W = RV = RQU = RQPX$, so that linear forms in $w_1, w_2, \ldots, w_n$ are also linear forms in $x_1, x_2, \ldots, x_n$. This gives $y_1, y_2, \ldots, y_n$ as linear forms in $x_1, x_2, \ldots, x_n$.

It is desirable to designate, by special names, certain types of linear transformations used in this process.

DEFINITION. *A linear transformation and its matrix will be called elementary if it is one of the following types:*

Type 1: $x_i = y_i \qquad (i \neq j, k)$,

$x_j = y_k,$

$x_k = y_j;$

Type 2: $x_i = y_i \qquad (i \neq j)$,

$x_j = y_j + cy_k$, where c is any number;

Type 3: $x_i = y_i \qquad (i \neq j)$,

$x_j = ty_j \qquad (t \neq 0)$.

It is obvious that each of these transformations is nonsingular. We shall find it more descriptive to refer to these types as permutative, additive, and multiplicative, respectively. Thus transformation (3.2.1) is an elementary permutative transformation, and transformation (3.2.3) is an elementary multiplicative transformation.

We observe that an elementary permutative matrix is one obtained from the identity matrix by the interchange of two rows (columns); an elementary additive matrix is one obtained from the identity matrix by adding to one row (column) a constant multiple of another row (column); and an elementary multiplicative matrix is one obtained from the identity matrix by multiplying a row (column) by a nonzero constant.

Illustration: The matrices

$$\begin{pmatrix} 1 & 0 & 0 \\ 0 & t & 0 \\ 0 & 0 & 1 \end{pmatrix} \text{ for } t \neq 0, \qquad \begin{pmatrix} 1 & 0 & c \\ 0 & 1 & 0 \\ 0 & 0 & 1 \end{pmatrix}, \quad \text{and} \quad \begin{pmatrix} 1 & 0 & 0 \\ 0 & 0 & 1 \\ 0 & 1 & 0 \end{pmatrix}$$

are elementary matrices. The first may be obtained from the identity matrix by multiplying the second row or the second column by $t \neq 0$. The second one may be obtained from the identity matrix by adding c times the third row to the first row or by adding c times the first column to the third column. The third one may be obtained from the identity matrix by interchanging the second and third rows or by interchanging the second and third columns. Also, the matrix

$$\begin{pmatrix} I_s & 0 & 0 \\ 0 & U & 0 \\ 0 & 0 & I_t \end{pmatrix}$$

is elementary if and only if U is elementary, as may be readily verified.

The transformation (3.2.5) is not an elementary transformation but has the same effect as applying a sequence of elementary additive transformations. Hence the matrix of (3.2.5) is a product of elementary matrices. Thus we see from (3.2.7) that, if A is a nonsingular matrix, there exists a matrix T_1 which is a product of elementary matrices and is such that

$$T_1 A = \begin{pmatrix} 1 & D_1 \\ 0 & D_2 \end{pmatrix}.$$

Assume now that there exists a matrix T_k which is a product of elementary matrices and such that

$$T_k A = \begin{pmatrix} I_k & A_1 \\ 0 & A_2 \end{pmatrix}.$$

Since T_kA is nonsingular, the matrix A_2 is nonsingular. Therefore there exists a matrix U_1 which is a product of elementary matrices and is such that

$$U_1A_2 = \begin{pmatrix} 1 & A_3 \\ 0 & A_4 \end{pmatrix}.$$

Then, writing

$$U = \begin{pmatrix} I_k & 0 \\ 0 & U_1 \end{pmatrix} \quad \text{and} \quad H = UT_kA,$$

we have

$$H = \begin{pmatrix} I_k & 0 \\ 0 & U_1 \end{pmatrix} \begin{pmatrix} I_k & A_1 \\ 0 & A_2 \end{pmatrix} = \begin{pmatrix} I_k & A_1 \\ 0 & U_1A_2 \end{pmatrix}.$$

Replacing U_1A_2 by its value above, we have

$$H = UT_kA = \begin{pmatrix} I_k & B_1 & B_2 \\ 0 & 1 & A_3 \\ 0 & 0 & A_4 \end{pmatrix},$$

where B_1 is the first column of A_1 and B_2 is the remaining columns of A_1. We write $B_1 = (b_i)$ $(i = 1, 2, \ldots, k)$. Now consider the transformation $W = HY$ and make the transformation $Z = GW$, given by

$$(3.2.8) \quad \begin{aligned} z_i &= w_i - b_iw_k + 1 & (i = 1, 2, \ldots, k), \\ z_i &= w_i & (i = k + 1, \ldots, n), \end{aligned}$$

which has the same effect as a sequence of elementary additive transformations. This gives $Z = GHY$, where

$$GH = \left(\begin{array}{cc|c} I_k & 0 & B_3 \\ 0 & 1 & A_3 \\ \hline 0 & 0 & A_4 \end{array} \right) = \begin{pmatrix} I_{k+1} & B_4 \\ 0 & A_4 \end{pmatrix}.$$

If we now define T_{k+1} to be GUT_k, then $GH = T_{k+1}A$. Thus by induction we have shown that, for a given nonsingular matrix A, there exists a matrix T_n, which is a product of elementary matrices, such that $T_nA = I$.

Each elementary matrix has an inverse which is an elementary matrix; consequently from $A = T_n^I$ it follows that A is a product of elementary matrices. We have established

THEOREM 3.2.1 *Every nonsingular matrix is a product of elementary matrices.*

We have used three elementary transformations here as a matter of convenience. That two of these would suffice is a consequence of

THEOREM 3.2.2 *An elementary permutative matrix is a product of elementary additive matrices and elementary multiplicative matrices.*

An elementary matrix coincides with the identity matrix except for, at most, two rows and two columns. Hence it is sufficient to establish theorem 3.2.2 for 2×2 matrices.

The elementary matrices of two rows are as follows:

$$\begin{pmatrix} 0 & 1 \\ 1 & 0 \end{pmatrix} \quad \text{(permutative)},$$

$$(3.2.9) \qquad \begin{pmatrix} 1 & c \\ 0 & 1 \end{pmatrix} \quad \text{or} \quad \begin{pmatrix} 1 & 0 \\ c & 1 \end{pmatrix} \quad \text{(additive)},$$

and

$$\begin{pmatrix} t & 0 \\ 0 & 1 \end{pmatrix} \quad \text{or} \quad \begin{pmatrix} 1 & 0 \\ 0 & t \end{pmatrix}, \qquad t \neq 0 \text{ (multiplicative)}.$$

It may be readily verified that

$$(3.2.10) \qquad \begin{pmatrix} 0 & 1 \\ 1 & 0 \end{pmatrix} = \begin{pmatrix} 1 & -1 \\ 0 & 1 \end{pmatrix} \begin{pmatrix} 1 & 0 \\ 1 & 1 \end{pmatrix} \begin{pmatrix} 1 & -1 \\ 0 & 1 \end{pmatrix} \begin{pmatrix} 1 & 0 \\ 0 & -1 \end{pmatrix}.$$

In the right member of (3.2.10) the first three matrices are additive and the fourth is multiplicative. This completes the proof of the theorem.

The fact that the elementary permutative matrix may be expressed as a product of elementary additive and elementary multiplicative matrices in several ways shows that the representation of an elementary permutative matrix in this manner is not unique.

EXERCISES

1. Write the inverse of each elementary matrix in (3.2.9) and show that it is elementary.

2. State how each elementary matrix in (3.2.9) may be obtained from the identity matrix by one operation on the rows; also by one operation on the columns.

3. Write

$$A = \begin{pmatrix} p & q \\ r & s \end{pmatrix}.$$

Multiply A on the left (right) by each elementary matrix in (3.2.9) and, in each case, state the effect on the rows (columns) of A.

4. Given

$$A = \begin{pmatrix} 2 & 3 \\ 5 & 7 \end{pmatrix} \quad \text{and} \quad B = \begin{pmatrix} 7 & 10 \\ 5 & 7 \end{pmatrix},$$

find E so that $EA = B$. Is E an elementary matrix?

5. Write the elementary permutative matrix

$$\begin{pmatrix} 1 & 0 & 0 & 0 \\ 0 & 0 & 0 & 1 \\ 0 & 0 & 1 & 0 \\ 0 & 1 & 0 & 0 \end{pmatrix}$$

as a product of elementary additive and elementary multiplicative matrices by using (3.2.10).

6. Show how the relation (3.2.10) may be used to write the general elementary permutative matrix as a product of three additive and one multiplicative elementary matrix.

7. Find a representation of

$$\begin{pmatrix} 0 & 1 \\ 1 & 0 \end{pmatrix}$$

as a product of four elementary additive and multiplicative matrices other than the one given in (3.2.10).

8. Solve for x, y, u, and v in the equation

$$\begin{pmatrix} x & y \\ u & v \end{pmatrix} \begin{pmatrix} 2 & 3 \\ 5 & 7 \end{pmatrix} = \begin{pmatrix} 1 & 0 \\ 0 & 1 \end{pmatrix}.$$

9. If A is a nonsingular matrix, how may A^I be used to determine X and Y such that $XA = B$ and $AY = B$?

CHAPTER 4

BILINEAR FORMS AND THE RANK OF A MATRIX

4.1 Bilinear Forms. Let $X = (x_i)$ and $Y = (y_j)$ $(i = 1, 2, \ldots, m;$ $j = 1, 2, \ldots, n)$ be one-column matrices and let $A = (a_{ij}) \neq 0$ be an $m \times n$ matrix. Then the 1×1 matrix $X^T A Y$ is called a *bilinear form* in the sets of variables $x_1, x_2, \ldots, x_m$ and $y_1, y_2, \ldots, y_n$. If we now indicate this bilinear form by f, we have

$$(4.1.1) \qquad f = X^T A Y = \sum_{i=1}^{m} \sum_{j=1}^{n} a_{ij} x_i y_j.$$

The form (4.1.1) may be written as a linear form in either of the sets with the coefficients linear forms in the other set. For example, the right member may be written

$$\sum_{i=1}^{m} \left(\sum_{j=1}^{n} a_{ij} y_j \right) x_i = \sum_{i=1}^{m} t_i x_i,$$

where

$$t_i = \sum_{j=1}^{n} a_{ij} y_j.$$

We also note that we may write the bilinear form f in the following way:

$$f = \sum_{j=1}^{n} \sum_{i=1}^{m} a_{ij} x_i y_j = \sum_{j=1}^{n} \left(\sum_{i=1}^{m} a_{ij} x_i \right) y_j.$$

Since f is a 1×1 matrix, we have $f = f^T = (X^T A Y)^T = Y^T A^T X$. That is, $X^T A Y$ and $Y^T A^T X$ are identical expressions except, perhaps, for the arrangement of the terms.

Since the form f may be written as a product of matrices in two different ways, it is clear that f could be associated with either the matrix A or the matrix A^T. However, it is customary to write f as $X^T A Y$ and to define A to be the *matrix of the form*.

Let us subject X and Y to nonsingular linear transformations $X = PU$ and $Y = QV$, where $U = (u_i)$ and $V = (v_j)$. Then the bilinear form f is transformed into the bilinear form $U^T P^T A Q V = U^T B V$, where B denotes $P^T A Q$. If we now apply the linear transformations $U = IX$, $V = IY$, we get a bilinear form $g = X^T BY$. The relationship between the bilinear forms f and g is expressed in the following definition.

DEFINITION. *A bilinear form $g = X^T BY$ is said to be equivalent to the bilinear form $f = X^T A Y$ if and only if f may be transformed into g by nonsingular linear transformation.*

Since all nonsingular linear transformations have inverses, it follows that g is equivalent to f if and only if f is equivalent to g. Hence we may simply say that f and g are equivalent and we write $f \overset{E}{=} g$. That $f \overset{E}{=} f$ follows by taking $P = I$ and $Q = I$ in the above. Also, if $f \overset{E}{=} g$ and $g \overset{E}{=} h$, then $f \overset{E}{=} h$ follows from the fact that the result of a sequence of nonsingular linear transformations is a nonsingular linear transformation. These properties are called *equivalence properties*. A relation is called an equivalence relation if it possesses the following properties:

Determinative: Either p is in relation to q or p is not in relation to q.

Reflexive: p is in relation to p for all p.

Symmetric: p in relation to q implies q in relation to p.

Transitive: p in relation to q and q in relation to r implies p in relation to r.

The student is familiar with numerous relations between mathematical elements such as "*is equal to*," "*is greater than*," "*is not equal to*," "*is congruent to*," "*is similar to*," and "*is a factor of*." Some of these are equivalence relations and some are not. For example, "is greater than" is both determinative and transitive but is neither symmetric nor reflexive and hence is not an equivalence relation. However, "is similar to" as applied to triangles is an equivalence relation.

DEFINITION. *Two $m \times n$ matrices are defined to be equivalent if their corresponding bilinear forms are equivalent.*

It follows that two $m \times n$ matrices, A and B, are equivalent if and only if there exist two nonsingular matrices, P and Q, such that $PAQ = B$. It is sometimes more convenient to indicate this relationship by $PA = BQ^I$. If A and B are equivalent, we write $A \overset{E}{=} B$.

THEOREM 4.1.1   *If $A_1 \overset{E}{=} B_1$ and $A_2 \overset{E}{=} B_2$, then*

$$\begin{pmatrix} A_1 & 0 \\ 0 & A_2 \end{pmatrix} \overset{E}{=} \begin{pmatrix} B_1 & 0 \\ 0 & B_2 \end{pmatrix}.$$

Since $A_1 \overset{E}{=} B_1$ and $A_2 \overset{E}{=} B_2$, there exist nonsingular matrices P_1, Q_1, P_2, and Q_2 such that $P_1 A_1 Q_1 = B_1$ and $P_2 A_2 Q_2 = B_2$. Then, by theorem 3.1.6 (Chapter 3),

$$\begin{pmatrix} P_1 & 0 \\ 0 & P_2 \end{pmatrix} \quad \text{and} \quad \begin{pmatrix} Q_1 & 0 \\ 0 & Q_2 \end{pmatrix}$$

are nonsingular and

$$\begin{pmatrix} P_1 & 0 \\ 0 & P_2 \end{pmatrix} \begin{pmatrix} A_1 & 0 \\ 0 & A_2 \end{pmatrix} \begin{pmatrix} Q_1 & 0 \\ 0 & Q_2 \end{pmatrix} = \begin{pmatrix} B_1 & 0 \\ 0 & B_2 \end{pmatrix}.$$

This completes the proof of theorem 4.1.1.

For future reference we state the corresponding theorem for bilinear forms. Let $f_1 = X_1^T A_1 Y_1$ and $g_1 = X_1^T B_1 Y_1$, where $X_1 = (x_i)$ and $Y_1 = (y_j)$ $(i = 1, 2, \ldots, s; j = 1, 2, \ldots, t)$, be equivalent bilinear forms and let $f_2 = X_2^T A_2 Y_2$ and $g_2 = X_2^T B_2 Y_2$, where $X_2 = (x_k)$ and $Y_2 = (y_l)$ $(k = s + 1, \ldots, m; l = t + 1, \ldots, n)$, be equivalent bilinear forms. Then

$$f = f_1 + f_2 = (X_1 \quad X_2) \begin{pmatrix} A_1 & 0 \\ 0 & A_2 \end{pmatrix} \begin{pmatrix} Y_1 \\ Y_2 \end{pmatrix}$$

and

$$g = g_1 + g_2 = (X_1 \quad X_2) \begin{pmatrix} B_1 & 0 \\ 0 & B_2 \end{pmatrix} \begin{pmatrix} Y_1 \\ Y_2 \end{pmatrix}$$

are equivalent bilinear forms.

We return now to the general bilinear form $f = X^T A Y$. If $A \neq 0$, it contains some nonzero element, say a_{st}. The nonsingular linear transformations

$$x_1 = u_s, \qquad\qquad y_1 = v_t,$$

(4.1.2) $\qquad x_s = \dfrac{1}{a_{st}} u_1, \qquad \text{and} \quad y_t = v_1,$

$$x_i = u_i \quad (i \neq 1, s) \qquad y_j = v_j \quad (j \neq 1, t)$$

transform $f = X^T A Y$ into $g = U^T B V$, where $b_{11} = 1$ in the matrix $B = (b_{ij})$. The nonsingular linear transformations

$$u_1 = x_1 - \sum_{i=2}^{m} b_{i1} x_i, \qquad v_1 = y_1 - \sum_{j=2}^{n} b_{1j} y_j,$$

(4.1.3) $\qquad\qquad\qquad\qquad \text{and}$

$$u_i = x_i \quad (i \neq 1) \qquad v_j = y_j \quad (j \neq 1)$$

transform g into

(4.1.4) $\qquad\qquad\qquad h = x_1 y_1 + f_1,$

where f_1 is either 0 or is a bilinear form in $x_2, x_3, \ldots, x_m; y_2, y_3, \ldots, y_n$. This establishes the following

LEMMA 4.1.1 *A bilinear form f in $x_1, x_2, \ldots, x_m$ and $y_1, y_2, \ldots, y_n$ is equivalent to $x_1y_1 + f_1$, where f_1 is either zero or a bilinear form in $x_2, x_3, \ldots, x_m$ and $y_2, y_3, \ldots, y_n$.*

Assume now that the bilinear form f is equivalent to $x_1y_1 + x_2y_2 + \cdots + x_ky_k + f_k$, $k \leq \min(m, n)$, where f_k is either zero or is a bilinear form in $x_{k+1}, \ldots, x_m$ and $y_{k+1}, \ldots, y_n$. If $f_k \neq 0$, it follows, from lemma 4.1.1, that f_k is equivalent to $x_{k+1}y_{k+1} + f_{k+1}$. Hence f is equivalent to $x_1y_1 + x_2y_2 + \cdots + x_{k+1}y_{k+1} + f_{k+1}$. If $f_{k+1} \neq 0$, the process may be repeated. However, $f_l = 0$ for some $l \leq \min(m, n)$ and the process terminates. Thus we have

THEOREM 4.1.2 *Every bilinear form in $x_1, x_2, \ldots, x_m$ and $y_1, y_2, \ldots, y_n$ is equivalent to $x_1y_1 + x_2y_2 + \cdots + x_ry_r$ for some r.*

The corresponding theorem for matrices is stated as

THEOREM 4.1.3 *Every nonzero $m \times n$ matrix is equivalent to a matrix of one of the following types:*

$$(4.1.5) \qquad \begin{pmatrix} I_r & 0 \\ 0 & 0 \end{pmatrix}, \qquad (I_m \quad 0), \qquad \begin{pmatrix} I_n \\ 0 \end{pmatrix}, \qquad I.$$

EXERCISES

1. Write the following bilinear forms as $X^T A Y$:

(a) $2x_1y_1 + 2x_1y_2 + x_2y_1 + x_2y_2,$
(b) $x_1y_2 - x_2y_3 + x_3y_1,$
(c) $x_1y_2 - 2x_1y_3 + x_2y_1.$

2. Write the product $Y^T A^T X$ for each form in Exercise 1 and perform the multiplication to show that, in each case, $Y^T A^T X = X^T A Y$.

3. Apply the steps used in proving theorem 4.1.2 to each bilinear form in Exercise 1 and obtain the equivalent form as given in theorem 4.1.2. Write matrices P and Q in each case so that PAQ will be in form (4.1.5).

4. Write

$$f = \sum_{i=1}^{3} \sum_{j=1}^{4} a_{ij} x_i y_j$$

as a linear form in x_1, x_2, x_3 with coefficients linear forms in y_1, y_2, y_3, y_4 and show that this is the same as $X^T(AY)$. Also, expand $X^T A Y$ by grouping it as $(X^T A)Y$ and expand $Y^T A^T X$ as $(Y^T A^T)X$ and as $Y^T(A^T X)$. Show that each of these expansions may be obtained by grouping the terms of f in a particular way.

5. Is the relation "is a factor of" an equivalence relation when applied to (a) nonzero elements of a field $\mathcal{F}$? (b) polynomials in x with coefficients in a field $\mathcal{F}$? (c) polynomials of degree 3 in x with coefficients in a field $\mathcal{F}$? Give reasons in each case.

6. Are the matrices A and B equivalent if there exist matrices P, Q such that $PA = QB$? Do the matrices given by

$$P = \begin{pmatrix} 1 & 0 & 0 \\ 0 & 1 & 1 \\ 1 & 0 & 0 \end{pmatrix}, \quad Q = \begin{pmatrix} 1 & 0 & 0 \\ 0 & 0 & 1 \\ 0 & 1 & 0 \end{pmatrix}, \quad A = \begin{pmatrix} 0 & 0 & 0 \\ 0 & 1 & 0 \\ 0 & 0 & 1 \end{pmatrix}, \quad B = \begin{pmatrix} 0 & 0 & 0 \\ 0 & 0 & 0 \\ 0 & 1 & 1 \end{pmatrix}$$

serve as an illustration?

4.2 Rank of a Matrix. We now establish a necessary and sufficient condition for two $m \times n$ matrices to be equivalent. First we prove

LEMMA 4.2.1 *If*

$$A = \begin{pmatrix} I_r & 0 \\ 0 & A_1 \end{pmatrix} \quad and \quad B = \begin{pmatrix} I_r & 0 \\ 0 & 0 \end{pmatrix}$$

are equivalent, then $A_1 = 0$ *and* $A = B$.

Let P and Q be nonsingular matrices such that $PA = BQ$. Partition P and Q regularly so that block multiplication of PA and BQ is defined. Then

$$PA = \begin{pmatrix} P_1 & P_2 \\ P_3 & P_4 \end{pmatrix}\begin{pmatrix} I_r & 0 \\ 0 & A_1 \end{pmatrix} = \begin{pmatrix} P_1 & P_2 A_1 \\ P_3 & P_4 A_1 \end{pmatrix}$$

and

$$BQ = \begin{pmatrix} I_r & 0 \\ 0 & 0 \end{pmatrix}\begin{pmatrix} Q_1 & Q_2 \\ Q_3 & Q_4 \end{pmatrix} = \begin{pmatrix} Q_1 & Q_2 \\ 0 & 0 \end{pmatrix}$$

and hence $P_3 = 0$. Therefore P is a nonsingular triangular block matrix. Hence P_4 is nonsingular and consequently $P_4 A_1 = 0$ implies that $A_1 = 0$.

As an immediate consequence of lemma 4.2.1, we have

THEOREM 4.2.1 *The bilinear forms* $x_1 y_1 + x_2 y_2 + \cdots + x_r y_r$ *and* $x_1 y_1 + x_2 y_2 + \cdots + x_s y_s$ *are equivalent if and only if* $r = s$.

Thus we see that there is a unique matrix of one of the types in (4.1.5) equivalent to every nonzero $m \times n$ matrix. This matrix is determined by the number, r, of ones appearing in the diagonal.

DEFINITION. *If A is a nonzero $m \times n$ matrix, the number of ones appearing in the equivalent matrix of type (4.1.5) is called the rank of A and also the rank of the bilinear form associated with A.*

The rank of the zero matrix is defined to be zero, and we have

THEOREM 4.2.2 *Two $m \times n$ matrices are equivalent if and only if they have the same rank.*

This theorem classifies all $m \times n$ matrices into sets of equivalent matrices. The number of such sets is one greater than the smaller of the numbers m and n. That is, if $n > m$, then r may assume all the values $0, 1, 2, \ldots, m$. The particular matrix of the type in (4.1.5) may be taken as the *representative* of the class, and we shall call it the *rank canonical* matrix of the class.

Illustration: Every 3×5 matrix is equivalent to one of the following:

$$C_0 = \begin{pmatrix} 0 & 0 & 0 & 0 & 0 \\ 0 & 0 & 0 & 0 & 0 \\ 0 & 0 & 0 & 0 & 0 \end{pmatrix}, \qquad C_1 = \begin{pmatrix} 1 & 0 & 0 & 0 & 0 \\ 0 & 0 & 0 & 0 & 0 \\ 0 & 0 & 0 & 0 & 0 \end{pmatrix},$$

$$C_2 = \begin{pmatrix} 1 & 0 & 0 & 0 & 0 \\ 0 & 1 & 0 & 0 & 0 \\ 0 & 0 & 0 & 0 & 0 \end{pmatrix}, \qquad C_3 = \begin{pmatrix} 1 & 0 & 0 & 0 & 0 \\ 0 & 1 & 0 & 0 & 0 \\ 0 & 0 & 1 & 0 & 0 \end{pmatrix}.$$

The symbol C_r, as used in the illustration above, will be used to denote the rank canonical matrix of a set of equivalent matrices of rank r. In most cases the context will indicate the dimensions of the matrix C_r. Whenever it is necessary to call attention to the dimensions of the matrix, this will be done in some appropriate manner. If C_r is an $m \times n$ matrix, then C_r^T is an $n \times m$ matrix which is the rank canonical matrix for the set of $n \times m$ matrices of rank r.

If A is an $m \times n$ matrix of rank r and $PAQ = C_r$, then $Q^T A^T P^T = C_r^T$. Consequently, A^T is of rank r. That is, the rank of A^T is always the same as the rank of A.

It may readily be shown for

$$A = \begin{pmatrix} A_1 & 0 \\ 0 & A_2 \end{pmatrix}$$

that the rank of A is the sum of the ranks of A_1 and A_2. The rank of A is often written $r(A)$, and we would write this result as $r(A) = r(A_1) + r(A_2)$. Let B be the diagonal block matrix

$$\begin{pmatrix} B_1 & 0 \\ 0 & B_2 \end{pmatrix}.$$

If any two of the matrices A, A_1, A_2 are equivalent respectively to the corresponding two of the matrices B, B_1, B_2, then the remaining matrix in the first set is equivalent to the remaining matrix in the second set.

If P and Q are nonsingular, then both PA and AQ are equivalent to A, and we state this as

THEOREM 4.2.3   *If A is multiplied on either side by a nonsingular matrix, the product has the same rank as A.*

We now investigate the rank of AB when A is of rank r and B is of rank s. Let P and Q be nonsingular matrices such that $PAQ = C_r$. The matrices AB and PAB have the same rank. But

$$PAB = C_r Q^I B = \begin{pmatrix} B_1 \\ 0 \end{pmatrix},$$

where B_1 is the first r rows of $Q^I B$. Hence the rank of AB is the same as the rank of B_1 and cannot exceed r. Similarly, the rank of AB cannot exceed the rank of B. This establishes

THEOREM 4.2.4   *The rank of the product of two matrices cannot exceed the rank of either matrix.*

EXERCISES

1. Write the rank canonical matrices for 3×3 matrices.

2. Write the rank canonical matrices for all 2×4 matrices and also for all 4×2 matrices.

3. Prove that the rank of

$$\begin{pmatrix} B_1 \\ 0 \end{pmatrix}$$

is the same as the rank of B_1.

4. If A_1 is of rank r_1 and A_2 is of rank r_2 and

$$A = \begin{pmatrix} A_1 & 0 \\ 0 & A_2 \end{pmatrix},$$

prove that A is of rank $r_1 + r_2$.

5. Extend the result of Exercise 4 to determine the rank of $A = $ diag. $\{A_1, A_2, \ldots, A_k\}$ where A_i is of rank r_i $(i = 1, 2, \ldots, k)$.

6. Let $P = $ diag. $\{P_1, P_2, \ldots, P_k\}$ and $Q = $ diag. $\{Q_1, Q_2, \ldots, Q_l\}$ be nonsingular matrices and let $A = (a_{ij})$ be partitioned into $A = (A_{\alpha\beta})$ $(\alpha = 1, 2, \ldots, k; \beta = 1, 2, \ldots, l)$ in such a way that $P_\alpha A_{\alpha\beta} Q_\beta$ is defined. If $PAQ = B$, and B is partitioned, in the same way as A, into $(B_{\alpha\beta})$, then is $B_{\alpha\beta}$ equivalent to $A_{\alpha\beta}$?

7. Prove that the rank of a matrix is not changed by the multiplication by a nonsingular matrix.

8. Prove that the rank of the matrix A is unique.

9. If a matrix contains a nonzero element, show that its rank cannot be zero.

10. If A is a $1 \times n$ matrix and B is an $n \times 1$ matrix, what limitations can be placed on $r(AB)$ and $r(BA)$?

4.3   Elementary Row and Column Transformations on a Matrix.   We have seen that two $m \times n$ matrices are equivalent if and only if they have the same rank.   Hence one method of establishing equivalence is to determine the rank canonical matrix of each.   This may be accomplished by multiplying each matrix on the left and right by a sequence of elementary matrices.

DEFINITION.   *The effect of multiplying a matrix, A, on the left (right) by an elementary matrix is called an elementary row (column) transformation on A.*

This effect is given by the following three theorems.   The proofs of these theorems are left as exercises.

THEOREM 4.3.1   *If A is multiplied on the left (right) by an elementary permutative matrix, the effect is to interchange two rows (columns) of A.*

THEOREM 4.3.2   *If A is multiplied on the left (right) by an elementary multiplicative matrix, the effect is to multiply each element of a row (column) of A by a nonzero number.*

THEOREM 4.3.3   *If A is multiplied on the left (right) by an elementary additive matrix, the effect is to add to a row (column) a multiple of another row (column).*

Thus, as we have seen under the definition of elementary matrix, an elementary matrix of each type is the result of making the corresponding *elementary row (column) transformation on I.*   From these results, the following condition for equivalence of two $m \times n$ matrices may be readily established.

THEOREM 4.3.4   *Two $m \times n$ matrices, A and B, are equivalent if and only if B may be obtained by applying a finite number of elementary row and column transformations on A.*

The above theorems (4.3.1, 4.3.2, 4.3.3, and 4.3.4) suggest a convenient method for determining the C_r for a given matrix A.   By this method, we also determine nonsingular matrices, P and Q, such that $PAQ = C_r$.

To establish this method we consider the $(m + n) \times (m + n)$ matrix, M, which may be written as the 2×2 block matrix,

$$M = \begin{pmatrix} I_m & A \\ 0 & I_n \end{pmatrix},$$

having the given matrix A in the upper right corner. The matrix M is equivalent to the matrix N, where

$$N = \begin{pmatrix} P & 0 \\ 0 & I_n \end{pmatrix} \begin{pmatrix} I_m & A \\ 0 & I_n \end{pmatrix} \begin{pmatrix} I_m & 0 \\ 0 & Q \end{pmatrix} = \begin{pmatrix} P & C_r \\ 0 & Q \end{pmatrix},$$

and where P and Q are any nonsingular matrices such that $PAQ = C_r$. The transformation from M to N may be accomplished by making elementary row transformations on the first m rows of M and elementary column transformations on the last n columns of M, thus replacing A by C_r. This method provides a convenient way for recording these row and column transformations, giving matrices P and Q such that $PAQ = C_r$. In particular, if A is nonsingular, then $PAQ = I$. From this it follows that $A = P^I Q^I$, and consequently A^I may be computed at once since $A^I = QP$.

Illustration: We now compute the C_r for the matrix A given by

$$A = \begin{pmatrix} 1 & 2 & 1 \\ 2 & 4 & 3 \end{pmatrix}.$$

$$M = \begin{pmatrix} I_2 & A \\ 0 & I_3 \end{pmatrix} = \left(\begin{array}{cc|ccc} 1 & 0 & 1 & 2 & 1 \\ 0 & 1 & 2 & 4 & 3 \\ \hline 0 & 0 & 1 & 0 & 0 \\ 0 & 0 & 0 & 1 & 0 \\ 0 & 0 & 0 & 0 & 1 \end{array} \right).$$

Subtract two times the first row from the second row; in the resulting matrix, interchange the fourth and fifth columns; in the matrix thus obtained, subtract the third column from the fourth and two times the third column from the fifth column. By these transformations, a matrix N of the type above is obtained and is given by

$$N = \left(\begin{array}{cc|ccc} 1 & 0 & 1 & 0 & 0 \\ -2 & 1 & 0 & 1 & 0 \\ \hline 0 & 0 & 1 & -1 & -2 \\ 0 & 0 & 0 & 0 & 1 \\ 0 & 0 & 0 & 1 & 0 \end{array} \right) = \begin{pmatrix} P & C_2 \\ 0 & Q \end{pmatrix}.$$

Hence

$$PAQ = \begin{pmatrix} 1 & 0 \\ -2 & 1 \end{pmatrix} \begin{pmatrix} 1 & 2 & 1 \\ 2 & 4 & 3 \end{pmatrix} \begin{pmatrix} 1 & -1 & -2 \\ 0 & 0 & 1 \\ 0 & 1 & 0 \end{pmatrix} = \begin{pmatrix} 1 & 0 & 0 \\ 0 & 1 & 0 \end{pmatrix} = C_2.$$

Note that, at each stage, the elementary transformation is applied to the matrix which was obtained by the preceding transformation. Obviously, other transformations might have been made to get a matrix of the same type as N above. In such a case, different matrices P and Q may have been obtained. In fact, in this case we may use only column transformations and thus obtain

$$P = I, \qquad Q = \begin{pmatrix} 3 & -1 & -2 \\ 0 & 0 & 1 \\ -2 & 1 & 0 \end{pmatrix}.$$

If A and B are equivalent matrices, we may wish to determine non-singular matrices P and Q such that $PAQ = B$. To do this, we determine nonsingular matrices R and S such that $RAS = C_r$ and nonsingular matrices U and V such that $UBV = C_r$. Then, from $RAS = UBV$, it follows that $U^I RAS V^I = B$. Hence we may use $P = U^I R$ and $Q = SV^I$.

EXERCISES

1. State the elementary row transformation which must be made on I to obtain each of the following elementary matrices.

$$E_1 = \begin{pmatrix} 0 & 1 & 0 \\ 1 & 0 & 0 \\ 0 & 0 & 1 \end{pmatrix}, \qquad E_2 = \begin{pmatrix} 1 & 0 & 0 \\ 0 & 1 & 0 \\ 2 & 0 & 1 \end{pmatrix},$$

$$E_3 = \begin{pmatrix} 1 & 0 & 0 \\ 0 & 3 & 0 \\ 0 & 0 & 1 \end{pmatrix}, \qquad E_4 = \begin{pmatrix} 0 & 0 & 1 \\ 0 & 1 & 0 \\ 1 & 0 & 0 \end{pmatrix}.$$

2. State the elementary column transformation which must be made on I to obtain each of the matrices in Exercise 1.

3. Given a matrix A, defined by

$$A = \begin{pmatrix} 2 & 3 & 1 \\ 0 & -1 & -5 \\ -2 & 7 & 0 \end{pmatrix}.$$

Compute E_iA and AE_i for each matrix E_i in Exercise 1. In each case state the elementary row or column transformation which could have been made on A to obtain the resulting matrix.

4. Prove theorems 4.3.1, 4.3.2, 4.3.3, and 4.3.4.

5. Use the method described and illustrated above to find the C_r which is equivalent to A, A being the matrix

$$\begin{pmatrix} 1 & 2 & 3 & -1 \\ -1 & -3 & 2 & 0 \end{pmatrix}.$$

Verify that the matrices P and Q thus obtained are such that $PAQ = C_r$.

6. Use the method above to find the C_r which is equivalent to

$$A = \begin{pmatrix} 2 & 3 \\ 5 & 7 \end{pmatrix},$$

thus showing that A is nonsingular. Verify that $QP = A^I$. Show by using elementary row transformations only that you get $Q = I$ and $P = A^I$.

7. Using the matrices P, Q, and A, of Exercise 6, show that $Q^TA^TP^T = I$.

8. Prove that any nonsingular matrix may be transformed into I by using elementary row transformations (elementary column transformations).

9. Let A be any nonsingular matrix and let P and Q be any two nonsingular matrices such that $QP = A^I$. Prove that $PAQ = I$.

10. Prove that $PC_rQ = C_r$ if and only if

$$P = \begin{pmatrix} P_1 & P_2 \\ 0 & P_3 \end{pmatrix} \quad \text{and} \quad Q = \begin{pmatrix} P_1^I & 0 \\ Q_1 & Q_2 \end{pmatrix},$$

where P_1 is a nonsingular matrix of order r.

11. If R, S, T, and U are nonsingular matrices such that $RAS = TAU = C_r$, prove that $T = PR$ and $U = SQ$, where P and Q are nonsingular matrices of the type given in Exercise 10.

12. Given nonsingular matrices P, Q, and R such that $PAQ = PAR = C_r$. Is Q necessarily equal to R if A is nonsingular; if A is singular?

13. Let A be a singular matrix and P and Q be nonsingular matrices such that $PAQ = C_r$. Determine the form of all matrices M such that $C_rM = 0$. Show how this may be used to determine all matrices B such that $AB = 0$.

14. Use the method of Exercise 13 to determine a 3×3 matrix, B, such that $AB = 0$, where

$$A = \begin{pmatrix} 1 & 2 & 3 \\ 2 & 1 & 1 \\ 3 & 3 & 4 \end{pmatrix}.$$

15. Determine the rank canonical matrix equivalent to each of the following and use the method of this section to find the inverse of each nonsingular matrix.

$$\begin{pmatrix} 2 & 1 \\ 1 & 1 \end{pmatrix}, \quad \begin{pmatrix} 3 & 7 \\ 2 & 5 \end{pmatrix}, \quad \begin{pmatrix} 3 & 5 \\ 2 & 3 \end{pmatrix}, \quad \begin{pmatrix} 4 & 3 \\ 5 & 7 \end{pmatrix}, \quad \begin{pmatrix} 2 & 7 \\ 5 & 3 \end{pmatrix},$$

$$\begin{pmatrix} 1 & 2 & 3 \\ 2 & 1 & 1 \\ 3 & 3 & 5 \end{pmatrix}, \quad \begin{pmatrix} 1 & 3 & 2 \\ 4 & 1 & 3 \\ 5 & 4 & 6 \end{pmatrix}, \quad \begin{pmatrix} 1 & 0 & 1 \\ 2 & 1 & -1 \\ 3 & 1 & 1 \end{pmatrix}, \quad \begin{pmatrix} 2 & 1 & 0 & 3 \\ 1 & 2 & 3 & 5 \\ 7 & 0 & 1 & -1 \end{pmatrix},$$

$$\begin{pmatrix} 2 & 1 & 3 & 0 & 1 \\ 1 & 1 & 0 & 1 & 2 \\ 0 & 0 & 3 & 5 & 0 \\ 0 & 0 & 1 & 2 & 2 \\ 0 & 0 & 4 & 7 & 3 \end{pmatrix}.$$

16. Use the matrices given in Exercise 3 and Exercise 5 and find P, Q such that

$$\begin{pmatrix} P & 0 \\ 0 & I \end{pmatrix} \begin{pmatrix} A & I \\ I & 0 \end{pmatrix} \begin{pmatrix} Q & 0 \\ 0 & I \end{pmatrix} = \begin{pmatrix} C_r & P \\ Q & 0 \end{pmatrix},$$

where the identity matrices are of the appropriate dimension. Are the matrices regularly partitioned?

CHAPTER 5

SYSTEMS OF LINEAR EQUATIONS

5.1 Introduction. Consider the following system of three equations in three unknowns:

$$3x_1 - 2x_2 + 2x_3 = k_1,$$

(5.1.1) $$4x_1 - 2x_2 + 3x_3 = k_2,$$

$$2x_1 - 3x_2 + x_3 = k_3.$$

The reader is familiar with several methods of solving such a system. For example, in section 3.2 (Chapter 3) we discussed the method of solving by elimination. By this method we obtained the value of each unknown separately. To check the solution thus obtained, it is necessary to verify that these values for the three unknowns satisfy each of the three equations.

The equations (5.1.1) may be written as a single equation in matrices. This equation is

(5.1.2)
$$\begin{pmatrix} 3 & -2 & 2 \\ 4 & -2 & 3 \\ 2 & -3 & 1 \end{pmatrix} \begin{pmatrix} x_1 \\ x_2 \\ x_3 \end{pmatrix} = \begin{pmatrix} k_1 \\ k_2 \\ k_3 \end{pmatrix}.$$

The 3×3 matrix in (5.1.2) is called the coefficient matrix. It may be readily verified that this matrix is nonsingular and that its inverse is

$$\begin{pmatrix} 7 & -4 & -2 \\ 2 & -1 & -1 \\ -8 & 5 & 2 \end{pmatrix}.$$

If we multiply both the left member and the right member of (5.1.2), on the left, by this inverse, we obtain

(5.1.3)
$$I \begin{pmatrix} x_1 \\ x_2 \\ x_3 \end{pmatrix} = \begin{pmatrix} 7 & -4 & -2 \\ 2 & -1 & -1 \\ -8 & 5 & 2 \end{pmatrix} \begin{pmatrix} k_1 \\ k_2 \\ k_3 \end{pmatrix}.$$

From (5.1.3), the value of each of the unknowns is immediately obtained. These values are

$$x_1 = 7k_1 - 4k_2 - 2k_3,$$

(5.1.4) $$x_2 = 2k_1 - k_2 - k_3,$$

$$x_3 = -8k_1 + 5k_2 + 2k_3.$$

The system (5.1.1) may be thought of as involving six unknowns, x_1, x_2, x_3, k_1, k_2, and k_3. In this case, (5.1.1) gives k_1, k_2, and k_3 in terms of x_1, x_2, and x_3; whereas (5.1.4) gives x_1, x_2, and x_3 in terms of k_1, k_2, and k_3.

It is obvious that for any system of equations, $AX = K$, where A is nonsingular, we may immediately write $X = A^I K$, and thus the system is solved by determining A^I. Furthermore, if the system $AX = K$ involves more unknowns than equations, then we may write it

$$(A_1 \quad A_2) \begin{pmatrix} X_1 \\ X_2 \end{pmatrix} = K,$$

where A_1 is square. Now, if A_1 is nonsingular, we have

$$X_1 = A_1^I K - A_1^I A_2 X_2.$$

Thus those unknowns in X_1 are expressed in terms of the unknowns in X_2. That is, the unknowns in X_2 may be assigned arbitrarily.

We now consider a system of m linear equations in n unknowns:

(5.1.5) $a_{i1}x_1 + a_{i2}x_2 + \cdots + a_{in}x_n = k_i \qquad (i = 1, 2, \ldots, m).$

We may write this system as the matrix equation

(5.1.6) $$AX = K,$$

where

$$A = (a_{ij}), \quad X = (x_j), \quad K = (k_i) \qquad (i = 1, 2, \ldots, m; j = 1, 2, \ldots, n).$$

Equation (5.1.6) has the same solutions as $PAX = PK$ for every nonsingular matrix P. Also, PAX is identical with $PAQQ^I X$ for every nonsingular matrix Q. We may now determine nonsingular matrices P and Q such that $PAQ = C_r$, where r is the rank of A. Use the P and Q thus determined and define H to be the matrix PK, and Y to be the matrix $Q^I X$. The equation $PAX = PK$ then becomes

(5.1.7) $$C_r Y = H.$$

We now partition

$$Y \text{ into } \begin{pmatrix} Y_1 \\ Y_2 \end{pmatrix} \text{ and } H \text{ into } \begin{pmatrix} H_1 \\ H_2 \end{pmatrix}$$

so that Y_1 and H_1 each has r rows. Then (5.1.7) becomes

$$\begin{pmatrix} Y_1 \\ 0 \end{pmatrix} = \begin{pmatrix} H_1 \\ H_2 \end{pmatrix},$$

which is true if and only if $Y_1 = H_1$ and $0 = H_2$. Hence (5.1.5) has no solution if $H_2 \neq 0$. If $H_2 = 0$, then the system (5.1.5) has solutions and they may be read immediately from the solution of (5.1.6), which is

$$X = Q \begin{pmatrix} H_1 \\ Y_2 \end{pmatrix},$$

where Y_2 is completely arbitrary.

Now we write $A^+ = (A \;\; K)$ and $C^+ = (C_r \;\; H)$. The matrices A^+ and C^+ are called the *augmented matrices* of (5.1.6) and (5.1.7), respectively. Let Q^+ denote the nonsingular matrix

$$\begin{pmatrix} Q & 0 \\ 0 & 1 \end{pmatrix}.$$

Then $PA^+Q^+ = C^+$. Hence we have $A \overset{\mathrm{E}}{=} C_r$ and $A^+ \overset{\mathrm{E}}{=} C^+$. We have seen that (5.1.7) has a solution if and only if C^+ has rank r. But C^+ has rank r if and only if A^+ has rank r. Hence we have

THEOREM 5.1.1 *A system of m linear equations in n unknowns has a solution if and only if the rank of the matrix of the system is the same as the rank of the augmented matrix.*

The solution of (5.1.6), when it exists, is given by

$$X = QY = Q \begin{pmatrix} H_1 \\ Y_2 \end{pmatrix} = Q \begin{pmatrix} P_1 K \\ Y_2 \end{pmatrix},$$

where P_1 is the matrix consisting of the first r rows of the matrix P, and Y_2 is an $(n - r) \times 1$ matrix having arbitrary elements. If $r = m$, the equations are always solvable and the number of arbitrary parameters is $n - r$.

Illustration: We consider the system

$$x_1 + 2x_2 + x_3 = k_1,$$

$$2x_1 + 4x_2 + 3x_3 = k_2.$$

The matrix of this system is given by

$$A = \begin{pmatrix} 1 & 2 & 1 \\ 2 & 4 & 3 \end{pmatrix}.$$

In the illustration of section 4.3 we found, for

$$P = \begin{pmatrix} 1 & 0 \\ -2 & 1 \end{pmatrix} \quad \text{and} \quad Q = \begin{pmatrix} 1 & -1 & -2 \\ 0 & 0 & 1 \\ 0 & 1 & 0 \end{pmatrix},$$

that we have $PAQ = C_2$. With this choice of P, we get

$$P_1 K = \begin{pmatrix} k_1 \\ -2k_1 + k_2 \end{pmatrix}$$

and hence

$$X = \begin{pmatrix} x_1 \\ x_2 \\ x_3 \end{pmatrix} = \begin{pmatrix} 1 & -1 & -2 \\ 0 & 0 & 1 \\ 0 & 1 & 0 \end{pmatrix} \begin{pmatrix} k_1 \\ -2k_1 + k_2 \\ y \end{pmatrix} = \begin{pmatrix} 3k_1 - k_2 - 2y \\ y \\ -2k_1 + k_2 \end{pmatrix},$$

where y is arbitrary.

EXERCISES

1. By the use of matrices, find solutions of the following systems of equations if solutions exist.

(a) $2x_1 + x_2 = 3,$

$3x_1 + 2x_2 = 5.$

(b) $x_1 - 3x_2 = 7,$

$-x_1 + 5x_2 = 11,$

$2x_1 - 7x_2 = 5.$

(c) $x_1 + x_2 = 3,$

$5x_1 + 5x_2 = 10.$

(d) $3x_1 + 5x_2 = 2,$

$x_1 + \frac{5}{3}x_2 = \frac{2}{3}.$

(e) $3x_1 + 2x_2 - x_3 = 1,$

$x_1 + x_2 + x_3 = 2,$

$2x_1 + x_2 - x_3 = -1.$

(f) $x_1 + x_2 - x_3 = 0,$

$2x_1 + 3x_2 + x_3 = 11.$

2. Show that the following system of equations has solutions and find all solutions.

$$2x_1 + 3x_2 + x_3 = 2,$$

$$x_1 - x_2 + 2x_3 = 1,$$

$$x_1 + 4x_2 - x_3 = 1,$$

$$3x_1 + 2x_2 + 3x_3 = 3.$$

3. Given the following set of linear forms, in x_1, x_2, x_3.

$$y_1 = x_1 + 2x_2 - x_3,$$

$$y_2 = x_1 - x_2 + 2x_3,$$

$$y_3 = 3x_1 + 3x_2 + x_3.$$

Solve for x_1, x_2, and x_3 as linear forms in y_1, y_2, and y_3.

4. Consider the equations in Exercise 3 as $Y = AX$. Write the system $Y = A^T X$ and solve this system for x_1, x_2, and x_3 as linear forms in y_1, y_2, and y_3.

5. In many fields of application, particularly in engineering and in statistics, an equation of the type $ax_1 + bx_2 + cx_3 = k$ is an observational equation where a, b, and c are either known "weights" or they are accepted "biases" and where k is the observed value. Find solutions, if such exist, for the following observational system.

$$2x_1 + 3x_2 - x_3 = k_1,$$

$$x_1 - 2x_2 + 3x_3 = k_2,$$

$$3x_1 + x_2 + 3x_3 = k_3,$$

where

(a) $k_1 = 2,$ $k_2 = 3,$ $k_3 = -5;$
(b) $k_1 = -1,$ $k_2 = 7,$ $k_3 = 14;$
(c) $k_1 = 5,$ $k_2 = 3,$ $k_3 = 0;$
(d) $k_1 = k_2 = k_3 = 0.$

6. Show that the system

$$x_1 + x_2 + x_3 = k_1,$$

$$2x_1 + x_2 - x_3 = k_2,$$

$$x_1 \qquad - 2x_3 = k_3$$

has a solution if and only if $k_1 - k_2 + k_3 = 0$.

7. Is it possible to spend one thousand dollars for one hundred chairs if the chairs are to be selected from \$5, \$7, and \$11 chairs? If so, in what quantities will each type be purchased?

5.2 Rank of Submatrices. Let A be an $m \times n$ nonzero matrix. By a permutation of the rows and a permutation of the columns of A, we may obtain an equivalent matrix

$$RAS = \begin{pmatrix} A_1 & A_2 \\ A_3 & A_4 \end{pmatrix},$$

where A_1 is any submatrix of A. Since A contains at least one nonzero element, A contains at least one nonsingular submatrix of some order. The following theorem will be referred to many times in our further study.

THEOREM 5.2.1　*If the submatrix A_1 of A is nonsingular, then A is equivalent to*

$$\begin{pmatrix} A_1 & 0 \\ 0 & A_5 \end{pmatrix}.$$

To show this, we observe that A is equivalent to RAS. Since A_1 is nonsingular, we may write

$$P = \begin{pmatrix} I_k & 0 \\ -A_3 A_1^I & I_{m-k} \end{pmatrix} \quad \text{and} \quad Q = \begin{pmatrix} I_k & -A_1^I A_2 \\ 0 & I_{n-k} \end{pmatrix},$$

where k is the number of rows of A_1. Then

$$PRASQ = \begin{pmatrix} A_1 & 0 \\ 0 & A_5 \end{pmatrix}$$

and the proof of the theorem is completed.

Suppose now that r is the order of one of the largest order nonsingular submatrices in A and let A_1 be a nonsingular submatrix of order r. There exist nonsingular matrices R and S, which are products of elementary permutative matrices, such that

$$RAS = \begin{pmatrix} A_1 & A_2 \\ A_3 & A_4 \end{pmatrix}.$$

Furthermore, all submatrices of order $(r + 1)$ in RAS are singular. We select, from RAS, the $(r + 1) \times (r + 1)$ submatrix containing A_1, elements from the ith row, and elements from the jth column, $i, j > r$. We indicate this $(r + 1) \times (r + 1)$ submatrix by

$$C_{ij} = \begin{pmatrix} A_1 & C_j \\ R_i & b_{ij} \end{pmatrix}.$$

By theorem 5.2.1, C_{ij} is equivalent to

$$\begin{pmatrix} A_1 & 0 \\ 0 & c_{ij} \end{pmatrix}$$

and, since C_{ij} is singular, $c_{ij} = 0$.

That is, there exists a unique matrix $C = (c_{ij})$ $(i = r + 1, \ldots, m;$ $j = 1, 2, \ldots, r)$ such that

(5.2.1)
$$\begin{pmatrix} I_r & 0 \\ -C & I_{n-r} \end{pmatrix} \begin{pmatrix} A_1 & A_2 \\ A_3 & A_4 \end{pmatrix} = \begin{pmatrix} A_1 & A_2 \\ 0 & 0 \end{pmatrix}.$$

Also, there exists a unique matrix D such that

(5.2.2)
$$\begin{pmatrix} A_1 & A_2 \\ 0 & 0 \end{pmatrix} \begin{pmatrix} I_r & D \\ 0 & I_{n-r} \end{pmatrix} = \begin{pmatrix} A_1 & 0 \\ 0 & 0 \end{pmatrix}.$$

The matrix D is obviously $-A_1^I A_2$. Since A_1 is nonsingular, the rank of A is r. The matrix C is obviously $-A_3 A_1^I$. The rows of $-A_3 A_1^I$ are the sets of c_{ij}'s referred to above. This establishes

THEOREM 5.2.2   *The rank of A is the order of any largest order nonsingular submatrix in A.*

From (5.2.1) we have

$$PRAS = \begin{pmatrix} A_1 & A_2 \\ 0 & 0 \end{pmatrix}.$$

Since S is a product of elementary permutative matrices,

$$PRASS^I = PRA = \begin{pmatrix} G \\ 0 \end{pmatrix},$$

where G is composed of the r rows of A containing the submatrix A_1. Similarly, there exists a nonsingular matrix N such that

$$N^T A^T = \begin{pmatrix} H^T \\ 0 \end{pmatrix},$$

where H^T is composed of the r rows of A^T containing A_1^T. Hence $AN = (H \quad 0)$, where H is composed of the r columns of A containing A_1. This may be stated as

THEOREM 5.2.3   *Let A be a matrix of rank r, then there exist nonsingular matrices M and N such that*

(5.2.3)
$$MA = \begin{pmatrix} G \\ 0 \end{pmatrix} \quad and \quad AN = (H \quad 0),$$

where G is composed of any r rows of A and H is composed of any r columns of A such that G and H each contain at least one nonsingular submatrix of order r.

Let A be an n-row nonsingular matrix and write

$$A = \begin{pmatrix} A_1 \\ A_2 \end{pmatrix},$$

where A_1 is the first $n-1$ rows of A. If A_1 is of rank r, there exist non-singular matrices P and Q such that $PA_1Q = C_r$ and hence

$$\begin{pmatrix} P & 0 \\ 0 & 1 \end{pmatrix}\begin{pmatrix} A_1 \\ A_2 \end{pmatrix} Q = \begin{pmatrix} PA_1Q \\ A_2Q \end{pmatrix} = \begin{pmatrix} C_r \\ A_2Q \end{pmatrix}.$$

By elementary row transformations this may be transformed into

$$\begin{pmatrix} I_r & 0 \\ 0 & A_3 \end{pmatrix},$$

where A_3 is of rank one. Hence the rank of A is $r+1$. But, since A is nonsingular, $r+1=n$. Consequently, $r=n-1$. Then it follows, from theorem 5.2.2, that A_1 has a nonsingular submatrix of order $n-1$. Hence every nonsingular matrix of order n contains a nonsingular submatrix of order $n-1$, and the following theorem is established.

THEOREM 5.2.4 *Let A be of rank $r > 0$, then A contains a nonsingular submatrix of k rows if $1 \leqq k \leqq r$.*

We return now to the system of m linear equations in n unknowns given in (5.1.5). Since A is of rank r, the equations may be so ordered that the matrix of the first r equations is of rank r. Then by a nonsingular linear transformation $x_k = y_{i_k}$ $(k = 1, 2, \ldots, n)$, where the i_k represents some permutation of $1, 2, \ldots, n$, the system becomes

$$(5.2.4) \qquad \begin{pmatrix} A_1 & A_2 \\ A_3 & A_4 \end{pmatrix}\begin{pmatrix} Y_1 \\ Y_2 \end{pmatrix} = \begin{pmatrix} K_1 \\ K_2 \end{pmatrix},$$

where A_1 is an r-row nonsingular matrix. If (5.2.4) has a solution, multiplication on the left by P, as defined in theorem 5.2.1, yields the equation

$$(5.2.5) \qquad (A_1 \quad A_2)\begin{pmatrix} Y_1 \\ Y_2 \end{pmatrix} = K_1,$$

which has the same solutions as (5.2.4). From (5.2.5), $A_1Y_1 + A_2Y_2 = K_1$ and hence $A_1Y_1 = K_1 - A_2Y_2$; that is, $Y_1 = A_1^I K_1 - A_1^I A_2 Y_2$, where the elements in Y_2 are some $n-r$ of the x's.

THEOREM 5.2.5 *If a system of m linear equations in n unknowns has a solution and r is the rank of the matrix of the system, then some $n-r$ of the unknowns may be assigned arbitrarily and the remaining r may then be determined uniquely.*

EXERCISES

1. Given the matrix A, where

$$A = \begin{pmatrix} 1 & 2 & 3 & 1 \\ 2 & 5 & 7 & 2 \\ 0 & 1 & 0 & 1 \\ 3 & 3 & 2 & 7 \end{pmatrix}.$$

Transform A into an equivalent matrix

$$\begin{pmatrix} A_1 & 0 \\ 0 & A_5 \end{pmatrix},$$

where A_1 is the nonsingular matrix in the upper left-hand corner of A and where (a) A_1 is of order 1, (b) A_1 is of order 2, and (c) A_1 is of order 3.

2. Use the matrix A in Exercise 1 and show, by applying theorem 5.2.1 and row and column transformations to the successive matrices obtained, that we can obtain the following matrices equivalent to A:

$$\begin{pmatrix} D_1 & 0 \\ 0 & A_5 \end{pmatrix}, \quad \begin{pmatrix} D_2 & 0 \\ 0 & A_6 \end{pmatrix}, \quad \begin{pmatrix} D_3 & 0 \\ 0 & A_7 \end{pmatrix},$$

where D_i is an $i \times i$ nonsingular diagonal matrix.

3. Prove theorem 4.1.3 (Chapter 4), using the methods of Exercise 2.

4. For the matrix A,

$$A = \begin{pmatrix} 1 & 3 & -1 & 2 \\ 0 & 2 & 1 & -3 \\ \hline 1 & 5 & 0 & -1 \\ 1 & 1 & -2 & 5 \end{pmatrix} = \begin{pmatrix} A_1 & A_2 \\ A_3 & A_4 \end{pmatrix},$$

determine P and Q such that

$$PAQ = \begin{pmatrix} A_2 & 0 \\ 0 & 0 \end{pmatrix}.$$

5. Given the system of equations

$$2x_1 + 5x_2 - x_3 = 2,$$

$$3x_1 + 7x_2 - 2x_3 = 7,$$

$$x_1 + 2x_2 - x_3 = 5.$$

Show that the system has a solution. Solve for x_1 and x_2 in terms of x_3; for x_1 and x_3 in terms of x_2; and for x_2 and x_3 in terms of x_1.

6. Given the system of equations

$$x_1 - 3x_2 - 2x_3 - 5x_4 = 7,$$

$$x_1 - 3x_2 + x_3 - 5x_4 = 0.$$

Determine which pairs of unknowns may be assigned arbitrarily, and in each case obtain a solution in terms of these.

5.3　The MURT Technique. When the concept of the rank of a matrix was introduced, it was soon evident that a simple, workable technique for finding the inverse matrix was available. A method for recording the elementary row transformations and the elementary column transformations necessary to transform a nonsingular matrix A into I was given. We found nonsingular matrices P and Q such that $PAQ = I$. From this it is seen that $PA = Q^I$ and, therefore, $QPA = QQ^I = I$. That is, $QP = A^I$. Since the multiplication of A on the left by the matrix QP constitutes only row transformations upon A, it is clear that nonsingular A can be transformed by row transformations alone into the identity matrix, I. It is this property which gives us a simpler technique for solving systems of linear equations.

We now suppose that the matrix equation $AX = K$ represents the system

$$x - 2y = 1,$$

$$2x - 3y = 3.$$

The augmented matrix of this system, indicated by A^+, is given by

$$A^+ = (A \quad K) = \begin{pmatrix} 1 & -2 & \bigm| & 1 \\ 2 & -3 & \bigm| & 3 \end{pmatrix},$$

and it is easily seen, by using row transformations alone, that

$$\begin{pmatrix} 1 & -2 & \bigm| & 1 \\ 2 & -3 & \bigm| & 3 \end{pmatrix} \overset{E}{=} \begin{pmatrix} 1 & -2 & \bigm| & 1 \\ 0 & 1 & \bigm| & 1 \end{pmatrix} \overset{E}{=} \begin{pmatrix} 1 & 0 & \bigm| & 3 \\ 0 & 1 & \bigm| & 1 \end{pmatrix}.$$

Each matrix of this set of equivalent matrices represents a system of linear equations having the same solution as the system represented by any other matrix of this set.

If we subtract two times the first row of A^+ from the second row, then the equivalent matrix

$$\begin{pmatrix} 1 & -2 & \bigm| & 1 \\ 0 & 1 & \bigm| & 1 \end{pmatrix}$$

is obtained and the system of equations represented by this matrix has a solution if and only if the original system of equations possesses a solution. This is true of every matrix obtained by row transformations upon the original augmented matrix.

Using *equivalent matrices under row transformations* to solve systems of linear equations is actually a systematic elimination process. By adding two times the last row of the matrix above to the first row, we get the last of the displayed equivalent matrices, namely,

$$\left(\begin{array}{cc|c} 1 & 0 & 3 \\ 0 & 1 & 1 \end{array}\right).$$

But this matrix represents the system

$$1x + 0y = 3,$$
$$0x + 1y = 1,$$

from which the unique solution may be read immediately.

The row transformations used may be represented by the elementary additive matrices

$$\begin{pmatrix} 1 & 0 \\ -2 & 1 \end{pmatrix} \quad \text{and} \quad \begin{pmatrix} 1 & 2 \\ 0 & 1 \end{pmatrix},$$

from which we see that

$$\begin{pmatrix} 1 & 0 \\ -2 & 1 \end{pmatrix}\left(\begin{array}{cc|c} 1 & -2 & 1 \\ 2 & -3 & 3 \end{array}\right) = \left(\begin{array}{cc|c} 1 & -2 & 1 \\ 0 & 1 & 1 \end{array}\right),$$

and that

$$\begin{pmatrix} 1 & 2 \\ 0 & 1 \end{pmatrix}\left(\begin{array}{cc|c} 1 & -2 & 1 \\ 0 & 1 & 1 \end{array}\right) = \left(\begin{array}{cc|c} 1 & 0 & 3 \\ 0 & 1 & 1 \end{array}\right).$$

Furthermore, it should be noted that the coefficient matrix, A, of the original system of equations is

$$\begin{pmatrix} 1 & -2 \\ 2 & -3 \end{pmatrix},$$

and that

$$\begin{pmatrix} 1 & 2 \\ 0 & 1 \end{pmatrix}\begin{pmatrix} 1 & 0 \\ -2 & 1 \end{pmatrix}\begin{pmatrix} 1 & -2 \\ 2 & -3 \end{pmatrix} = \begin{pmatrix} 1 & 0 \\ 0 & 1 \end{pmatrix}.$$

That is,

$$\begin{pmatrix} 1 & 2 \\ 0 & 1 \end{pmatrix}\begin{pmatrix} 1 & 0 \\ -2 & 1 \end{pmatrix} = \begin{pmatrix} -3 & 2 \\ -2 & 1 \end{pmatrix} = A^I.$$

This system of equations, $AX = K$, could be solved by using the A^I technique, but the MURT technique, that is, the "Matrices Under Row Transformations" technique, has the advantage of applying the row transformations, necessary to obtain the A^I, directly to the augmented matrix. Furthermore, it has the advantage of being applicable even though A is nonsquare or square but singular. In these cases one obtains the rank canonical form, C_r, of A and thus determines the solution, solutions, or nonexistence of solutions from this form.

Illustration: Determine the solution of the system

$$3x + 5y - 4z = -16,$$

$$x + 2y - 4z = -14,$$

$$2x + 3y + z = 1.$$

The augmented matrix representing this system is

$$\begin{pmatrix} 3 & 5 & -4 & -16 \\ 1 & 2 & -4 & -14 \\ 2 & 3 & 1 & 1 \end{pmatrix}.$$

It is easily seen that interchanging row one and row two yields an equivalent matrix having the element 1 in the leading position. Subtracting three times the first row from the second in this resulting matrix and subtracting two times the first row from the third row in the following matrix yields

$$\begin{pmatrix} 3 & 5 & -4 & -16 \\ 1 & 2 & -4 & -14 \\ 2 & 3 & 1 & 1 \end{pmatrix} \overset{E}{=} \begin{pmatrix} 1 & 2 & -4 & -14 \\ 3 & 5 & -4 & -16 \\ 2 & 3 & 1 & 1 \end{pmatrix}$$

$$\overset{E}{=} \begin{pmatrix} 1 & 2 & -4 & -14 \\ 0 & -1 & 8 & 26 \\ 2 & 3 & 1 & 1 \end{pmatrix} \overset{E}{=} \begin{pmatrix} 1 & 2 & -4 & -14 \\ 0 & -1 & 8 & 26 \\ 0 & -1 & 9 & 29 \end{pmatrix}.$$

By row transformations alone we get successively the following equivalent matrices:

$$\begin{pmatrix} 1 & 2 & -4 & -14 \\ 0 & -1 & 8 & 26 \\ 0 & -1 & 9 & 29 \end{pmatrix} \overset{E}{=} \begin{pmatrix} 1 & 2 & -4 & -14 \\ 0 & 1 & -8 & -26 \\ 0 & -1 & 9 & 29 \end{pmatrix} \overset{E}{=} \begin{pmatrix} 1 & 2 & -4 & -14 \\ 0 & 1 & -8 & -26 \\ 0 & 0 & 1 & 3 \end{pmatrix}$$

$$\overset{E}{=} \begin{pmatrix} 1 & 0 & 12 & 38 \\ 0 & 1 & -8 & -26 \\ 0 & 0 & 1 & 3 \end{pmatrix} \overset{E}{=} \begin{pmatrix} 1 & 0 & 12 & 38 \\ 0 & 1 & 0 & -2 \\ 0 & 0 & 1 & 3 \end{pmatrix} \overset{E}{=} \begin{pmatrix} 1 & 0 & 0 & 2 \\ 0 & 1 & 0 & -2 \\ 0 & 0 & 1 & 3 \end{pmatrix}.$$

This last matrix represents the system

$$1x + 0y + 0z = 2,$$

$$0x + 1y + 0z = -2,$$

$$0x + 0y + 1z = 3,$$

from which the only possible solution of this system and thus the original system can be read.

Illustration: The following represent four readings taken in a pre-liminary testing program. The equipment is known to be in acceptable working condition. Are the readings consistent?

$$x + .3y = 1.7,$$
$$2x + .4y = 3,$$
$$x - y = -.8,$$
$$3x - 2y = 22.3.$$

Here the augmented matrix A^+ is given by

$$A^+ = (A \ K) = \begin{pmatrix} 1 & .3 & 1.7 \\ 2 & .4 & 3 \\ 1 & -1 & -.8 \\ 3 & -2 & 22.3 \end{pmatrix}$$

and, by row transformations alone, we get

$$A^+ \overset{E}{=} \begin{pmatrix} 1 & .3 & 1.7 \\ 0 & -.2 & -.4 \\ 1 & -1 & -.8 \\ 3 & -2 & 22.3 \end{pmatrix} \overset{E}{=} \begin{pmatrix} 1 & .3 & 1.7 \\ 0 & 2 & 4 \\ 1 & -1 & -.8 \\ 3 & -2 & 22.3 \end{pmatrix}$$

$$\overset{E}{=} \begin{pmatrix} 1 & .3 & 1.7 \\ 0 & 1 & 2 \\ 1 & -1 & -.8 \\ 3 & -2 & 22.3 \end{pmatrix} \overset{E}{=} \begin{pmatrix} 1 & 0 & 1.1 \\ 0 & 1 & 2 \\ 1 & -1 & -.8 \\ 3 & -2 & 22.3 \end{pmatrix}$$

$$\overset{E}{=} \begin{pmatrix} 1 & 0 & 1.1 \\ 0 & 1 & 2 \\ 0 & -1 & -1.9 \\ 3 & -2 & 22.3 \end{pmatrix} \overset{E}{=} \begin{pmatrix} 1 & 0 & 1.1 \\ 0 & 1 & 2 \\ 0 & 1 & 1.9 \\ 3 & -2 & 22.3 \end{pmatrix}$$

$$\overset{E}{=} \begin{pmatrix} 1 & 0 & 1.1 \\ 0 & 1 & 2 \\ 0 & 1 & 1.9 \\ 0 & -2 & 19 \end{pmatrix} \overset{E}{=} \begin{pmatrix} 1 & 0 & 1.1 \\ 0 & 1 & 2 \\ 0 & 1 & 1.9 \\ 0 & 1 & -9.5 \end{pmatrix}.$$

From the last matrix above it is seen that the readings yield $x = 1.1$, and successively, for this x, $y = 2$, $y = 1.9$, and $y = -9.5$. It appears from this that the read values of y, namely, $y = 2$ and $y = 1.9$, are sufficiently close to lead one to believe that these are consistent readings, depending, of course, upon the acceptable error. However, the reading $y = -9.5$ differs sufficiently from the other two values to warrant an investigation. There are many other aspects of this problem. If one were asked merely to examine the four equations for possible solution, then the report must be that they form an inconsistent system, possessing no solution. The first two equations are consistent, having $x = 1.1$, $y = 2$. The third is almost satisfied by these values, being close enough that one might suspect the laboratory experimenter of "not reading between the lines," whereas the fourth equation is such that the experimenter might be suspected of gross negligence or of maximum incompetence. It is not our purpose to determine the "best solution" by the process of least squares or by any of the various methods sometimes applied. It is imperative that the reader understand that a different approach to this problem may render an entirely different interpretation of the readings. For example, if more confidence is placed in the third and fourth readings, then the MURT technique gives

$$A^+ \overset{\mathrm{E}}{=} \begin{pmatrix} 1 & -1 & -.8 \\ 1 & .3 & 1.7 \\ 2 & .4 & 3 \\ 3 & -2 & 22.3 \end{pmatrix} \overset{\mathrm{E}}{=} \begin{pmatrix} 1 & -1 & -.8 \\ 0 & 1.3 & 2.5 \\ 0 & 2.4 & 4.6 \\ 0 & 1 & 24.7 \end{pmatrix}$$

$$\overset{\mathrm{E}}{=} \begin{pmatrix} 1 & 0 & 16.7 \\ 0 & 1 & 24.7 \\ 0 & 0 & -29.6 \\ 0 & 0 & -54.6 \end{pmatrix},$$

where calculations are carried out to one place and the best left decimal approximation is used. The conclusion is the same in each case; that is, inconsistent equations. If the last two equations represent consistent readings, then the first two equations were obtained under adverse circumstances.

If the MURT technique is applied to the general equation $AX = K$, $A = (a_{ij})$ $(i = 1, 2, \ldots, m; j = 1, 2, \ldots, n)$, then the augmented matrix $A^+ = (A \ K)$ may be transformed into several patterns depending upon the rank of A^+ and the rank of A. It is easy to state the theorems pertaining to the various cases by using the final rank canonical matrix or near-rank canonical matrix.

The simple case is given by $AX = K$, where A is an $n \times n$ nonsingular coefficient matrix, and thus

$$A^+ = (A \quad K) \overset{\mathrm{E}}{=} (I \quad H),$$

from which it is obvious that

$$x_i = h_i \qquad (i = 1, 2, \ldots, n).$$

If $m < n$ and $r(A) = m$, we may have

$$A^+ = (A \quad K) \overset{\mathrm{E}}{=} (I_m \quad B \quad H),$$

where $x_i = h_i - (b_{i1}x_{m+1} + b_{i2}x_{m+2} + \cdots + b_{i,n-m}x_n)$. Thus the $x_1, x_2, \ldots, x_m$ are represented in terms of the h_i and the $n - m$ remaining x_i which are completely independent.

If $r(A^+) > r(A) = r$, then we may get the pattern

$$A^+ = (A \quad K) \overset{\mathrm{E}}{=} \begin{pmatrix} I_r & B & H_1 \\ 0 & 0 & H_2 \end{pmatrix},$$

where it is immediately obvious that the system has no solution. However, the first r equations represented by the final matrix obtained under the MURT technique has a solution which may be represented in terms of the last $(n - r)$ x_i and the h_i. The last $m - r$ equations form the inconsistencies of the system and in the case of applied work may be examined to see if they differ sufficiently from the other equations to cause concern. Here, again, the question of "error" and "best solution" does not concern us at this time.

It is interesting and important to note that the MURT technique enables the solver to investigate the individual equation for discrepancies, particularly in the systems for which no solution exists, the inconsistent systems, and in systems containing many solutions, that is, those containing what are ordinarily called dependent equations. This is important in applied work.

It is also interesting to note that the MURT technique is actually what the name implies: the technique of applying the elementary additive matrices, the elementary permutative matrices, and the elementary multiplicative matrices, one at a time, to the rows of the augmented matrix of a system of equations until the appropriate C_r form is obtained in the upper left position and of reading, from this, the solutions of the original system and all systems equivalent to the original system. The technique may be described as the process of exchanging one system of equations for an equivalent system and repeating this process until a solution becomes obvious.

The simplicity of the process lies partly in omitting all irrelevant parts, the x_i, the equal signs, etc., working only with the augmented matrix.

The student will be misled if he comes to believe that all systems of equations consist of simple equations having integral coefficients. In practice one is more likely to encounter equations similar to

$$3.1273251x_1 + 2.2123798x_2 + \cdots + 8.7123456x_{21} = 2.2122127,$$

$$\dots\dots\dots\dots\dots\dots\dots\dots\dots\dots\dots\dots\dots\dots\dots\dots ,$$

$$\dots\dots\dots\dots\dots\dots\dots\dots\dots\dots\dots\dots\dots\dots\dots\dots$$

With systems of this type one must concern himself with round-off errors and approximate solutions and must set up some criteria for the acceptability of solutions.

EXERCISES

Use the MURT technique to solve the following systems of equations.

1. $x + 2y = 5,$
   $3x - y = 1.$

2. $x - y = 3,$
   $3x + 2y = 19.$

3. $2x - 5y = 0,$
   $x + y = 0.$

4. $2x - y = 8,$
   $x + 2y = 9.$

5. $2x + 3y = 2,$
   $3x + 2y = 2.$

6. $2x + 3y = 2,$
   $6x - 9y = 0.$

7. $x + y - z = 1,$
   $2x - y + z = 0,$
   $3x - 2y + 4z = 5.$

8. $x - y + z = 2,$
   $2x + 3y - z = 5,$
   $3x - y + 2z = 7.$

9. $4x + 2y - z - w = -2,$
   $x + y + z - w = 2,$
   $3x - y + 2z - w = 3,$
   $2x - z = -3.$

10. $\dfrac{2}{x} + \dfrac{3}{y} + \dfrac{4}{z} = -2,$

   $-\dfrac{2}{x} + \dfrac{9}{y} - \dfrac{8}{z} = 10,$

   $\dfrac{6}{x} + \dfrac{6}{y} + \dfrac{12}{z} = -7.$

Check the following systems of equations for solutions.

11. $x + y - z = 0,$
   $2x - 3y - 5z = 7,$
   $4x + 3y + 2z = 5,$
   $3x + 2y + 2z = 8,$

12. $x + y = 7,$
   $x + 2y = 8,$
   $2x - 3y = 9.$

13. $2x + 3y + z = 4,$
$3x - y + 2z = 13.$

14. $\dfrac{3}{x} - \dfrac{4}{y} + \dfrac{6}{z} = 1,$

$-\dfrac{3}{x} + \dfrac{4}{y} - \dfrac{6}{z} = -1,$

$\dfrac{9}{x} + \dfrac{8}{y} - \dfrac{12}{z} = 3.$

15. $x + 2y = 5,$
$3x + 6y = 15.$

16. $x = 0,$
$3x + 2y = 2,$
$x + 3y - z = 1,$
$-5x - y + z - 2u = 3,$
$3x - 2y + 3z - u - 5v = 15,$
$x - y + z - u + v - w = -5.$

17. $x + y + z + w = 1,$
$2x + y - z + w = 1.$

18. $x + y + z = 0,$
$3x + y + 6z = 0,$
$x + 5y - 5z = 0.$

19. $3x + 2y - 5z = 8,$
$x + y = 3.$

20. $x + y = 5,$
$2x - 3y = 0,$
$3x - 2y = 5,$
$5x - 5y = 5,$
$x - y = 5,$
$2x + 2y = 5.$

Examine the following matrices, using the MURT technique to determine which represent the augmented matrix of a system of equations having a solution or solutions.

21. $\begin{pmatrix} 1 & 1 & 1 & \bigm| & 0 \\ 2 & -1 & -1 & \bigm| & 0 \\ 1 & -1 & -1 & \bigm| & 0 \end{pmatrix}$

22. $\begin{pmatrix} 1 & 1 & 1 & 0 & 0 & \bigm| & -7 \\ 0 & 0 & 1 & 1 & 1 & \bigm| & 3 \\ 1 & 0 & 1 & 0 & 1 & \bigm| & 5 \\ 0 & 1 & 0 & 1 & 1 & \bigm| & 19 \\ 1 & 1 & 0 & 1 & 0 & \bigm| & 7 \end{pmatrix}$

23. $\begin{pmatrix} 1 & 1 & 1 & 1 & \bigm| & -1 \\ -1 & 3 & 1 & 2 & \bigm| & 0 \\ 3 & -1 & -2 & 1 & \bigm| & 6 \\ -2 & 2 & -1 & 3 & \bigm| & 2 \end{pmatrix}.$

24. $\begin{pmatrix} 1 & 0 & 0 & 1 & \bigm| & 3 \\ 0 & 1 & -1 & 1 & \bigm| & 1 \\ 1 & 1 & 0 & 0 & \bigm| & 4 \\ 0 & 0 & 1 & 1 & \bigm| & 2 \end{pmatrix}.$

25. $\begin{pmatrix} -3 & 4 & 5 & 0 & | & 2 \\ 0 & -3 & -2 & 1 & | & -4 \\ 2 & 0 & 3 & 4 & | & -4 \\ 4 & 2 & 0 & -1 & | & 7 \end{pmatrix}.$ 　　26. $\begin{pmatrix} 1 & 2 & 3 & 4 & | & 5 \\ 2 & 3 & 4 & 5 & | & 1 \\ 3 & 4 & 5 & 1 & | & 2 \\ 4 & 5 & 1 & 2 & | & 3 \end{pmatrix}.$

27. $\begin{pmatrix} 1 & 2 & 3 \\ 4 & 5 & 6 \\ 7 & 8 & 9 \end{pmatrix}.$ 　　28. $\begin{pmatrix} 0 & 1 & -2 & | & 5 \\ -1 & 0 & 3 & | & 7 \\ 2 & -3 & 0 & | & 9 \end{pmatrix}.$

29. $\begin{pmatrix} \binom{5}{0} & \binom{5}{1} & \binom{5}{2} & \binom{5}{3} & \binom{5}{4} & | & \binom{5}{5} \\ 0 & \binom{4}{0} & \binom{4}{1} & \binom{4}{2} & \binom{4}{3} & | & \binom{4}{4} \\ 0 & 0 & \binom{3}{0} & \binom{3}{1} & \binom{3}{2} & | & \binom{3}{3} \\ 0 & 0 & 0 & \binom{2}{0} & \binom{2}{1} & | & \binom{2}{2} \\ 0 & 0 & 0 & 0 & \binom{1}{0} & | & \binom{1}{1} \end{pmatrix},$ where $\binom{i}{j} = \dfrac{i!}{j!(i-j)!}.$

30. $\begin{pmatrix} 0 & 1 & 0 & | & 0 \\ -1 & 0 & 1 & | & 0 \\ 0 & -1 & 0 & | & 1 \\ 0 & 0 & -1 & | & 0 \end{pmatrix}.$

CHAPTER 6

CONGRUENCE OF SQUARE MATRICES

6.1 Introduction. We now consider some special properties of bilinear forms where the matrices of the forms are square. Such a bilinear form may be written

$$(6.1.1) \qquad f = X^T A Y,$$

where $X = (x_i)$, $Y = (y_j)$, and $A = (a_{ij})$ $(i, j = 1, 2, \ldots, n)$. If the linear transformations $X = PU$ and $Y = PV$ are applied to (6.1.1), then X and Y are said to be transformed *cogrediently*. If $g = X^T B Y$, then f and g are equivalent under cogredient transformations if and only if there exists a nonsingular matrix P such that

$$(6.1.2) \qquad B = P^T A P.$$

DEFINITION. *A square matrix B is said to be congruent to the square matrix A if there exists a nonsingular matrix P such that $B = P^T A P$.*

We shall indicate that B is congruent to A by writing $B \overset{c}{=} A$. It may be shown that "is congruent to" is an equivalence relation. The verification of this is left as an exercise. Since $B \overset{c}{=} A$ implies $A \overset{c}{=} B$, we say that A and B are congruent. If $B \overset{c}{=} A$, then obviously $B \overset{E}{=} A$ and hence it is necessary that A and B have the same rank. We shall not go into the sufficient conditions for two general matrices to be congruent but shall restrict our study to certain special types of matrices. From theorem 3.1.6 (Chapter 3), the nonsingular matrix P may be written as the product $E_1 E_2 \cdots E_k$, where the E_i are elementary matrices. Consequently $P^T = E_k^T E_{k-1}^T \cdots E_1^T$. Hence $P^T A P = E_k^T E_{k-1}^T \cdots E_2^T E_1^T A E_1 E_2 \cdots E_k$. If E is any elementary matrix, then the matrix $E^T A E$ may be obtained by making a certain elementary row transformation on A followed by the corresponding elementary column transformation. We shall call the result of these two transformations an *elementary cogredient transformation*. Hence

THEOREM 6.1.1 *The matrix B is congruent to A if and only if B is obtained from A by a finite number of elementary cogredient transformations.*

6.2 Symmetric Matrices and Skew Matrices. We have defined A to be symmetric if $A^T = A$ and to be skew if $A^T = -A$. If $B = P^T A P$, then $B^T = P^T A^T P$. From this we readily obtain

THEOREM 6.2.1 *If the matrix B is congruent to the matrix A, then B is symmetric if and only if A is symmetric and B is skew if and only if A is skew.*

Illustration: To illustrate one part of theorem 6.2.1, we use

$$A = \begin{pmatrix} a & b \\ b & c \end{pmatrix} \quad \text{and} \quad P = \begin{pmatrix} 1 & 2 \\ 3 & 5 \end{pmatrix}.$$

Then

$$P^T A P = \begin{pmatrix} 1 & 3 \\ 2 & 5 \end{pmatrix} \begin{pmatrix} a & b \\ b & c \end{pmatrix} \begin{pmatrix} 1 & 2 \\ 3 & 5 \end{pmatrix}$$

$$= \begin{pmatrix} a + 6b + 9c & 2a + 11b + 15c \\ 2a + 11b + 15c & 4a + 20b + 25c \end{pmatrix}.$$

Obviously, if $P^T A P = B$, then $P^{TI} B P^I = A$. Since A is transformed cogrediently, if A is symmetric then B is also symmetric.

In the study of symmetric and skew matrices, certain submatrices are of particular importance. We now define what we call *principal submatrices* of any general square matrix.

DEFINITION. *If A is any square matrix, then any submatrix obtained from A by deleting the same number of rows as columns and by always deleting the column containing a_{ii} whenever the row containing a_{ii} is deleted is called a principal submatrix of A.*

Illustration: For the matrix

$$A = \begin{pmatrix} 1 & 2 & 5 \\ -1 & 0 & 7 \\ 3 & -2 & 8 \end{pmatrix},$$

the principal submatrices of order two are

$$\begin{pmatrix} 1 & 2 \\ -1 & 0 \end{pmatrix}, \quad \begin{pmatrix} 1 & 5 \\ 3 & 8 \end{pmatrix}, \quad \text{and} \quad \begin{pmatrix} 0 & 7 \\ -2 & 8 \end{pmatrix}.$$

We note that the diagonal elements of any principal submatrix are diagonal elements of A. The principal submatrices of order one are (1), (0), and (8).

Let A be any symmetric (or skew) matrix of rank r. Then, by theorem 5.2.2, A contains an r-row nonsingular submatrix S. There exists a nonsingular matrix M such that

$$MA = \begin{pmatrix} G \\ 0 \end{pmatrix},$$

where G is composed of those rows of A containing S. Then, since A is symmetric (or skew),

$$MAM^T = \begin{pmatrix} A_1 & 0 \\ 0 & 0 \end{pmatrix},$$

where A_1 is an $r \times r$ nonsingular principal submatrix of A. The principal submatrix A_1 is symmetric and is that principal submatrix in the r rows containing S. Similarly, there exists a nonsingular matrix N such that

$$N^T A N = \begin{pmatrix} A_2 & 0 \\ 0 & 0 \end{pmatrix},$$

where A_2 is that principal submatrix in the r columns containing S. The submatrix A_2 is also of rank r.

In the above, both A_1 and A_2 are principal submatrices of A and we have

THEOREM 6.2.2   *Let A be a symmetric (or skew) matrix of rank r, and let S be any r-row nonsingular submatrix of A, then the principal submatrix in the r rows containing S and the principal submatrix in the r columns containing S are nonsingular.*

COROLLARY.   *If a symmetric (or skew) matrix of rank r has a nonsingular r-row submatrix which is not a principal submatrix, then at least two of its r-row principal submatrices are nonsingular.*

We state the following theorem without proof.

THEOREM 6.2.3   *Let*

$$A = \begin{pmatrix} A_1 & 0 \\ 0 & A_2 \end{pmatrix} \quad and \quad B = \begin{pmatrix} B_1 & 0 \\ 0 & B_2 \end{pmatrix}.$$

If $B_1 \overset{c}{=} A_1$ and $B_2 \overset{c}{=} A_2$, then $B \overset{c}{=} A$.

We shall now obtain a canonical form for matrices congruent to a given skew matrix. Let $A = (a_{ij})$ be an $n \times n$ skew matrix. Since $a_{ji} = -a_{ij}$ $(i, j = 1, 2, \ldots, n)$, it follows that $a_{ii} = -a_{ii} = 0$ $(i = 1, 2, \ldots, n)$.

Hence it follows from theorem 6.2.2 that A cannot be of rank one. If $A \neq 0$, then A contains at least one nonzero element, a_{pq}, and consequently the principal submatrix

$$\begin{pmatrix} 0 & a_{pq} \\ -a_{pq} & 0 \end{pmatrix}$$

is nonsingular. By elementary cogredient permutative transformations on A we may obtain a matrix having this submatrix in the upper left corner. If, in the matrix thus obtained, we divide the elements of the first row and the elements of the first column by a_{pq}, we get a matrix

$$B = \begin{pmatrix} E & A_1 \\ -A_1^T & A_2 \end{pmatrix}, \quad \text{where} \quad E = \begin{pmatrix} 0 & 1 \\ -1 & 0 \end{pmatrix}.$$

This matrix B is congruent to A.

If

$$P = \begin{pmatrix} I_2 & -E^I A_2 \\ 0 & I_{n-2} \end{pmatrix}, \quad \text{then} \quad P^T B P = \begin{pmatrix} E & 0 \\ 0 & B_1 \end{pmatrix},$$

where B_1 is skew. If B_1 is not zero, then a matrix congruent to A may be obtained by replacing B_1 by

$$\begin{pmatrix} E & 0 \\ 0 & B_2 \end{pmatrix},$$

which is congruent to B_1. This process may be continued as long as there is a nonzero matrix in the lower right corner. The rank of A is the sum of the ranks of the E's. The matrix E is of rank two. Hence we have

THEOREM 6.2.4 *Every skew matrix $A \neq 0$ is congruent to diag.* $\{E, E, \ldots, E, 0, \ldots, 0\}$, *where*

$$E = \begin{pmatrix} 0 & 1 \\ -1 & 0 \end{pmatrix}$$

and the rank of A is twice the number of E's appearing in this diagonal block matrix.

COROLLARY. *Two n-row skew matrices are congruent if and only if they are equivalent.*

If A is a skew matrix, then it follows from theorem 6.2.4 that the corresponding bilinear form $X^T A Y$ may be transformed by nonsingular cogredient transformations into

$$(6.2.1) \quad x_1 y_2 - x_2 y_1 + x_3 y_4 - x_4 y_3 + - \cdots + x_{2t-1} y_{2t} - x_{2t} y_{2t-1},$$

where $2t$ is the rank of A.

Let

$$A \overset{c}{=} \begin{pmatrix} A_1 & 0 \\ 0 & 0 \end{pmatrix} \quad \text{and} \quad B \overset{c}{=} \begin{pmatrix} B_1 & 0 \\ 0 & 0 \end{pmatrix},$$

where A_1 and B_1 are nonsingular r-row matrices. If $A \overset{c}{=} B$, there exists a nonsingular matrix

$$P = \begin{pmatrix} P_1 & P_2 \\ P_3 & P_4 \end{pmatrix}$$

such that

$$\begin{pmatrix} P_1^T & P_3^T \\ P_2^T & P_4^T \end{pmatrix} \begin{pmatrix} A_1 & 0 \\ 0 & 0 \end{pmatrix} \begin{pmatrix} P_1 & P_2 \\ P_3 & P_4 \end{pmatrix} = \begin{pmatrix} B_1 & 0 \\ 0 & 0 \end{pmatrix},$$

and it follows that

$$\begin{pmatrix} P_1^T A_1 P_1 & P_1^T A_1 P_2 \\ P_2^T A_1 P_1 & P_2^T A_1 P_2 \end{pmatrix} = \begin{pmatrix} B_1 & 0 \\ 0 & 0 \end{pmatrix}.$$

Then $P_1^T A_1 P_1 = B_1$, and P_1 is nonsingular since B_1 is nonsingular. Hence $A_1 \overset{c}{=} B_1$. Conversely, if $A_1 \overset{c}{=} B_1$, then there exists a nonsingular matrix P_1 such that $P_1^T A_1 P_1 = B_1$. Then

$$\begin{pmatrix} P_1^T & 0 \\ 0 & I \end{pmatrix} \begin{pmatrix} A_1 & 0 \\ 0 & 0 \end{pmatrix} \begin{pmatrix} P_1 & 0 \\ 0 & I \end{pmatrix} = \begin{pmatrix} B_1 & 0 \\ 0 & 0 \end{pmatrix}.$$

Consequently $A \overset{c}{=} B$, and we have

THEOREM 6.2.5 *Let*

$$A \overset{c}{=} \begin{pmatrix} A_1 & 0 \\ 0 & 0 \end{pmatrix} \quad \text{and} \quad B \overset{c}{=} \begin{pmatrix} B_1 & 0 \\ 0 & 0 \end{pmatrix},$$

where A_1 and B_1 are nonsingular matrices, then $A \overset{c}{=} B$ if and only if $A_1 \overset{c}{=} B_1$.

If A is a symmetric matrix of rank r, it follows from theorem 6.2.2 that A contains a nonsingular r-row principal submatrix A_1 and that

$$(6.2.2) \qquad A \overset{c}{=} \begin{pmatrix} A_1 & 0 \\ 0 & 0 \end{pmatrix}.$$

Thus we have

COROLLARY. *If A and B are symmetric matrices of rank r, then $A \overset{c}{=} B$ if any nonsingular r-row principal submatrix of A is congruent to a nonsingular r-row principal submatrix of B. Also, if $A \overset{c}{=} B$, each nonsingular r-row principal submatrix of A is congruent to every nonsingular r-row principal submatrix of B.*

We have just shown that any problem involving congruence of symmetric matrices may be reduced to a problem involving the congruence of *nonsingular* symmetric matrices. That is, in order to establish conditions for two symmetric matrices to be congruent, it is sufficient to consider only nonsingular symmetric matrices.

If A_1 in (6.2.2) has a nonzero diagonal element, c_1, then A_1 may be transformed by an elementary cogredient permutative transformation into

$$B_1 = \begin{pmatrix} c_1 & B_2 \\ B_2^T & B_4 \end{pmatrix}.$$

If

$$P = \begin{pmatrix} 1 & -(1/c_1)B_2 \\ 0 & I_{r-1} \end{pmatrix},$$

then

$$P^T B_1 P = \begin{pmatrix} c_1 & 0 \\ 0 & A_2 \end{pmatrix}.$$

The matrix A_2 is nonsingular and symmetric. If A_2 has a nonzero diagonal element, the process may be repeated to get

$$A_2 \overset{c}{=} \begin{pmatrix} c_2 & 0 \\ 0 & A_3 \end{pmatrix}.$$

This process may be continued to obtain $A_1 \overset{c}{=}$ diag. $\{c_1, c_2, \ldots, c_r\}$ or

$$A_1 \overset{c}{=} \begin{pmatrix} C & 0 \\ 0 & A_i \end{pmatrix},$$

where C is a nonsingular diagonal matrix of $i - 1$ rows and A_i has all diagonal elements zero. Then, since A_i is nonsingular, it has a nonzero element, k, in the pth row of the first column. It should be noted that the element in the pth column of the first row of A_i is also k. By adding the pth row of A_i to the first row of A_i and then adding the pth column of the resulting matrix to its first column we obtain a matrix B_i congruent to A_i and having as its leading diagonal element $2k$. We write $2k = c_i$ and, since $c_i \neq 0$, we proceed as above. Thus, by induction, we obtain

THEOREM 6.2.6   *Every symmetric matrix A of rank r is congruent to diag.* $\{c_1, c_2, \ldots, c_r, 0, \ldots, 0\}$, *where $c_i \neq 0$ $(i = 1, 2, \ldots, r)$.*

This may be applied to obtain a corresponding result on symmetric bilinear forms. Let $f = X^T A Y$, where A is symmetric and of rank r. Then f may be transformed by nonsingular cogredient transformation into $c_1 x_1 y_1 + c_2 x_2 y_2 + \cdots + c_r x_r y_r$, where $c_i \neq 0$ $(i = 1, 2, \ldots, r)$.

EXERCISES

Given the matrix A, defined by

$$A = \begin{pmatrix} 1 & 2 & 3 \\ 2 & -1 & 1 \\ 3 & 1 & 4 \end{pmatrix}.$$

1. Determine a nonsingular matrix P such that

$$P^T A P = \begin{pmatrix} 1 & 2 & 0 \\ 2 & -1 & 0 \\ 0 & 0 & 0 \end{pmatrix}.$$

2. Determine a nonsingular matrix P such that

$$P^T A P = \begin{pmatrix} -1 & 1 & 0 \\ 1 & 4 & 0 \\ 0 & 0 & 0 \end{pmatrix}.$$

3. Write the bilinear form $f = X^T A Y$ and determine a nonsingular matrix P such that $X = PU$, $Y = PV$ transforms f into $u_1 v_1 + 3u_1 v_2 + 3u_2 v_1 + 4u_2 v_2$.

4. Determine a nonsingular matrix P such that $X = PU$, $Y = PV$ transforms f of Exercise 3 into $u_1 v_1 + u_2 v_2$.

5. Show that the matrix P, used in the proof of theorem 6.2.5, is a triangular block matrix.

6. Apply elementary cogredient transformations to the matrix given by

$$B = \begin{pmatrix} 0 & 0 & 1 & 2 \\ 0 & 0 & 3 & 1 \\ -1 & -3 & 0 & -1 \\ -2 & -1 & 1 & 0 \end{pmatrix}$$

to obtain a congruent matrix of the type given by theorem 6.2.4. Write the corresponding matrix P determined by these transformations and show that

$$P^T B P = \begin{pmatrix} 0 & 1 & 0 & 0 \\ -1 & 0 & 0 & 0 \\ 0 & 0 & 0 & 1 \\ 0 & 0 & -1 & 0 \end{pmatrix}.$$

CHAPTER 7

QUADRATIC FORMS

7.1 Introduction. Let B denote the $n \times n$ matrix (b_{ij}) and write $X = (x_i)$ $(i = 1, 2, \ldots, n)$. Write $f = X^T B X$. Then

$$f = \sum_{i,j=1}^{n} b_{ij} x_i x_j,$$

and we call f a quadratic form. Since we may write B, uniquely, as $B = A + K$, where A is symmetric and K is skew, then $f = X^T B X = X^T A X + X^T K X$. But, since

$$X^T K X = \sum_{i,j=1}^{n} x_i k_{ij} x_j$$

and since $k_{ij} = -k_{ji}$, it follows that $X^T K X = 0$ and therefore $f = X^T B X = X^T A X$, where A is symmetric. Since for the form f the matrix A is unique, we shall call A the matrix of the form. We recall that A is $\frac{1}{2}(B + B^T)$.

We define the rank of the form f to be the rank of the matrix A. There is a one-to-one correspondence between the quadratic forms in n variables and the n-row symmetric matrices.

We define a quadratic form g in $x_1, x_2, \ldots, x_n$ to be equivalent to f if and only if f may be transformed into g by nonsingular linear transformations. That is, if there exists a nonsingular matrix P such that, when we apply, to f, the transformation $X = PU$ followed by the transformation $U = IX$, the resulting form is g, then g is equivalent to f. We call the bilinear form having the same matrix as the quadratic form f the *corresponding bilinear form* of f. It follows that two quadratic forms are equivalent if and only if their corresponding bilinear forms are equivalent under cogredient transformations. From theorem 6.2.6, we have

THEOREM 7.1.1 *Every quadratic form of rank r is equivalent to* $c_1 x_1^2 + c_2 x_2^2 + \cdots + c_r x_r^2$, *where* $c_i \neq 0$ $(i = 1, 2, \ldots, r)$.

That is, every quadratic form in n variables and of rank r may be written as a nonsingular quadratic form in r variables.

EXERCISES

1. Write the quadratic form whose matrix is given by

$$A = \begin{pmatrix} 2 & 1 & -1 \\ 1 & 3 & 5 \\ -1 & 5 & 8 \end{pmatrix}.$$

2. Given

$$K = \begin{pmatrix} 0 & 1 & -3 & 5 \\ -1 & 0 & 2 & -4 \\ 3 & -2 & 0 & 6 \\ -5 & 4 & -6 & 0 \end{pmatrix},$$

show that $X^T K X = 0$. Show how the result given by (6.2.1) may be used to prove $X^T K X = 0$ for all skew matrices K.

3. Given

$$B = \begin{pmatrix} 1 & 4 & 2 \\ 0 & 5 & 6 \\ 0 & 0 & 3 \end{pmatrix} \quad \text{and} \quad C = \begin{pmatrix} 1 & 3 & 3 \\ 1 & 5 & 4 \\ -1 & 2 & 3 \end{pmatrix},$$

show that $X^T B X$ and $X^T C X$ represent the same quadratic form and find the matrix of the form.

4. Given the quadratic form $f = x_1^2 + 3x_1x_2 + 5x_2^2 + 7x_2x_3$, write the matrix of f.

5. Show that the quadratic form

$$f = x_1^2 + 4x_1x_2 + 6x_1x_3 - x_2^2 + 2x_2x_3 + 4x_3^2$$

is equivalent to $g = x_1^2 + x_2^2$ and determine a nonsingular transformation which carries f into g.

7.2 Real Quadratic Forms. Up to this point we have not found it necessary to restrict the elements of our matrices to any particular number field. In our definitions of elementary transformations and equivalence of matrices we assumed that the field was the complex number field. If we have a matrix A with elements in a particular field $\mathcal{F}$ and if we restrict the multipliers c and t in the elementary transformation matrices to belong to this field $\mathcal{F}$, then any matrix B obtained from A by multiplying A by a finite number of these elementary matrices will also have its elements in $\mathcal{F}$. These matrices A and B are said to be equivalent over this field $\mathcal{F}$. A similar definition may be made for congruence of matrices over the field $\mathcal{F}$.

It may be readily shown, using arguments similar to those used in theorem 6.2.6, that every symmetric matrix A, of rank r, having elements in a field $\mathcal{F}$ is congruent over $\mathcal{F}$ to diag. $\{c_1, c_2, \ldots, c_r, 0, 0, \ldots, 0\}$, where c_i is a nonzero element of $\mathcal{F}$ for $i = 1, 2, \ldots, r$. For brevity, we shall refer to a matrix all of whose elements belong to the field of real numbers as a *real matrix*. Hence, if A is a real symmetric matrix of rank r and if $f = X^T A X$, then f is called a real quadratic form and f may be transformed by real nonsingular linear transformations into $a_1 x_1^2 + a_2 x_2^2 + \cdots + a_r x_r^2$ with real nonzero a_i $(i = 1, 2, \ldots, r)$. From theorem 6.2.5, it follows that we need consider only the matrix diag. $\{a_1, a_2, \ldots, a_r\}$ which may be transformed by elementary permutative cogredient transformations into diag. $\{b_1, b_2, \ldots, b_s, -b_{s+1}, \ldots, -b_r\}$, where $b_i > 0$. If we now divide both the ith row and the ith column of this matrix by $\sqrt{b_i}$, which amounts to performing real elementary multiplicative cogredient transformations, then we get diag. $\{a_1, a_2, \ldots, a_r\} \overset{c}{=}$ diag. $\{I_s, -I_{r-s}\}$, where the congruence is over the field of real numbers.

Next we show that s, the number of positive coefficients in this form, is unique. To show this, we shall prove that if $s \neq t$ then

$$f(x) = x_1^2 + x_2^2 + \cdots + x_s^2 - x_{s+1}^2 - \cdots - x_r^2$$

and

$$g(x) = x_1^2 + x_2^2 + \cdots + x_t^2 - x_{t+1}^2 - \cdots - x_r^2$$

are not equivalent under real transformations. Suppose that the real nonsingular transformation

$$(7.2.1) \quad x_i = p_{i1} y_1 + p_{i2} y_2 + \cdots + p_{ir} y_r \quad (i = 1, 2, \ldots, r)$$

applied to $f(x)$ yields $g(y)$. If, in $g(y)$, we substitute any set of numbers for $y_1, \ldots, y_r$ and if, in $f(x)$, we substitute the corresponding values of $x_1, x_2, \ldots, x_r$ obtained from (7.2.1), then the values obtained for f and g must be the same. There is no loss of generality in assuming $s > t$. If we select $y_1 = y_2 = \cdots = y_t = 0$, we may then determine $y_{t+1}, \ldots, y_r$ so that $x_{s+1} = x_{s+2} = \cdots = x_r = 0$. Since $r - s < r - t$, the $r - s$ equations

$$p_{i t+1} y_{t+1} + \cdots + p_{in} y_r = 0 \quad (i = s + 1, \ldots, r)$$

will have a nontrivial solution which we denote by $y_j = v_j$ $(j = t + 1, \ldots, r)$. These values, substituted in (7.2.1), yield corresponding values for x_i which we denote by $x_i = u_i$ $(i = 1, 2, \ldots, s)$. For this particular choice of the y_j, the value of $g(y)$ is $-v_{t+1}^2 - \cdots - v_r^2 < 0$ since not all v_i are zero. The corresponding values of the x_i, substituted in $f(x)$, yield $u_1^2 + u_2^2 + \cdots + u_s^2 \geq 0$. Hence, if $s > t$, the resulting numbers are not equal and consequently the forms $f(x)$ and $g(x)$ are not equivalent under real transformations. A similar argument holds for the assumption $s < t$.

Thus we see that, if we apply real elementary cogredient transformations to a real symmetric matrix A to obtain a real diagonal matrix, the number of positive terms in the diagonal matrix is independent of the particular transformations used on A.

DEFINITION. *The number of positive elements in a real diagonal matrix congruent over the field of real numbers to the real symmetric matrix A is called the index of the matrix A. The index of a real quadratic form is defined to be the index of the matrix of the form.*

From the preceding discussion and definition, we have

THEOREM 7.2.1 *Two real symmetric matrices of order n are congruent over the field of real numbers if and only if they have the same rank and the same index.*

DEFINITION. *A real quadratic form, $f = X^T A X$, and its matrix, A, are called* positive (negative) definite *if f is positive (negative) for all X with real elements, not all zero. We call f and its matrix* semidefinite *if f does not assume both positive and negative values for X with real elements, and we call f and its matrix* indefinite *if f assumes a positive value for some X with real elements and also a negative value for some X with real elements.*

If A is positive definite (semidefinite), then $-A$ is negative definite (semidefinite). A real symmetric matrix, A, is positive semidefinite if and only if it is singular and its index is the same as its rank; it is positive definite if and only if it is nonsingular and its index is the same as its order. Hence we have

THEOREM 7.2.2 *A real symmetric matrix A is positive (negative) definite if and only if it is congruent over the real field to I $(-I)$.*

Let P be any real nonsingular $n \times n$ matrix and write the linear transformation $Y = PX$. Then

$$Y^T Y = X^T P^T P X = \sum_{i=1}^{n} y_i^2,$$

and hence we have

THEOREM 7.2.3 *If P is a real nonsingular matrix, then $P^T P$ is positive definite.*

If A is a real symmetric positive definite matrix, then there exists a real nonsingular matrix P such that $P^T A P = I$ and hence $A = P^{TI} P^I = Q^T Q$, where $Q = P^I$. The matrices P and Q are obviously not unique. For example, see the following illustration.

Illustration: If

$$P = \begin{pmatrix} 1 & 2 & 1 \\ 2 & 0 & 1 \\ -1 & 2 & 1 \end{pmatrix} \quad \text{and} \quad Q = \begin{pmatrix} 2 & 0 & 1 \\ 1 & 2 & 1 \\ -1 & 2 & 1 \end{pmatrix},$$

then

$$A = \begin{pmatrix} 6 & 0 & 0 \\ 0 & 8 & 4 \\ 0 & 4 & 3 \end{pmatrix},$$

where $P^T P = Q^T Q = A$. It is obvious, too, that $P^{TI} A P^I = Q^{TI} A Q^I = I$. Thus, for $R^T A R = I$, R is not unique.

THEOREM 7.2.4 *If A is a real positive definite symmetric matrix, there exists a real nonsingular matrix Q such that $A = Q^T Q$.*

Suppose that A is a real positive definite symmetric matrix. Then there exist real nonsingular matrices P and Q such that $P^T A P = I$ and $A = Q^T Q$ and hence $P^T Q^T Q P = I$. The matrix QP, therefore, has the property that $(QP)^T = (QP)^I$.

Illustration: If

$$P = \begin{pmatrix} -3 & 2 \\ 2 & -1 \end{pmatrix} \quad \text{and} \quad Q = \begin{pmatrix} \frac{11}{5} & \frac{18}{5} \\ -\frac{2}{5} & -\frac{1}{5} \end{pmatrix},$$

then

$$QP = \begin{pmatrix} \frac{3}{5} & \frac{4}{5} \\ \frac{4}{5} & -\frac{3}{5} \end{pmatrix} \quad \text{and} \quad (QP)^T = (QP)^I.$$

Also, in this case, $QP = P^I Q^I$, as may be easily verified.

DEFINITION. *If a matrix R is such that $R^T = R^I$, we say that R is orthogonal.*

If R and S are two orthogonal matrices, then $(RS)^T RS = S^T R^T RS = S^T I S = S^T S = I$ and $(RS)^T = (RS)^I$. Thus we have

THEOREM 7.2.5 *The product of two orthogonal matrices is an orthogonal matrix.*

Let A be a real positive definite symmetric matrix and write $f = X^T A X$. If, in X, we assign certain elements zero and call the matrix of the remaining elements X_1, then, for this choice of elements in X, $f = X_1^T A_1 X_1$, where A_1 is a principal submatrix of A. But, since $f > 0$ for all real $X \neq 0$, $X_1^T A_1 X_1 > 0$ for all real $X_1 \neq 0$ and hence A_1 is positive definite. Thus we have

THEOREM 7.2.6 *Every principal submatrix of a real positive definite symmetric matrix is a positive definite symmetric matrix.*

Let A be a real symmetric matrix having a nonsingular principal submatrix A_1 of order r. If all principal submatrices of A of orders $r + 1$ and $r + 2$ which contain A_1 are singular, we shall show that A is of rank r. There is no loss of generality in writing

$$A = \begin{pmatrix} A_1 & A_2 \\ A_2^T & A_3 \end{pmatrix}.$$

Indicate by B_i those principal submatrices of order $r + 1$ which contain A_1, and by B_{ij} those of order $r + 2$ which contain A_1. In general, we have

$$B_i = \begin{pmatrix} A_1 & K_i \\ K_i^T & a_{ii} \end{pmatrix} \quad \text{and} \quad B_{ij} = \begin{pmatrix} A_1 & K_i & K_j \\ K_i^T & a_{ii} & a_{ij} \\ K_j^T & a_{ij} & a_{jj} \end{pmatrix},$$

where K_i and K_j are one-column matrices given by $K_i = (a_{ti})$, $K_j = (a_{tj})$ $(r < i < j; t = 1, 2, \ldots, r)$. By hypothesis, B_i and B_{ij} are singular. We now obtain triangular block matrices equivalent to B_i and B_{ij}. Thus we see that

$$\begin{pmatrix} I & 0 \\ -K_i^T A_1^I & 1 \end{pmatrix}\begin{pmatrix} A_1 & K_i \\ K_i^T & a_{ii} \end{pmatrix} = \begin{pmatrix} A_1 & K_i \\ 0 & a_{ii} - K_i^T A_1^I K_i \end{pmatrix},$$

and, since B_i is singular and A_1 is nonsingular, we have $a_{ii} - K_i^T A_1^I K_i = 0$ for $i > r$. We may now replace, in A, the a_{ii} by $K_i^T A_1^I K_i$ for $i > r$. Then we have

$$B_{ij} \overset{\text{E}}{=} \begin{pmatrix} I & 0 & 0 \\ -K_i^T A_1^I & 1 & 0 \\ -K_j^T A_1^I & 0 & 1 \end{pmatrix}\begin{pmatrix} A_1 & K_i & K_j \\ K_i^T & K_i^T A_1^I K_i & a_{ij} \\ K_j^T & a_{ij} & K_j^T A_1^I K_j \end{pmatrix}$$

$$= \begin{pmatrix} A_1 & K_i & K_j \\ 0 & 0 & a_{ij} - K_i^T A_1^I K_j \\ 0 & a_{ij} - K_j^T A_1^I K_i & 0 \end{pmatrix}.$$

But $K_i^T A_1^I K_j = (K_i^T A_1^I K_j)^T = K_j^T A_1^I K_i$ and, since B_{ij} is singular, it follows that $a_{ij} - K_i^T A_1^I K_j = 0$ for $i, j > r$. However, since $A_2 = (K_{r+1}, K_{r+2}, \ldots, K_n)$, and $(a_{ij}) = K_i^T A_1^I K_j$ $(i, j = r + 1, r + 2, \ldots, n)$, it follows that $A_3 = A_2^T A_1^I A_2$. We now have

$$A \overset{c}{=} \begin{pmatrix} I_r & 0 \\ -A_2^T A_1^I & I_{n-r} \end{pmatrix} \begin{pmatrix} A_1 & A_2 \\ A_2^T & A_2^T A_1^I A_2 \end{pmatrix} \begin{pmatrix} I_r & -A_1^I A_2 \\ 0 & I_{n-r} \end{pmatrix} = \begin{pmatrix} A_1 & 0 \\ 0 & 0 \end{pmatrix},$$

and hence A is of rank r. Thus we have proved

THEOREM 7.2.7 *Let A be a real symmetric matrix having a nonsingular principal submatrix, A_1, of order r. If all principal submatrices of orders $r + 1$ and $r + 2$ which have A_1 as a submatrix are singular, then A is of rank r.*

It may be easily shown that, if all principal submatrices of order one and all principal submatrices of order two of a symmetric matrix A are singular, then $A = 0$.

A real symmetric nonsingular matrix A is said to be *regularly arranged* if no two consecutive ones of the principal submatrices of orders $1, 2, \ldots, n$ in the upper left-hand corner are singular. Since A is nonsingular, there is a nonsingular principal submatrix either of order one or of order two. This submatrix may be moved to the upper left-hand corner by a cogredient permutative transformation. Applying theorem 7.2.7, if there is a nonsingular principal submatrix, A_1, of order $r < n - 1$ in the upper left-hand corner, then there is a nonsingular principal submatrix of either order $r + 1$ or order $r + 2$ containing A_1. Hence we have

THEOREM 7.2.8 *Every nonsingular real symmetric matrix A may be regularly arranged by applying cogredient permutative transformations to A.*

EXERCISES

1. Show that the following real quadratic forms are equivalent under real transformations:

   (a) $x_1^2 - x_2^2 + x_3^2 + 2x_1x_3$,
   (b) $x_1^2 - x_2^2$,
   (c) $2x_1x_3 + x_3^2 - 2x_1x_2 - x_2^2$.

2. Show by substituting $x_1 = ay_1 + by_2$, $x_2 = cy_1 + dy_2$ in $x_1^2 + x_2^2$ that it is not possible to obtain $y_1^2 - y_2^2$ for a, b, c, and d all real.

3. Show that the following matrices are congruent:

$$\begin{pmatrix} 1 & 2 & 3 \\ 2 & 1 & 3 \\ 3 & 3 & 6 \end{pmatrix}, \quad \begin{pmatrix} 1 & 2 & 3 \\ 2 & 2 & 4 \\ 3 & 4 & 7 \end{pmatrix}, \quad \begin{pmatrix} 2 & 1 & 3 \\ 1 & -1 & 0 \\ 3 & 0 & 3 \end{pmatrix}.$$

4. Show that

$$\begin{pmatrix} 2 & 1 & 3 \\ 1 & 3 & 4 \\ 3 & 4 & 8 \end{pmatrix}$$

is a positive definite matrix.

5. Given $A = (a_{ij})$ $(i,j = 1, 2, \ldots, n)$. Show that A is orthogonal if and only if

$$\sum_{j=1}^{n} a_{ij}^2 = 1 \qquad (i = 1, 2, \ldots, n)$$

and

$$\sum_{j=1}^{n} a_{ij}a_{kj} = 0 \qquad (i \neq k).$$

6. If A is an orthogonal matrix, show that A^T is orthogonal and state the problem corresponding to Exercise 5 in terms of the elements of the columns of A.

7. Use Exercise 5 to compute two different orthogonal matrices each having as first row $(\frac{4}{9} \quad \frac{4}{9} \quad \frac{7}{9})$.

8. Write two different orthogonal matrices of order three having elements in the first column proportional to 3, 4, and 12.

9. If A is a skew matrix such that $I - A$ is nonsingular, show that $(I - A)^I(I + A)$ is orthogonal.

10. Use the result in Exercise 9 to obtain two 3×3 orthogonal matrices.

11. If B is an orthogonal matrix such that $B + I$ is nonsingular, show that $(B - I)(B + I)^I$ is skew.

12. Let $A = (B - I)(B + I)^I$, where B is as defined in Exercise 11. Show that $I - A$ is nonsingular, and thus show that all orthogonal matrices B such that $B + I$ is nonsingular are given by $(I - A)^I(I + A)$, where A is skew and $I - A$ is nonsingular.

13. Let the first row of a matrix A be $(a_{11} \ a_{12} \ \ldots \ a_{1n})$, and let the remaining $n - 1$ rows be such that

$$\sum_{j=1}^{n} a_{ij}a_{kj} = 0 \qquad (i \neq k; i, k = 1, 2, \ldots, n).$$

Show that AA^T is diagonal. Write

$$s_i^2 = \sum_{j=1}^{n} a_{ij}^2$$

and show that, if $s_i \neq 0$ $(i = 1, 2, \ldots, n)$, and $S = \text{diag.} \{s_1^{-1}, s_2^{-1}, \ldots, s_n^{-1}\}$, then SA is orthogonal. Use this method to construct numerical examples of orthogonal matrices.

14. Given the orthogonal matrix, B, defined by

$$B = \begin{pmatrix} \frac{2}{7} & -\frac{3}{7} & \frac{6}{7} \\ \frac{3}{7} & \frac{6}{7} & \frac{2}{7} \\ -\frac{6}{7} & \frac{2}{7} & \frac{3}{7} \end{pmatrix},$$

determine A so that $(I - A)B = (I + A)$ and show that $I - A$ is nonsingular and that A is skew and hence $B = (I - A)^I(I + A)$.

15. If P is an $m \times n$ matrix, $m > n$; and, if the rank of P is n, show that $P^T P$ is a positive definite symmetric matrix.

16. If A is an $n \times n$ real positive semidefinite matrix of rank r, show that $A = Q^T Q$, where Q is an $r \times n$ matrix of rank r.

17. If W is an orthogonal matrix and if $Q = WP$, show that PQ^I is orthogonal for nonsingular P.

CHAPTER 8

LINEAR VECTOR SPACE OVER A FIELD

8.1 Introduction. The ordered pair of real numbers x_1, x_2 forming the elements of the 1×2 matrix $(x_1 \; x_2)$ is commonly used as the symbol to represent a point, X, in two-space, Fig. 8.1, Fig. 8.2. Also associated with

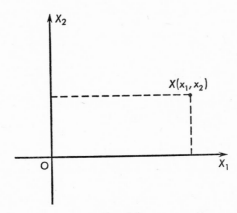

FIG. 8.1.

this matrix is the vector $\overrightarrow{OX}$, which is sometimes indicated by $(x_1 \; x_2)$, the matrix itself. Interpreted as a vector, $(x_1 \; x_2)$ is called a *two-space vector*, or a *two-dimensional vector*. In three-space the same interpretation may be given the ordered triplet $(x_1 \; x_2 \; x_3)$. That is, it may be used as a 1×3 matrix to represent a point in three-space, or to indicate a vector directed from the origin to the point identified in three-space. These interpretations are familiar ones, and the terms *three-space vector* and *three-dimensional vector* for $(x_1 \; x_2 \; x_3)$ are in common usage.

We now consider vectors X_1 and X_2 in two-space. In order to distinguish the coordinates of the endpoint of vector X_1 from those of vector X_2 we use the notation

$$X_1 = (x_{11} \; x_{12}),$$

and

$$X_2 = (x_{21} \; x_{22}).$$

99

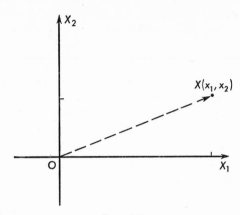

Fig. 8.2.

By applying the well-known parallelogram law for the addition of vectors, it is seen that

$$X_1 + X_2 = (x_{11} + x_{21} \quad x_{12} + x_{22}),$$

which is the sum of X_1 and X_2, considering them as matrices.

Similarly, the sum of the vectors

$$X_1 = (x_{11} \quad x_{12} \quad x_{13})$$

and

$$X_2 = (x_{21} \quad x_{22} \quad x_{23})$$

is given by

$$X_1 + X_2 = (x_{11} + x_{21} \quad x_{12} + x_{22} \quad x_{13} + x_{23}).$$

If k is a scalar and X is the matrix $(x_1 \ x_2 \ x_3)$, then

$$kX = k(x_1 \quad x_2 \quad x_3) = (kx_1 \quad kx_2 \quad kx_3),$$

which is the usual treatment of the familiar operation in physics and engineering known as multiplying a vector by a real number.

8.2 Generalization to n-Dimensional Vectors. It is convenient and easy to represent a real vector of two dimensions or of three dimensions by a geometric model. An n-dimensional vector for $n > 3$ does not lend itself to such geometric representation. Nevertheless, such vectors are significant in many branches of mathematics, even when the elements x_{ij} are complex numbers.

DEFINITION. *An n-dimensional vector X over a number field $\mathcal{F}$ is an ordered set $x_1, x_2, \ldots, x_n$, where x_i belong to $\mathcal{F}$, $i = 1, 2, \ldots, n$. The x_i are called the* elements *or* components *of the vector X.*

It will be convenient for us to utilize the conventional matrix notation for the representation of an n-dimensional vector X having elements $x_i \, \epsilon \, \mathcal{F}$,

$i = 1, 2, \ldots, n.$ Thus we shall symbolize the n-dimensional vector as a $1 \times n$ matrix and denote this in the usual manner $(x_1 \ x_2 \ \ldots \ x_n)$.

To consider the totality of all n-dimensional vectors over a number field $\mathcal{F}$ we state the following

DEFINITION. *If $V_n(\mathcal{F})$ represents the set of all vectors*

$$X_i = (x_{i1} \ \ x_{i2} \ \ \ldots \ \ x_{in}), \quad x_{ij} \, \epsilon \, \mathcal{F},$$

for fixed n, then $V_n(\mathcal{F})$ is called the n-dimensional vector space over $\mathcal{F}$.

For the vectors

$$X_1 = (x_{11} \ \ x_{12} \ \ \ldots \ \ x_{1n}),$$

$$X_2 = (x_{21} \ \ x_{22} \ \ \ldots \ \ x_{2n}),$$

$$\cdots\cdots\cdots\cdots\cdots\cdots\cdots$$

of $V_n(\mathcal{F})$ the sum $X_i + X_j$ is defined to be the vector

$$(x_{i1} + x_{j1} \ \ x_{i2} + x_{j2} \ \ \ldots \ \ x_{in} + x_{jn})$$

and is thus a vector of $V_n(\mathcal{F})$. And, for each $c \, \epsilon \, \mathcal{F}$, the vector representing the scalar product cX_i is defined to be $(cx_{i1} \ cx_{i2} \ \ldots \ cx_{in})$, which also belongs to $V_n(\mathcal{F})$. It is immediately obvious that these operations are identical with the corresponding ones for matrices and that $V_n(\mathcal{F})$ is closed with respect to these two operations.

Since addition is now defined and since two vectors are equal if and only if their corresponding components are equal, it is easy to see that for X_i, X_j in $V_n(\mathcal{F})$ then there exists a unique Y in $V_n(\mathcal{F})$ such that $X_i + Y = X_j$. In particular, the unique vector $Y = (0, 0, \ldots, 0)$ satisfies the condition $X_i + Y = X_i$ and is denoted by the single symbol 0. There is no ambiguity in this notation.

DEFINITION. *The vector Y of $V_n(\mathcal{F})$ having the property that $X_i + Y = X_i$ for all X_i of $V_n(\mathcal{F})$ is called the zero vector of $V_n(\mathcal{F})$.*

The vectors belonging to $V_n(\mathcal{F})$ are often referred to as the elements of $V_n(\mathcal{F})$ and, in particular, the zero vector of $V_n(\mathcal{F})$ is referred to as the *zero element* of $V_n(\mathcal{F})$.

We note that, since $1 \, \epsilon \, \mathcal{F}$, then $1 \cdot X_i$ belongs to $V_n(\mathcal{F})$ and actually $1 \cdot X_i = X_i$. Also, $-1 \, \epsilon \, \mathcal{F}$ and $-1 \cdot X_i \, \epsilon \, V_n(\mathcal{F})$. Clearly, for the sake of consistency, we must indicate $-1 \cdot X_i$ by $-X_i$, and we see that $-X_i$ is the unique negative (sometimes called "additive inverse") of X_i and that $X_i + (-X_i) = 0$.

Since addition of vectors and the multiplication of a vector by a scalar are defined in the same way as these operations are defined for matrices, the various laws established for matrices are valid for vectors. It should be pointed out that the product of two vectors is not defined. However, using the matrix notation, the product of the matrices X_i and X_j^T, that is, $X_i X_j^T$, is useful in the study of vectors, and we shall have occasion to use this product in future work.

DEFINITION. *A set V of vectors in $V_n(\mathcal{F})$ is called a linear vector space over $\mathcal{F}$, or a subspace of $V_n(\mathcal{F})$, if the set V is closed with respect to addition and with respect to scalar multiplication by elements in $\mathcal{F}$.*

For example, if $V_3(\mathcal{F})$ is used to designate the linear vector space consisting of the set of all 1×3 matrices $(a_1\ a_2\ a_3)$ with real elements, then the subset, V, consisting of all matrices $(b_1\ b_2\ 0)$ with real elements is a subspace of $V_3(\mathcal{F})$. Furthermore, the linear vector space $V_3(\mathcal{F})$ is itself a subspace of $V_3(\mathcal{C})$, where $\mathcal{C}$ is the field of complex numbers.

It is obvious that $V_n(\mathcal{F})$ is itself a subspace of $V_n(\mathcal{F})$. If V is a subspace of $V_n(\mathcal{F})$ but V does not contain all the vectors of $V_n(\mathcal{F})$, then V is said to be a proper subspace of $V_n(\mathcal{F})$. From this it is seen that $V_n(\mathcal{F})$ is a proper subspace of $V_n(\mathcal{C})$. It is evident that V contains the zero vector as does every n-dimensional linear vector space, for, since $0 \in \mathcal{F}$ and V is closed with respect to scalar multiplication, then for every $X_i \in V$ we have $0 \cdot X_i = 0$ and $0 \in V$. Actually, the zero vector constitutes a subspace of $V_n(\mathcal{F})$, and thus we have a subspace of $V_n(\mathcal{F})$ composed of a single vector.

An important question which often arises is how may one select a linear subspace V from a linear vector space $V_n(\mathcal{F})$. The following, easily established, theorem will indicate one way in which this may be done.

THEOREM 8.2.1   *If $X_1, X_2, \ldots, X_m$ are m vectors belonging to $V_n(\mathcal{F})$, then the set V consisting of all linear combinations*

$$\sum_{i=1}^{m} c_i X_i, \quad c_i \in \mathcal{F},$$

is a linear vector space over $\mathcal{F}$.

The set V is obviously closed with respect to addition and scalar multiplication. Verification of this is left as an exercise.

From the theorem above it will be noted that, if $X_1, X_2, \ldots, X_m$ are m n-dimensional vectors over a number field $\mathcal{F}$, then the set of all linear forms in the $X_i, i = 1, 2, \ldots, m$, with coefficients in $\mathcal{F}$ is a linear vector space over $\mathcal{F}$. This set, V, of all linear forms in the X_i is said to be *generated* by the vectors $X_1, X_2, \ldots, X_m$. The set of vectors $X_1, X_2, \ldots, X_m$ is said to *span* the linear vector space so determined. We indicate this by writing

$$V = \{X_1, X_2, \ldots, X_m\} \text{ over } \mathcal{F}.$$

Obviously the subspace V is unaffected by a permutation of the generating elements.

Illustration: $V_1 = \{X_1, X_2\}$, $V_2 = \{Y_1, Y_2\}$, where $X_1 = (1\ 1\ 2)$, $X_2 = (1\ 2\ 0)$, and $Y_1 = (2\ 3\ 2)$, $Y_2 = (0\ -1\ 2)$. Since $Y_1 = X_1 + X_2$ and $Y_2 = X_1 - X_2$ and also $X_1 = \frac{1}{2}Y_1 + \frac{1}{2}Y_2$ and $X_2 = \frac{1}{2}Y_1 - \frac{1}{2}Y_2$, thus every element of V_1 belongs to V_2 and every element of V_2 belongs to V_1. The relationship between the X_i and Y_j could be expressed as

$$\begin{pmatrix} 1 & 1 \\ 1 & -1 \end{pmatrix}\begin{pmatrix} X_1 \\ X_2 \end{pmatrix} = \begin{pmatrix} Y_1 \\ Y_2 \end{pmatrix}.$$

DEFINITION. *If V_1 and V_2 are subspaces of $V_n(\mathcal{F})$, then they are identical if and only if each is a subspace of the other.*

EXERCISES

1. Given $V = \{X_1, X_2\}$ over the field of real numbers, where $X_1 = (1\ 1\ 2)$ and $X_2 = (1\ 2\ 0)$, determine which of the following vectors belong to V.

(a) $(1\ 0\ 4)$.
(b) $(1\ 1\ 3)$.
(c) $(a\ 2a\ 0)$.
(d) $(2\ 4\ 0)$.
(e) $(a\ b\ 2c)$.
(f) $(a + b\ \ a + 2b\ \ 2a)$.

2. Let $V_1 = \{X_1, X_2\}$ over $\mathcal{F}$ and $V_2 = \{Y_1, Y_2\}$ over $\mathcal{F}$, where $X_1 = (1\ 0\ 0)$, $X_2 = (0\ 1\ 0)$, $Y_1 = (0\ 1\ 0)$, $Y_2 = (0\ 0\ 1)$. Show that V_1 and V_2 are not identical.

3. Let $V_1 = \{X_1, X_2\}$ over $\mathcal{F}$, $V_2 = \{X_1, Y_2\}$ over $\mathcal{F}$, where Y_2 does not belong to V_1. Show that V_1 and V_2 are not identical.

4. Show that the product of any element of $\mathcal{F}$ by the zero element of $V_n(\mathcal{F})$ is the zero element of $V_n(\mathcal{F})$.

5. Show that the product of the zero element of $\mathcal{F}$ by any element of $V_n(\mathcal{F})$ is the zero element of $V_n(\mathcal{F})$.

6. For the vectors, X_i, of $V_n(\mathcal{F})$ show that

(a) $X_i + X_j = X_j + X_i$,
(b) $X_i + (X_j + X_k) = (X_i + X_j) + X_k$,
(c) $c(X_i + X_j) = cX_i + cX_j$,
(d) $(c_1 + c_2)X_i = c_1X_i + c_2X_i$,
(e) $(c_1c_2)X_i = c_1(c_2X_i)$.

7. Prove theorem 8.2.1.

8. Let $V = \{X_1, X_2, \ldots, X_m\}$ over $\mathcal{F}$ and let P be any elementary permutative matrix. If $PX = Y$, where

$$X = \begin{pmatrix} X_1 \\ X_2 \\ \vdots \\ X_m \end{pmatrix}, \qquad Y = \begin{pmatrix} Y_1 \\ Y_2 \\ \vdots \\ Y_m \end{pmatrix},$$

prove that $V = \{Y_1, Y_2, \ldots, Y_m\}$ over $\mathcal{F}$.

9. In Exercise 8 above, if P is any nonsingular matrix having elements in $\mathcal{F}$, prove that $V = \{Y_1, Y_2, \ldots, Y_m\}$ over $\mathcal{F}$.

8.3 Linear Dependence, Linear Independence, Bases.

We have noted that every linear vector space $V_n(\mathcal{F})$ contains a unique zero element and that every subspace V of $V_n(\mathcal{F})$ also contains this zero vector. In fact, the zero element of the subspace $V = \{X_1, X_2, \ldots, X_m\}$ over $\mathcal{F}$ is the particular linear combination $OX_1 + OX_2 + \cdots + OX_m$. It is quite possible that

$$\sum_{i=1}^{m} c_i X_i = 0, \qquad c_i \in \mathcal{F},$$

where at least one c_i is not zero. In this case the X_i, $i = 1, 2, \ldots, m$, are said to be *linearly dependent over* $\mathcal{F}$. If the zero element of V is represented in only one way as a linear form in the X_i, $i = 1, 2, \ldots, m$, with coefficients in $\mathcal{F}$, then we say that the X_i, $i = 1, 2, \ldots, m$, are *linearly independent over* $\mathcal{F}$. That is, if

$$\sum_{i=1}^{m} c_i X_i = 0$$

implies that $c_1 = c_2 = \cdots = c_m = 0$, then the X_i are linearly independent over $\mathcal{F}$.

Illustration: Given the three vectors, components in the real number field $\mathcal{F}$,

$$X_1 = (1 \quad 3 \quad 5),$$
$$X_2 = (2 \quad -1 \quad 4),$$
$$X_3 = (4 \quad -9 \quad 2),$$

then $2X_1 - 3X_2 + X_3 = (0 \ 0 \ 0) = 0$ shows that the X_i are linearly dependent over $\mathcal{F}$.

Illustration: Given the vectors, with components in the real number field $\mathcal{F}$,

$$X_1 = (1 \quad 0 \quad 0 \quad 0),$$
$$X_2 = (0 \quad 1 \quad 0 \quad 0),$$
$$X_3 = (0 \quad 0 \quad 1 \quad 0),$$
$$X_4 = (0 \quad 0 \quad 0 \quad 1),$$

then

$$\sum_{i=1}^{4} c_i X_i \text{ is the vector } (c_1 \quad c_2 \quad c_3 \quad c_4);$$

and if this vector is zero then $c_1 = c_2 = c_3 = c_4 = 0$, which implies that the X_i are linearly independent over $\mathcal{F}$.

Basic to the idea of linear independence and linear dependence we have

THEOREM 8.3.1   *If m vectors $X_1, X_2, \ldots, X_m$ are linearly dependent over $\mathcal{F}$, then it is always possible to express some one of them as a linear form in the remaining $m - 1$ vectors, having coefficients in $\mathcal{F}$.*

For, there exists $a_i \in \mathcal{F}$ such that

$$\sum_{i=1}^{m} a_i X_i = 0,$$

where at least one of the coefficients, say a_k, is not zero.   Hence X_k may be expressed as a linear form in the remaining vectors.

THEOREM 8.3.2   *If m vectors $X_1, X_2, \ldots, X_m$ are linearly independent over $\mathcal{F}$ whereas the $m + 1$ vectors $X_1, X_2, \ldots, X_m, X_{m+1}$ are linearly dependent over $\mathcal{F}$, then X_{m+1} is a linear form in the $X_1, X_2, \ldots, X_m$ with coefficients in $\mathcal{F}$.*

Since the $m + 1$ vectors are linearly dependent over $\mathcal{F}$, there exist $a_i \in \mathcal{F}$ such that

$$\sum_{i=1}^{m+1} a_i X_i = 0,$$

where not all a_i are zero.   And, in particular, a_{m+1} is not zero; otherwise the m vectors $X_1, X_2, \ldots, X_m$ are linearly dependent over $\mathcal{F}$.   It follows then that

$$X_{m+1} = \sum_{i=1}^{m} \frac{-a_i}{a_{m+1}} X_i$$

and the theorem is established.

The concept of linearly dependent and linearly independent sets of vectors is an important one and we shall now devote some attention to determining which of these properties a given set of vectors possesses and to the study of the significance of this property.   We shall now make the following observations, all of which may be easily verified.

(1) The zero vector constitutes a linearly dependent set over every number field.

(2) Any nonzero vector constitutes a linearly independent set over every number field.

(3) If the vectors of a given set are linearly dependent over a number field, then the vectors of any set containing the given set as a subset are linearly dependent over the same number field.   In particular, it is easy to see that, if a given set of vectors contains the zero vector, then the vectors of the set are linearly dependent over every number field.   More generally, if a set of vectors contains a subset of vectors which are linearly dependent

over a field $\mathcal{F}$, then all the vectors of the set are linearly dependent over $\mathcal{F}$.

(4) If the vectors of a set are linearly dependent over a number field $\mathcal{F}$, then they may be linearly independent over a subfield of $\mathcal{F}$. For example, the one-dimensional vectors 1 and i are linearly dependent over the field of complex numbers but are linearly independent over the field of real numbers.

From these observations we have the following

THEOREM 8.3.3   *If the set of m vectors $X_1, X_2, \ldots, X_m$ contains a subset comprised of r vectors linearly dependent over $\mathcal{F}$, for $r < m$, then the vectors $X_1, X_2, \ldots, X_m$ are linearly dependent over $\mathcal{F}$.*

Consider the vector space $V = \{X_1, X_2, \ldots, X_m\}$ over $\mathcal{F}$. We have observed that each element of V may be expressed in the form

$$\sum_{i=1}^{m} a_i X_i.$$

We now inquire whether or not such a representation is unique. Suppose that the vector

$$\sum_{i=1}^{m} a_i X_i$$

may also be represented by

$$\sum_{i=1}^{m} b_i X_i,$$

then

$$\sum_{i=1}^{m} a_i X_i = \sum_{i=1}^{m} b_i X_i$$

and thus

$$\sum_{i=1}^{m} (a_i - b_i) X_i = 0.$$

Now, if the X_i are linearly independent over $\mathcal{F}$, then each coefficient, $a_i - b_i$, must be zero and we have $a_i = b_i$ for $i = 1, 2, \ldots, m$. Thus, in this case, each vector of V is represented uniquely as a linear form in the X_i. Now suppose that $V = \{X_1, X_2, \ldots, X_m\}$ over $\mathcal{F}$ has the property that every vector X belonging to V has a unique representation as a linear form in the $X_1, X_2, \ldots, X_m$ with coefficients in $\mathcal{F}$. Then

$$\sum_{i=1}^{m} O X_i$$

is the only representation of the zero vector of V and consequently

$$\sum_{i=1}^{m} a_i X_i = 0$$

implies $a_i = 0$ for $i = 1, 2, \ldots, m$. Thus the $X_1, X_2, \ldots, X_m$ are linearly independent over $\mathcal{F}$, and we have established the following

THEOREM 8.3.4 *If $V = \{X_1, X_2, \ldots, X_m\}$ over $\mathcal{F}$, then a necessary and sufficient condition that every X of V be represented uniquely as a linear form in the $X_1, X_2, \ldots, X_m$ with coefficients in $\mathcal{F}$ is that the $X_1, X_2, \ldots, X_m$ be linearly independent over $\mathcal{F}$.*

For every X of V we have $X + 0 = X$. There exist $a_i \,\epsilon\, \mathcal{F}$ such that

$$\sum_{i=1}^{m} a_i X_i = 0,$$

where not all a_i are zero if and only if $X_1, X_2, \ldots, X_m$ are linearly dependent over $\mathcal{F}$. It follows that every X of V has more than one representation if and only if $X_i, i = 1, 2, \ldots, m$, are linearly dependent over $\mathcal{F}$. We now have

THEOREM 8.3.5 *If $V = \{X_1, X_2, \ldots, X_m\}$ over $\mathcal{F}$, then a necessary and sufficient condition that every vector $X \,\epsilon\, V$ be expressible as a linear form in the $X_1, X_2, \ldots, X_m$ over $\mathcal{F}$ in more than one way is that the vectors $X_1, X_2, \ldots, X_m$ be linearly dependent over $\mathcal{F}$.*

We have seen that, if the generating X_i of $V = \{X_1, X_2, \ldots, X_m\}$ over $\mathcal{F}$ are linearly independent over $\mathcal{F}$, then every vector of V is expressed uniquely as a linear form in the generating elements having coefficients in the field $\mathcal{F}$. Moreover, we have seen that, if the generating X_i of V are linearly dependent over $\mathcal{F}$, then, in this case, each vector of V is expressible in more than one way as a linear form in the generating elements having coefficients in $\mathcal{F}$. This leads us to inquire whether or not it is always possible to select a subset of the generating elements X_i which are linearly independent over $\mathcal{F}$ and which will generate the set V.

We shall now show that, if the generating X_i of $V = \{X_1, X_2, \ldots, X_m\}$ over $\mathcal{F}$ are linearly dependent over $\mathcal{F}$, then some r of these X_i are linearly independent over $\mathcal{F}$ and, moreover, these r vectors generate the space V except when V is the *null* space, that is, contains only the zero vector. If V is not the null space, then some one of the generating vectors, say X_p, is not zero. If $aX_p = 0$, then $a = 0$ and thus this vector X_p constitutes a one-member set linearly independent over $\mathcal{F}$. If among the generators X_i there are k vectors which are linearly independent over $\mathcal{F}$, we may without loss of generality and for simplicity of notation choose the first k, namely $X_1, X_2, \ldots, X_k$. If each of the remaining generating elements of V is now a linear combination of these $X_1, X_2, \ldots, X_k$, then every element of V is a linear combination of these and we may write $V = \{X_1, X_2, \ldots, X_k\}$ over $\mathcal{F}$. But, if there is some element, say X_{k+1}, of V which is not a linear combination of the elements $X_1, X_2, \ldots, X_k$, then the vectors $X_1, X_2, \ldots, X_k, X_{k+1}$ are linearly independent over $\mathcal{F}$. For, if

$$\sum_{i=1}^{k+1} a_i X_i = 0, \qquad a_i \text{ not all zero,}$$

then a_{k+1} must differ from zero since $X_1, X_2, \ldots, X_k$ are linearly independent over $\mathcal{F}$. Consequently, X_{k+1} is a linear form in $X_1, X_2, \ldots, X_m$; this contradicts the hypothesis that X_{k+1} is not a linear combination of the X_i, $i = 1, 2, \ldots, k$. Thus we may obtain a subset $X_1, X_2, \ldots, X_r$, $r < m$, which will have the property that these X_i, for $i = 1, 2, \ldots, r$, are linearly independent over $\mathcal{F}$ and that each remaining generating vector is a linear combination of these with coefficients in $\mathcal{F}$. Thus we see that we may write $V = \{X_1, X_2, \ldots, X_r\}$ over $\mathcal{F}$. We have now demonstrated that every vector space $V = \{X_1, X_2, \ldots, X_m\}$ over $\mathcal{F}$ may be generated by a set of vectors linearly independent over $\mathcal{F}$. For this reason we introduce the term *basis* and give the following

DEFINITION. Basis. *A set of vectors $X_1, X_2, \ldots, X_m$ of $V_n(\mathcal{F})$ is said to constitute a* basis *for the subspace $V = \{X_1, X_2, \ldots, X_m\}$ over $\mathcal{F}$ if the vectors $X_1, X_2, \ldots, X_m$ are linearly independent over $\mathcal{F}$.*

If the generating elements of V constitute a basis for V, then we indicate this by writing the generating elements in square brackets, and in this case we have

$$V = [X_1, X_2, \ldots, X_m] \text{ over } \mathcal{F}.$$

We have established

THEOREM 8.3.6 *If V is a linear vector space over $\mathcal{F}$ generated by the vectors $X_1, X_2, \ldots, X_m$ not all of which are zero, then some r of these generating vectors form a basis for V over $\mathcal{F}$ where $1 \leq r \leq m$.*

It is clear from the proof of the previous theorem that a basis for V cannot contain more than r vectors if it contains the particular basis vectors $X_1, X_2, \ldots, X_r$ from the generating vectors, since any other vector of V is a linear combination of these. We have actually shown that any k vector linearly independent over $\mathcal{F}$ and belonging to the generators $X_1, X_2, \ldots, X_m$ of V is a subset of a basis for the vector space V.

There are still several questions as yet unanswered. For example:

(1) Is it possible to have more than one basis for a vector space?

(2) Is there any relation between different bases of the same vector space and, if so, knowing one basis, how may we determine another?

(3) If it is possible to select two different bases for a vector space, must each basis contain the same number of vectors?

(4) Is it possible to determine the number of vectors constituting a basis for a given linear vector space?

We consider the first question above in the following illustration.

Illustration: Different bases. If the components of the vectors of the three-dimensional vector space V belong to the real number field $\mathcal{F}$, then the vectors

$$X_1 = (1 \quad 0 \quad 0),$$

$$X_2 = (0 \quad 1 \quad 0),$$

$$X_3 = (0 \quad 0 \quad 1)$$

constitute a basis for V over the real number field and we have

$$V = [X_1, X_2, X_3] \text{ over } \mathcal{F}.$$

But the vectors $2X_1, 2X_2, 2X_3$ also constitute a basis for V, and we see immediately that the number of different bases is certainly not limited. Consider now the vector $X_4 = (3 \quad 2 \quad 1)$. It follows that

$$V = [X_1, X_2, X_4] \text{ over } \mathcal{F}.$$

Since $X_3 = (-3)X_1 + (-2)X_2 + X_4$, then any vector of V expressible as a linear form in the X_1, X_2, X_3 with coefficients in $\mathcal{F}$ may be expressed as a linear form in X_1, X_2, X_4 with coefficients in $\mathcal{F}$. That is, if

$$X = \sum_{i=1}^{3} a_i X_i,$$

then also

$$X = a_1 X_1 + a_2 X_2 + a_3((-3)X_1 + (-2)X_2 + X_4)$$
$$= (a_1 - 3)X_1 + (a_2 - 2)X_2 + a_3 X_4.$$

This is a linear form in X_1, X_2, X_4 with coefficients in $\mathcal{F}$, and $a_1 X_1 + a_2 X_2 + a_4 X_4 = 0$ implies $a_1 = a_2 = a_4 = 0$.

Illustration: The ordered pair of real numbers (a, b), regarded as a complex number, may be expressed as $a + bi$. Every complex number may be expressed as $a + bi$, where the a and b are elements of the real number field. In this notation the elements 1 and i would constitute a basis for the set of complex numbers over the field of real numbers, since 1 and i are linearly independent over the field of real numbers. Written another way, the basis elements 1 and i could be $1 + 0i$ and $0 + 1i$. Considered as ordered pairs of real numbers, then, the basis elements would be $C_1 = (1\ 0)$ and $C_2 = (0\ 1)$, and, if C represents the complex number field and $\mathcal{R}$ represents the real number field, $C = [C_1, C_2]$ over $\mathcal{R}$. The elements $C_3 = (1\ 1)$ and $C_4 = (1\ 2)$ are related to the C_1 and C_2 in that $C_1 = 2C_3 - C_4$ and $C_2 = (-1)C_3 + C_4$. It is readily determined that C_3 and C_4 are linearly independent over $\mathcal{R}$ and thus form a basis for C and we have $C = [C_3, C_4]$ over $\mathcal{R}$.

We shall now show the relationship which one basis of a particular vector space over $\mathcal{F}$ bears to another basis of this same vector space. From the preceding illustration, in which $X_1 = (1\ 0\ 0)$, $X_2 = (0\ 1\ 0)$, $X_3 = (0\ 0\ 1)$, and $X_4 = (3\ 2\ 1)$, we saw that both X_1, X_2, X_3 and X_1, X_2, X_4 formed bases for V over $\mathcal{F}$. If we denote these, in matrix fashion, by

$$X = \begin{pmatrix} X_1 \\ X_2 \\ X_3 \end{pmatrix}, \qquad Y = \begin{pmatrix} X_1 \\ X_2 \\ X_4 \end{pmatrix},$$

then it is easy to see that $PX = Y$ and that $X = P^I Y$, where P is the nonsingular matrix

$$\begin{pmatrix} 1 & 0 & 0 \\ 0 & 1 & 0 \\ 3 & 2 & 1 \end{pmatrix}.$$

It is easy to find the nonsingular 2×2 matrix P which will transform the basis C_1, C_2 into the basis C_3, C_4 used above to generate the complex numbers.

It will be convenient in the discussion to follow to write the generating vectors of V as a matrix X having the generating elements as rows. That is,

$$X = \begin{pmatrix} X_1 \\ X_2 \\ \vdots \\ X_m \end{pmatrix}.$$

This matrix is said to be a matrix of the space V, and the space V is often referred to as the *row space* of X.

We now make the general

DEFINITION. *A matrix Y with s rows and n columns is said to be a matrix of V if each row of Y is an element of V.*

We have seen that a certain number of the generating vectors of a linear vector space $V_n(\mathcal{F})$ constitute a basis for the space. If $V =$

$[X_1, X_2, \ldots, X_r]$ over $\mathcal{F}$ and $Y_1, Y_2, \ldots, Y_s$ are vectors of V, we may ask under what conditions do these also constitute a basis for V. Since

$$Y_i = \sum_{j=1}^{r} p_{ij}X_j, \quad \text{for} \quad i = 1, 2, \ldots, s; \quad p_{ij} \epsilon \mathcal{F},$$

we may write $Y = PX$, where X and Y are matrices of V and $P = (p_{ij})$. If $s > r$, there exists a nonzero vector $A = (a_1 \; a_2 \; \ldots \; a_s)$ such that $AP = 0$, and hence

$$AY = \sum_{i=1}^{s} a_iY_i = 0.$$

Consequently, the $Y_1, Y_2, \ldots, Y_s$ are linearly dependent over $\mathcal{F}$ and do not form a basis for V. Thus we have shown that the number of elements in one basis cannot be greater than the number of elements in any other basis.

THEOREM 8.3.7   *The number of elements in a basis for V is unique.*

DEFINITION.   *The number of elements in the basis of a linear space is called the* order *of the linear space over $\mathcal{F}$.*

It is sufficient now to consider only the case when $r = s$. The matrix P is now square. If P is singular, then it is possible to determine the vector $A \neq 0$ so that $AP = 0$ and, hence, $Y_1, Y_2, \ldots, Y_r$ are linearly dependent over $\mathcal{F}$ and do not form a basis for V. Hence, if $Y_1, Y_2, \ldots, Y_r$ form a basis, then P must necessarily be nonsingular. If P is nonsingular, then, since $AY = 0$ implies that $APX = 0$, and since $X_1, X_2, \ldots, X_r$ are linearly independent over $\mathcal{F}$, we must have $AP = 0$ and, hence, $A = 0$. It follows that the $Y_1, Y_2, \ldots, Y_r$ are linearly independent over $\mathcal{F}$ if P is nonsingular. Also, $X = P^I Y$. That is, the X_i, for $i = 1, 2, \ldots, r$, belong to the space $W = \{Y_1, Y_2, \ldots, Y_r\}$ over $\mathcal{F}$. Consequently, W and V are identical. We have shown that W has a basis consisting of some of its generating elements. We have also shown that the number of elements in the basis is r. Hence $W = [Y_1, Y_2, \ldots, Y_r]$ over $\mathcal{F}$.

THEOREM 8.3.8   *If the order of the linear space V is r, then any r elements of V which are linearly independent over $\mathcal{F}$ constitute a basis for V.*

It follows from the preceding discussion that the row space of a matrix X is identical with the row space of PX for every nonsingular matrix P. If X is of rank r, there exists a nonsingular matrix P such that

$$PX = \begin{pmatrix} G \\ 0 \end{pmatrix},$$

where G consists of a certain r rows of X and is of rank r. The order of the row space of PX cannot exceed r since these are at most r nonzero rows. Partition G so that

$$G = \begin{pmatrix} X_1 \\ X_2 \\ \vdots \\ X_r \end{pmatrix}.$$

Since G is of rank r, we may have $AG = 0$ only if $A = 0$ and, hence, $X_1, X_2, \ldots, X_r$ are linearly independent over $\mathcal{F}$ and thus constitute a basis for the row space of PX. We have established

THEOREM 8.3.9   *The order of the row space of a matrix X is identical with the rank of X.*

EXERCISES

1. Given the vectors $X_1 = (3\ 6)$, $X_2 = (2\ 4)$, determine all real numbers c_1 and c_2 such that $c_1X_1 + c_2X_2 = 0$.

2. Given the vectors $X_1 = (1\ 2)$, $X_2 = (1\ 3)$, determine all real numbers c_1 and c_2 such that $c_1X_1 + c_2X_2 = 0$.

3. Show that the vectors $(1\ 0)$ and $(0\ 1)$ form a basis of the space generated by X_1 and X_2 of Exercise 2 above. Find the nonsingular matrix P which will transform either of these bases into the other.

4. Given the general vector X of the space $V = \{X_1, X_2\}$ over a number field where X_1 and X_2 are the vectors of Exercise 1, determine a basis for the space V.

5. Determine the conditions under which $c_1X_1 + c_2X_2 = 0$ if $X_1 = (3)$, $X_2 = (5)$ and describe the vector space $V = \{X_1, X_2\}$ over a number field.

6. Given $V = \{X_1, X_2, X_3\}$ over a number field, where $X_1 = (1\ 2\ 3)$, $X_2 = (2\ 3\ 1)$, $X_3 = (3\ 1\ 2)$, for what c_i does

$$\sum_{i=1}^{3} c_iX_i = 0?$$

If the matrix X, having as its rows the elements X_1, X_2, and X_3, is nonsingular, determine P such that $PX = I$. Partition I to get

$$I = \begin{pmatrix} E_1 \\ E_2 \\ E_3 \end{pmatrix}$$

and express E_i as a linear combination of the X_i and express X_i as a linear combination of the E_i by using the matrix P and its inverse.

7. Given the system of equations

$$x_1 + 3x_2 = 5,$$

$$2x_1 + 6x_2 = 10,$$

show that the row space of the augmented matrix is of order one.

8. Discuss the order of the row space of the augmented matrix of the system

$$a_{11}x_1 + a_{12}x_2 = k_1,$$

$$a_{21}x_1 + a_{22}x_2 = k_2,$$

where the a_{ij} are elements of a number field.

9. Discuss the order of the row space of the augmented matrix of the $m \times n$ system of equations $AX = K$, where the elements of $(A \ K)$ belong to a number field.

10. Express a necessary and sufficient condition for the system of linear equations $AX = K$ to have a solution in terms of the row space of A and the row space of $(A \ K)$.

11. Find a basis for and determine the order of each vector space over the field of real numbers generated by the vectors

(a) (1 3 5),

   (5 3 1),

   (0 0 0).

(b) (1 0 0),

   (1 2 0),

   (1 2 3).

(c) (0 2   0 0),

   (1 1   0 0),

   (0 0 −1 0).

(d) (1 0 1 0),

   (0 1 0 1).

(e) (3   1   −5),

   (1 −2 −12),

   (2   3   7),

   (4   4   2).

(f) (1 2 3 4),

   (3 2 1 4),

   (0 4 0 4),

   (1 2 0 4).

(g) (1 2 3),

   (3 2 1),

   (1 3 2),

   (3 1 2),

   (2 1 3),

   (2 3 1).

(h) (1 1 1),

   (2 2 2),

   (3 3 3).

12. Extend the idea of linear dependence and linear independence to the set having 2×2 matrices A_i as elements of the set and where the elements of the A_i

belong to a number field. In this connection specifically what would be meant by order, generators, basis?

8.4 Linear Mapping of Vector Spaces. If X_i is an element of $V_n(\mathcal{F})$ and $A = (a_{ij})$ is an $n \times m$ matrix with elements in $\mathcal{F}$, then X_iA is an element Y_i of $V_m(\mathcal{F})$. We say that the matrix A maps the vector X_i of $V_n(\mathcal{F})$ into the vector Y_i of $V_m(\mathcal{F})$. Such a mapping of vectors of $V_n(\mathcal{F})$ into vectors of $V_m(\mathcal{F})$ is said to be linear since it has the property that $aX_i + bX_j$ is mapped into $aY_i + bY_j$ for a, $b \,\epsilon\, \mathcal{F}$, where A maps X_i into Y_i and X_j into Y_j. The vectors of V, a linear vector subspace of $V_n(\mathcal{F})$, are mapped by A into the vectors of W, a linear vector subspace of $V_m(\mathcal{F})$. The vector space V has a basis $X_1, X_2, \ldots, X_r$, and the mapping of the vectors of V by A is completely determined by the mapping of these basis vectors because of the linear property of the mapping. That is, the vector

$$\sum_{i=1}^{r} c_iX_i, \quad c_i \,\epsilon\, \mathcal{F},$$

is mapped into

$$\sum_{i=1}^{r} c_iY_i$$

if X_i is mapped into Y_i for $i = 1, 2, \ldots, r$. Writing

$$X = \begin{pmatrix} X_1 \\ X_2 \\ \cdot \\ \cdot \\ X_r \end{pmatrix} \quad \text{and} \quad Y = \begin{pmatrix} Y_1 \\ Y_2 \\ \cdot \\ \cdot \\ Y_r \end{pmatrix},$$

we have

$$XA = Y \quad \text{and} \quad CXA = CY$$

for $C = (c_1, c_2, \ldots, c_r)$. The vectors $Y_1, Y_2, \ldots, Y_r$ do not generally constitute a basis for W, the row space of Y. If $W = [Z_1, Z_2, \ldots, Z_s]$ over $\mathcal{F}$ and if we write

$$Z = \begin{pmatrix} Z_1 \\ Z_2 \\ \cdot \\ \cdot \\ Z_s \end{pmatrix},$$

then there exists an $r \times s$ matrix Q such that $Y = QZ$. We now have $XA = QZ$, where the rows of X constitute a basis for V and the rows of Z constitute a basis for W. If P is an $r \times r$ nonsingular matrix and R is an $s \times s$ nonsingular matrix, then the rows of PX constitute a basis for V

and the rows of RZ constitute a basis for W. Writing $H = PX$ and $K = RZ$, it follows from $XA = QZ$ that

$$P^I HA = QR^I K,$$

which may be written

$$HA = PQR^I K.$$

That is, if A maps X into QZ, then A maps H into $PQR^I K$. In particular, if A is such that W is identical with V, we have a linear mapping of V onto itself. In this case we may choose $Z = X$ and we have

$$XA = QX.$$

If now we have $H = PX$, where P is nonsingular, we then get

$$HA = PQP^I H.$$

We have shown that, if X has rows which constitute a basis for V and if A maps X into QX and if H is another matrix whose elements constitute a basis for V given by $H = PX$, then A maps H into $PQP^I H$. We say that the matrices Q and PQP^I are similar.

EXERCISES

1. If

$$A = \begin{pmatrix} 1 & 2 & -1 \\ 3 & 0 & 2 \end{pmatrix},$$

determine the vectors of V_3 into which $(1\ 2)$ and $(2\ 1)$ are mapped by A.

2. If

$$A = \begin{pmatrix} 1 & 1 & 0 \\ -1 & 1 & 2 \\ 0 & 2 & 1 \end{pmatrix},$$

show that A maps V_3 onto itself.

3. If

$$A = \begin{pmatrix} 0 & 1 & 0 \\ 1 & 0 & 0 \\ 0 & 0 & 1 \end{pmatrix}$$

and V is a subspace of V_3 of order two, then show that A maps V onto V. If

$$X = \begin{pmatrix} 1 & 0 & 0 \\ 0 & 1 & 0 \end{pmatrix}, \quad H = \begin{pmatrix} 1 & 2 & 0 \\ 2 & 1 & 0 \end{pmatrix}, \quad XA = QX, \quad \text{and} \quad H = PX,$$

then show that $PQP^I = Q$.

4. Show that A and B are similar for the particular matrices

$$A = \begin{pmatrix} 1 & 2 \\ 3 & 4 \end{pmatrix} \quad \text{and} \quad B = \begin{pmatrix} -3 & 11 \\ -2 & 8 \end{pmatrix}.$$

5. If

$$A = \begin{pmatrix} 1 & 2 \\ 3 & 4 \end{pmatrix} \quad \text{and} \quad B = \begin{pmatrix} -3 & 11 \\ -2 & 8 \end{pmatrix},$$

find the general X such that $XA = BX$.

CHAPTER 9

DETERMINANTS OF SQUARE MATRICES

9.1 Ordered Elements, Permutations, and Inversions. We have seen that a matrix consists of a set of elements, arranged in a definite manner. The arrangement of the elements is basic in the concept of a matrix. For example, a $1 \times n$ matrix is simply an ordered set of n elements which may be arranged in $n!$ ways. That is, $n!$ distinct $1 \times n$ matrices may be formed from these n distinct elements. In many cases the n elements $a_1, a_2, \ldots, a_n$ shall be assigned one of the $n!$ possible permutations of these elements as the desirable order for these elements. For example, we may select the order

$$(9.1.1) \qquad a_1, a_2, \ldots, a_p, \ldots, a_q, \ldots, a_n,$$

where $p < q$, or the order

$$a_n, a_{n-1}, \ldots, a_i, \ldots, a_j, \ldots, a_2, a_1,$$

where $i > j$. It may sometimes be preferable to select one of the remaining $(n! - 2)$ different permutations of these elements as the desired order. We refer to the particular arrangement, order, or permutation desired as the *normal order* of these elements. This normal order is sometimes referred to as the natural order, reference order, common order, fixed order, assigned order, designated order, or desired order.

DEFINITION. *Any n elements a_i $(i = 1, 2, \ldots, n)$, with the assigned normal order $a_1, a_2, \ldots, a_p, \ldots, a_q, \ldots, a_n, p < q$, is said to possess an* inversion *if the elements have been permuted from this normal order by interchanging any two adjacent elements. Any permutation of these elements is said to possess as many inversions as there are inversion pairs $[a_q, a_p]$, where $p < q$.*

Illustration: For $n = 6$, the arrangement $a_1, a_2, a_3, a_4, a_5, a_6$, being the assigned normal order for these six elements, has no inversions. The permutation $a_1, a_2, a_4, a_3, a_5, a_6$ possesses one inversion; for the adjacent elements a_3, a_4 have been interchanged and we have the one inversion pair $[a_4, a_3]$. The permutation $a_1, a_6, a_5, a_3, a_4, a_2$ has nine inversions since it has nine inversion pairs $[a_q, a_p]$, $p < q$. These are: $[a_6, a_5]$, $[a_6, a_3]$, $[a_6, a_2]$, $[a_6, a_4]$, $[a_5, a_3]$, $[a_5, a_4]$, $[a_5, a_2]$, $[a_3, a_2]$, and $[a_4, a_2]$.

Obviously any permutation of the elements of an ordered set possesses either no inversions or a positive number of inversions.

We now consider the general permutation

$$(9.1.2) \qquad a_{i_1}, a_{i_2}, \ldots, a_{i_{p-1}}, a_{i_p}, a_{i_{p+1}}, \ldots, a_{i_{q-1}}, a_{i_q}, \ldots, a_{i_n},$$

of the n elements a_i $(i = 1, 2, \ldots, n)$, having the normal order

$$(9.1.3) \qquad a_1, a_2, \ldots, a_j, \ldots, a_k, \ldots, a_n \qquad (j < k).$$

As a matter of convenience, let t denote the number of inversions in (9.1.2). If, in (9.1.2), the two elements $a_{i_{p-1}}$ and a_{i_p} are interchanged, it is clear that the number of inversions in the new permutation is $t + 1$ or $t - 1$; for this does not affect inversions with respect to elements either preceding or following this pair. If $i_p < i_{p-1}$, then by definition the inversion pair $[a_{i_{p-1}}, a_{i_p}]$ counts as one of the t inversions possessed by (9.1.2). Interchanging these two elements gives the pair $a_{i_p}, a_{i_{p-1}}$. But these elements are in normal order since $i_p < i_{p-1}$ and $a_{i_p}, a_{i_{p-1}}$ is not an inversion pair. Thus the new permutation contains $t - 1$ inversions. Similarly, in case $i_{p-1} < i_p$, the new permutation will contain $t + 1$ inversions. We consider next the interchange of the two nonadjacent elements a_{i_p} and a_{i_q}. This transformation does not affect the inversions with respect to those elements either preceding a_{i_p} or following a_{i_q}. For reference, let us suppose there are m elements between a_{i_p} and a_{i_q}. The interchange of a_{i_p} with each of the m elements $a_{i_{p+1}}, a_{i_{p+2}}, \ldots, a_{i_{q-1}}$ immediately following a_{i_p} changes the number of inversions in (9.1.2) m times, each time increasing by one or decreasing by one the number of inversions possessed in the immediately preceding permutation. This gives the permutation

$$(9.1.4) \qquad a_{i_1}, a_{i_2}, \ldots, a_{i_{p-1}}, a_{i_{p+1}}, \ldots, a_{i_p}, a_{i_q}, \ldots, a_{i_n}.$$

The interchange of the two elements a_{i_p} and a_{i_q} changes the number of inversions in (9.1.4), either increasing this number by one or decreasing it by one. Finally, interchanging a_{i_q} with the m elements $a_{i_{q-1}}, a_{i_{q-2}}, \ldots, a_{i_{p+1}}$ changes the number of inversions m additional times. This gives the permutation

$$(9.1.5) \quad a_{i_1}, a_{i_2}, \ldots, a_{i_{p-1}}, a_{i_q}, a_{i_{p+1}}, \ldots, a_{i_{q-1}}, a_{i_p}, a_{i_{q+1}}, \ldots, a_{i_n}.$$

Thus, interchanging the elements a_{i_p} and a_{i_q} of (9.1.2) gives (9.1.5) and changes the number of inversions by unity $2m + 1$ times. Let r be the number of increases in inversions in these $2m + 1$ changes. Then $2m + 1 - r$ represents the number of decreases in inversions in these same $2m + 1$ changes. Thus the number of inversions in (9.1.5) is $t + 2(r - m) - 1$, and we have established

THEOREM 9.1.1 *The interchange of two elements of any permutation of n ordered elements changes the number of inversions by an odd number.*

We now consider the two permutations,

(9.1.6) $a_{i_1}, a_{i_2}, \ldots, a_{i_n}$

and

(9.1.7) $a_{j_1}, a_{j_2}, \ldots, a_{j_n},$

of the ordered elements $a_1, a_2, \ldots, a_n$. Let s denote the number of inversions in (9.1.6) and t the number of inversions in (9.1.7). It is obvious that the number of pairs of elements which may be interchanged in (9.1.6) to produce (9.1.7) is not unique. By theorem 9.1.1, the interchange of one pair of elements in (9.1.6) will give a new permutation which will contain $s - 2k_\nu - 1$ inversions where, of course, k_ν may be positive or negative but must always satisfy the condition that $s \geqq 2k_\nu + 1$. If (9.1.7) is obtained from (9.1.6) by the interchange of p pairs of elements, then

(9.1.8) $t = s - \sum_{\nu=1}^{p} (2k_\nu + 1) = s - 2 \sum_{\nu=1}^{p} k_\nu - p,$

and, if (9.1.7) is also obtained from (9.1.6) by the interchange of q pairs of elements, then

(9.1.9) $t = s - \sum_{\nu=1}^{q} (2l_\nu + 1) = s - 2 \sum_{\nu=1}^{q} l_\nu - q.$

From (9.1.8) and (9.1.9) it follows that

(9.1.10) $p + q = 2 \left\{ s - t - \sum_{\nu=1}^{p} k_\nu - \sum_{\nu=1}^{q} l_\nu \right\}.$

By (9.1.10) it is seen that p and q are either both even numbers or both odd numbers. We shall describe this property as *parity*. If the sum of p and q is even, then p and q are said to have the same parity. If their sum is odd, they are said to have (or to be of) different parity. It follows immediately that the integers p and q have the same parity if and only if $(-1)^p = (-1)^q$. We have proved

> **THEOREM 9.1.2** *If the permutation $a_{j_1}, a_{j_2}, \ldots, a_{j_n}$ may be obtained from the $a_{i_1}, a_{i_2}, \ldots, a_{i_n}$ by the interchange of an even (odd) number of pairs of elements, then the permutation $a_{j_1}, a_{j_2}, \ldots, a_{j_n}$ can be obtained from $a_{i_1}, a_{i_2}, \ldots, a_{i_n}$ only by the interchange of an even (odd) number of pairs of elements.*

Our primary concern in dealing with the number of inversions in a permutation of a set of ordered elements will usually be whether the number of inversions is even or odd. In most cases we shall not be interested in the actual number of inversions. It is easily seen from (9.1.10) that *the task of ascertaining whether the permutation (9.1.6) contains an even*

*or an odd number of inversions may be replaced by that of ascertaining the
number of pairs of elements which may be interchanged in* (9.1.6) *in order to
obtain the elements of* (9.1.6) *in normal order.* Thus, if (9.1.7) were in
normal order, then $t = 0$ and we would have, from (9.1.8),

$$s = \sum_{\nu=1}^{p} (2k_\nu + 1) = 0.$$

This gives

(9.1.11) $(-1)^s = (-1) \sum_{\nu=1}^{p} (2k_\nu + 1) = (-1)^p.$

Thus we have, from (9.1.11),

THEOREM 9.1.3   *If the permutation* $a_{i_1}, a_{i_2}, \ldots, a_{i_n}$ *has s inversions and
if this permutation may be put in normal order by the interchange of the
elements of p pairs of elements, then s and p have the same parity.*

Illustration of theorem 9.1.3:   Consider the permutation

(9.1.12)   1, 2, 7, 4, 5, 6, 3, 8

of the first eight positive integers, where their normal order is that of
the natural numbers.   The interchange of the elements 3 and 7 puts
the eight elements in normal order.   By theorem 9.1.3 it is seen immediately that (9.1.12) has an odd number of inversions.   That (9.1.12)
actually possesses seven inversions is easily seen by listing its seven
inversion pairs or the seven inequalities.

(9.1.13) $7 > 4$, $7 > 5$, $7 > 6$, $7 > 3$, $4 > 3$, $5 > 3$, $6 > 3$.

The elements of a matrix are located within the matrix by the use of
double subscripts.   The first subscript indicates the row and the second
subscript indicates the column in which the element is found.   We now
consider n pairs of numbers,

(9.1.14) $1i_1, 2i_2, \ldots, ti_t, \ldots, ni_n,$

and call the numbers $1, 2, \ldots, n$ the row subscripts, and $i_1, i_2, \ldots, i_n$ the
column subscripts.   The column subscripts are the first n positive integers
$1, 2, \ldots, n$ in some order.   It is clear, then, that both the set of row subscripts and the set of column subscripts of (9.1.14) may have a well-defined
normal order which we define to be the order $1, 2, \ldots, n$ for both sets.
The following theorem is an immediate consequence of theorem 9.1.1.

THEOREM 9.1.4   *If a permutation of the pairs of subscripts in* (9.1.14)
*changes the number of inversions in the row subscripts by p and changes
the number of inversions in the column subscripts by q, then p and q have
the same parity.*

The following corollary is an obvious consequence of theorem 9.1.4.

COROLLARY. If *the pairs of ordered elements* $1i_1$, $2i_2$, . . . , ni_n *have no inversions in the row indicators and i inversions in the column indicators* and if *these pairs are permuted to obtain the arrangement* $j_1k_1, j_2k_2, \ldots, j_nk_n$, *where there are now j inversions in the row indicators and k inversions in the column indicators* and furthermore, if *the pairs of either of these arrangements are permuted to obtain the set* $l_1 1, l_2 2, \ldots, l_n n$ *having l inversions in the row indicators and no inversions in the column indicators, then* $(-1)^i = (-1)^{j+k} = (-1)^l$.

EXERCISES

1. Determine the number of inversion pairs in each of the following permutations where the normal order is the order of the positive integers in ascending order; descending order.

(a) 1, 2, 4, 3, 5, 7, 6.
(b) 7, 5, 6, 3, 4, 1, 2.
(c) 1, 7, 3, 5, 4, 6, 2.

2. In each of the permutations in Exercise 1 interchange the numbers 5 and 6 and determine the number of inversion pairs in each. Verify, in each case, that the number of inversion pairs is thus changed by an odd number.

3. In Exercise 1, start with any number k in the permutation and interchange it with adjacent elements in order to move it into the kth position in a permutation. Repeat this process until each element is in its normal position. Verify that the number of such interchanges required is of the same parity as the number of inversion pairs in the original arrangement.

4. In Exercise 1, interchange the element k with the element in the kth position. Continue until the elements are in the normal order. Verify that the number of such interchanges is of the same parity as the number of inversion pairs in the original permutation.

5. Given the number pairs

$$(1, 4), \quad (5, 7), \quad (3, 2), \quad (7, 6), \quad (2, 1), \quad (6, 5), \quad (4, 3).$$

Let the normal order of the first elements be 1, 2, . . . , n and the normal order of the second elements be 1, 2, . . . , n.

(a) Determine the number of inversions, p, in the first elements.

(b) Determine the number of inversions, q, in the second elements.

(c) Permute the pairs so that the first elements are in normal order and then find the number of inversions, r, in the second elements.

(d) Permute the pairs so that the second elements are in normal order and determine the number of inversions, s, in the first elements.

Note that r, s, and $p + q$ are either all even or all odd. How does this verify theorem 9.1.4 and its corollary for this set of pairs?

6. Is *"has the same parity as"* an equivalence relation?

7. Prove that the number of distinct permutations of n distinct elements is $n!$.

8. Given mn distinct elements, how many distinct $m \times n$ matrices can be written using these and only these elements?

9. Show that exactly half of the $n!$ permutations of n distinct elements, $n > 1$, has an odd number of inversions.

10. Show that the maximum number of inversions in n ordered elements is given by $[n(n-1)]/2$.

11. Show that any arrangement of n elements may be rearranged in their normal order by the interchange of adjacent elements at most $[n(n-1)]/2$. Verify this by using the permutation 4, 7, 9, 2, 5, 1, 6, 8, 3 of the natural numbers and by performing the transposition of 1 interchanged with 5, indicated by $(1, 5)$. Follow this with the transpositions $(1, 2)$, $(1, 9)$, $(1, 7)$, $(1, 4)$. Continue with $(2, 9)$, etc., until the original set is in the assigned normal order $1, 2, \ldots, 9$.

12. Show that the permutation $a_{i_1}, a_{i_2}, \ldots, a_{i_n}$ of the natural numbers $1, 2, \ldots, n$ has an even or an odd number of inversions depending upon whether
$$\prod_{\substack{k,l=1 \\ k<l}}^{n} (a_{i_k} - a_{i_l})$$
is positive or negative.

9.2 Determinant, Determinantal Polynomial. We have seen that there is associated with every matrix a unique integer, positive or zero, which we call the rank of the matrix. Also there is associated with every square matrix a homogeneous function of its elements which is called the *determinantal polynomial*. By definition, the determinantal polynomial of the square matrix A, given by

$$(9.2.1) \qquad \begin{pmatrix} a_{11} & a_{12} & \ldots & a_{1n} \\ a_{21} & a_{22} & \ldots & a_{2n} \\ \cdots\cdots\cdots\cdots\cdots \\ a_{n1} & a_{n2} & \ldots & a_{nn} \end{pmatrix},$$

is

$$(9.2.2) \qquad \sum_{p(i_t)} (-1)^i a_{1i_1} \cdot a_{2i_2} \cdots a_{ni_n},$$

where the $i_1, i_2, \ldots, i_n$ are the column subscripts $1, 2, \ldots, n$ in some order, i is the number of inversions in this permutation, and where the algebraic sum is to be taken over all possible permutations of these subscripts. This range of summation is indicated by $p(i_t)$. It is sometimes desirable to indicate (9.2.2) by the matrix array in (9.2.1), using vertical bars instead of the usual parentheses and to call this displayed array the determinant of the matrix A. That is, $|A|$ is read "the determinant of A," and we write

(9.2.3)
$$|A| = \begin{vmatrix} a_{11} & a_{12} & \cdots & a_{1n} \\ a_{21} & a_{22} & \cdots & a_{2n} \\ \cdots\cdots\cdots\cdots\cdots \\ a_{n1} & a_{n2} & \cdots & a_{nn} \end{vmatrix}.$$

The determinantal polynomial (9.2.2) is said to be the expansion of the determinant given by (9.2.3). The value of (9.2.2) is called the value of the determinant (9.2.3). The determinant (9.2.3) of the matrix (9.2.1) is often written in other ways. For example, some standard notations are:

(9.2.4) $|A| = |a_{ij}|,$

(9.2.5) $|A| = |a_{11}a_{22} \ldots a_{nn}|,$

(9.2.6) $|A| = |a_{11}a_{12} \ldots a_{1n}|.$

The symbol $|A|$ is also used to denote the value of the determinant, and it will be clear from the context which is intended. We may write the determinantal polynomial in the more compact form

(9.2.7) $$|A| = \sum_{p(i_t)} (-1)^i \prod_{t=1}^{n} a_{t i_t}.$$

In general, the terminology used in matrices applies also to determinants. That is, the a_{ij} of $|A|$ are the elements of the determinant. The elements $a_{11}, a_{22}, \ldots, a_{nn}$ are the elements of the principal diagonal. The elements $a_{1n}, a_{2n-1}, \ldots, a_{n1}$ constitute the *secondary diagonal*. The elements $a_{i1}, a_{i2}, \ldots, a_{in}$ form the ith row, and the elements $a_{1j}, a_{2j}, \ldots, a_{nj}$ form the jth column. When we speak of any operation between the rows of a determinant, this operation is applied to the rows, considering them to be $1 \times n$ matrices. For example, in the determinant $|a_{ij}|$, if we add the sth row to the tth row, then we get a determinant identical with $|a_{ij}|$ except that the tth row is replaced by the $1 \times n$ matrix $(a_{t1} + a_{s1}, a_{t2} + a_{s2}, \ldots, a_{tn} + a_{sn})$. We say that the sth row of $|A|$ is multiplied by the scalar k if and only if the sth row of $|A|$ is replaced by the $1 \times n$ matrix $(ka_{s1}, ka_{s2}, \ldots, ka_{sn})$. By the expression $k|A|$ we shall *always* mean the product of k by the value of the determinant and shall *never* mean the determinant of the matrix kA.

An $n \times n$ determinant is said to be of order n. Every square submatrix of the square matrix A has a determinant which is called a subdeterminant of the determinant of A. Later we shall show that $|A| \cdot |B| = |AB|$. That is, determinantal arrays may be multiplied in exactly the same manner as matrix arrays. However, $|A| + |B|$ and $|A + B|$ are not necessarily equal.

An examination of the determinantal polynomial (9.2.2) reveals that each term, $(-1)^i a_{1i_1} a_{2i_2} \ldots a_{ni_n}$, in the expansion, contains one and only one element from each row. Since the column subscripts $i_1, i_2, \ldots, i_n$ are the integers $1, 2, \ldots, n$, in some order, this term also contains one and only one element from each column. By the corollary of theorem 9.1.4 we note that

$$\sum_{p(j_t)} (-1)^j a_{j_1 1} a_{j_2 2} \ldots a_{j_n n}$$

is another pattern in which we may write the determinantal polynomial. Also,

$$\sum_{p(j_s, k_t)} (-1)^{j+k} a_{j_1 k_1} a_{j_2 k_2} \ldots a_{j_n k_n}$$

gives the value of the determinant, but here we must be very careful or an inclusion of duplicate terms will be made.

Illustration: Using the general 4×4 determinant $|a_{ij}|$, we see that, by (9.2.2), we would have $(-1)^3 a_{12} a_{24} a_{31} a_{43}$ as one term in the determinantal polynomial. If we use the expansion

$$\sum_{p(j_t)} (-1)^j a_{j_1 1} a_{j_2 2} \ldots a_{j_n n},$$

the corresponding term is $(-1)^3 a_{31} a_{12} a_{43} a_{24}$. However, the elements $a_{12}, a_{24}, a_{31}, a_{43}$ may be arranged in 4! different orders, and the term in

$$\sum_{p(j_s, k_t)} (-1)^{j+k} a_{j_1 k_1} a_{j_2 k_2} \ldots a_{j_n k_n}$$

consisting of these elements may be any one of these 4! arrangements. For example, $(-1)^{4+1} a_{31} a_{43} a_{12} a_{24}$, $(-1)^{5+4} a_{43} a_{24} a_{31} a_{12}$, and $(-1)^{1+4} a_{24} a_{12} a_{31} a_{43}$ show only three choices of the twenty-four different arrangements from which we may select the representative of the product obtained from the elements in the 1st row and 2nd column, 2nd row and 4th column, 3rd row and 1st column, 4th row and 3rd column. Obviously only one such representation may be used in obtaining the value of the determinant.

As an immediate consequence of the definition of the value of a determinant we have the following theorems.

THEOREM 9.2.1   *If any row of a determinant contains only zero elements, then the value of the determinant is zero.*

THEOREM 9.2.2   *The value of the determinant of the identity matrix is 1.*

THEOREM 9.2.3   *The value of the determinant of a triangular matrix is the product of the diagonal elements of the matrix.*

COROLLARY. *The value of the determinant of a diagonal matrix is the product of the diagonal elements of the matrix.*

THEOREM 9.2.4 *If in the determinant* $|a_{ij}|$ *we write the elements of the rth row as* $a_{rk} = \alpha_{rk} + \beta_{rk}$ $(k = 1, 2, \ldots, n)$, *then* $|a_{ij}|$ *is equal to the sum of the two determinants, each identical with* $|a_{ij}|$ *except that the rth row of one has the elements* $\alpha_{r1}, \alpha_{r2}, \ldots, \alpha_{rn}$ *and the rth row of the other has the elements* $\beta_{r1}, \beta_{r2}, \ldots, \beta_{rn}$.

For, if $a_{rk} = \alpha_{rk} + \beta_{rk}$ $(k = 1, 2, \ldots, n)$, in $|a_{ij}|$, then

$$\sum_{p(i_t)} (-1)^i a_{1i_1} a_{2i_2} \ldots a_{ri_r} \ldots a_{ni_n}$$

is actually

$$\sum_{p(i_t)} (-1)^i a_{1i_1} a_{2i_2} \ldots (\alpha_{ri_r} + \beta_{ri_r}) \ldots a_{ni_n},$$

which may be written

$$\sum_{p(i_t)} (-1)^i a_{1i_1} a_{2i_2} \ldots \alpha_{ri_r} \ldots a_{ni_n} + \sum_{p(i_t)} (-1)^i a_{1i_1} a_{2i_2} \ldots \beta_{ri_r} \ldots a_{ni_n},$$

and this completes the proof. The reader may generalize this result.

Illustration of theorem 9.2.4:   Given the determinant

$$\begin{vmatrix} a_{11} & a_{12} & a_{13} \\ a_{21} & a_{22} & a_{23} \\ a_{31} & a_{32} & a_{33} \end{vmatrix},$$

where $a_{21} = \alpha_{21} + \beta_{21}$, $a_{22} = \alpha_{22} + \beta_{22}$, $a_{23} = \alpha_{23} + \beta_{23}$; then

$$\begin{vmatrix} a_{11} & a_{12} & a_{13} \\ a_{21} & a_{22} & a_{23} \\ a_{31} & a_{32} & a_{33} \end{vmatrix} = \begin{vmatrix} a_{11} & a_{12} & a_{13} \\ \alpha_{21} + \beta_{21} & \alpha_{22} + \beta_{22} & \alpha_{23} + \beta_{23} \\ a_{31} & a_{32} & a_{33} \end{vmatrix}.$$

It follows that

$$\begin{vmatrix} a_{11} & a_{12} & a_{13} \\ a_{21} & a_{22} & a_{23} \\ a_{31} & a_{32} & a_{33} \end{vmatrix}$$

$$= \sum_{p(i_t)} (-1)^i a_{1i_1} a_{2i_2} a_{3i_3} = \sum_{p(i_t)} (-1)^i a_{1i_1} (\alpha_{2i_2} + \beta_{2i_2}) a_{3i_3}$$

$$= \sum_{p(i_t)} (-1)^i a_{1i_1} \alpha_{2i_2} a_{3i_3} + \sum_{p(i_t)} (-1)^i a_{1i_1} \beta_{2i_2} a_{3i_3}$$

$$= \begin{vmatrix} a_{11} & a_{12} & a_{13} \\ \alpha_{21} & \alpha_{22} & \alpha_{23} \\ a_{31} & a_{32} & a_{33} \end{vmatrix} + \begin{vmatrix} a_{11} & a_{12} & a_{13} \\ \beta_{21} & \beta_{22} & \beta_{23} \\ a_{31} & a_{32} & a_{33} \end{vmatrix}.$$

In a similar manner

$$\begin{vmatrix} \alpha_{11} + \beta_{11} & \alpha_{12} + \beta_{12} \\ \alpha_{21} + \beta_{21} & \alpha_{22} + \beta_{22} \end{vmatrix}$$

may be shown to be

$$\begin{vmatrix} \alpha_{11} & \alpha_{12} \\ \alpha_{21} & \alpha_{22} \end{vmatrix} + \begin{vmatrix} \alpha_{11} & \beta_{12} \\ \alpha_{21} & \beta_{22} \end{vmatrix} + \begin{vmatrix} \beta_{11} & \alpha_{12} \\ \beta_{21} & \alpha_{22} \end{vmatrix} + \begin{vmatrix} \beta_{11} & \beta_{12} \\ \beta_{21} & \beta_{22} \end{vmatrix}.$$

Since

$$\sum_{p(i_t)} (-1)^i a_{1i_1} a_{2i_2} \ldots k a_{ri_r} \ldots a_{ni_n} = k \sum_{p(i_t)} (-1)^i \prod_{\lambda=1}^{n} a_{\lambda i \lambda},$$

we have

THEOREM 9.2.5　*If the matrix B is obtained from the matrix A by replacing the rth row of A by* $k(a_{r1} \ a_{r2} \ \ldots \ a_{rn})$, *then* $|B| = k|A|$.

Suppose that the rth and sth rows of $|A|$, where $r < s$, are such that $(a_{r1} \ a_{r2} \ \ldots \ a_{rn}) = k(a_{s1} \ a_{s2} \ \ldots \ a_{sn})$ and, furthermore, suppose that we expand $k|A|$ in the following manner.

$$(9.2.8) \qquad |A| = \sum_{p(i_t)} (-1)^i a_{1i_1} a_{2i_2} \ldots a_{ri_r} \ldots (k a_{si_s}) \ldots a_{ni_n}.$$

The general term in the determinantal polynomial (9.2.8) is $(-1)^p a_{1i_1} a_{2i_2} \ldots a_{ri_r} \ldots k a_{si_s} \ldots a_{ni_n}$. In this expansion there must also exist the term $(-1)^q a_{1i_1} a_{2i_2} \ldots a_{ri_s} \ldots k a_{si_r} \ldots a_{ni_n}$. These terms are numerically equal since $a_{ri_r} = k a_{si_r}$ and $a_{ri_s} = k a_{si_s}$. However, the number of inversions in the column subscripts of either of these differs from the number of inversions in the column subscripts of the other. It is obvious that p and q are of different parity, and, therefore, the sum of these two terms is zero. Since the terms in (9.2.8) may be uniquely paired so that the sum of each pair is zero, we have

THEOREM 9.2.6　*If one row of a determinant is a constant times another row, then the value of the determinant is zero.*

If two rows are identical, then theorem 9.2.6 is usually stated as follows:

COROLLARY.　*If two rows of a determinant are identical, then the value of the determinant is zero.*

EXERCISES

1. Write the determinantal polynomials for the general determinants, $|a_{ij}|$, of orders one, two, three, and four.
2. How many terms are in the determinantal polynomial of an nth order determinant?

3. Determine the sign of each of the following products occurring in the expansion of the determinant, $|a_{ij}|$, of order six.

(a) $a_{12}a_{26}a_{33}a_{41}a_{54}a_{65}$.　　　　　　　(b) $a_{63}a_{51}a_{42}a_{36}a_{25}a_{14}$.

(c) $a_{32}a_{16}a_{51}a_{24}a_{65}a_{43}$.　　　　　　　(d) $a_{61}a_{52}a_{43}a_{34}a_{25}a_{16}$.

4. In the expansion of the nth order determinant, $|a_{ij}|$, determine the sign of the term containing the elements of the secondary diagonal.

5. In the expansions of the third and fourth order determinants of Exercise 1 write the determinantal polynomials as a linear form in the elements of the (a) second row; (b) third column. In each case express the coefficients of the elements in these linear forms as determinants and show that they are sub-determinants of the original determinant.

6. Show, by expanding each determinant and comparing the results, that

$$\begin{vmatrix} a_1 & a_2 & a_3 \\ k_1 + l_1 & k_2 + l_2 & k_3 + l_3 \\ c_1 & c_2 & c_3 \end{vmatrix} = \begin{vmatrix} a_1 & a_2 & a_3 \\ k_1 & k_2 & k_3 \\ c_1 & c_2 & c_3 \end{vmatrix} + \begin{vmatrix} a_1 & a_2 & a_3 \\ l_1 & l_2 & l_3 \\ c_1 & c_2 & c_3 \end{vmatrix}.$$

7. Show, by expansion, that

$$\begin{vmatrix} a_1 & a_2 & a_3 \\ b_1 & b_2 & b_3 \\ kc_1 & kc_2 & kc_3 \end{vmatrix} = k \begin{vmatrix} a_1 & a_2 & a_3 \\ b_1 & b_2 & b_3 \\ c_1 & c_2 & c_3 \end{vmatrix}.$$

8. In Exercise 7, verify that the value of the determinant is zero in case $c_i = b_i$ ($i = 1, 2, 3$).

9. If A and B are $n \times n$ triangular matrices of like pattern, prove $|AB| = |A| \cdot |B|$.

9.3 Determinants of Equivalent Matrices.

If A and B are equivalent $n \times n$ matrices, then there exist nonsingular matrices P and Q such that $PAQ = B$. The matrices P and Q may each be expressed as a product of elementary transformation matrices. At this stage we shall consider the equivalent matrices A and B, where $PA = B$ and where P is an elementary permutative matrix. Let P be the elementary permutative matrix obtained from I by interchanging the rth and sth rows. Then PA is the matrix obtained from A by interchanging the rth and sth rows of A. The normal order of the row subscripts has been changed from

$$1, \quad 2, \quad \ldots, \quad r-1, \quad r, \quad r+1, \quad \ldots, \quad s-1, \quad s, \quad s+1, \quad \ldots, \quad n$$

in A to

$$1, \quad 2, \quad \ldots, \quad r-1, \quad s, \quad r+1, \quad \ldots, \quad s-1, \quad r, \quad s+1, \quad \ldots, \quad n$$

in the matrix B. However, the normal order of the column subscripts has been left unaltered. Let

$$(-1)^p a_{1i_1} a_{2i_2} \ldots a_{r-1,i_{r-1}} a_{r i_r} a_{r+1,i_{r+1}} \ldots a_{s-1,i_{s-1}} a_{s i_s} a_{s+1,i_{s+1}} \ldots a_{n i_n}$$

be any term in the expansion of $|A|$. The term in the expansion of the determinant $|B|$ containing these same elements is

$$(-1)^q a_{1i_1} a_{2i_2} \cdots a_{r-1,i_{r-1}} a_{si_s} a_{r+1,i_{r+1}} \cdots a_{s-1,i_{s-1}} a_{ri_r} a_{s+1,i_{s+1}} \cdots a_{ni_n},$$

where the row subscripts are in normal order in each case. But p and q are of different parity, and consequently $|B| = -|A|$. Since we are interested in the effect of the elementary permutative transformation of P on A, we sum up the results as

THEOREM 9.3.1   *If B is the matrix PA, where P is an elementary permutative matrix, then $|PA| = |B| = -|A|$.*

Since theorem 9.3.1 is true for all A, let A be the identity matrix, and we have the following

COROLLARY.   *If P is an elementary permutative matrix, then $|P| = -1$.*

From this corollary and theorem 9.3.1, $|PA| = |B| = -|A| = |P| \cdot |A|$. This gives an important result which we state as

THEOREM 9.3.2   *The determinant of the product of an elementary permutative matrix P by any matrix A is the product of the determinant of P by the determinant of A.*

Suppose now that P is an elementary multiplicative matrix obtained from I by multiplying the rth row by k. Then, by the corollary of theorem 9.2.3, $|P| = k$. The matrix PA is obtained from the matrix A by replacing the rth row of A by k times the rth row of A, and hence, by theorem 9.2.5, the determinant of PA is equal to $k|A|$. Hence we have

THEOREM 9.3.3   *If P is an elementary multiplicative matrix, then $|PA| = |P| \cdot |A|$.*

We now consider the elementary additive matrix P obtained from the identity matrix by adding k times the sth row to the rth row. The matrix PA is the matrix obtained from $A = (a_{ij})$ by adding k times the sth row to the rth row. That is, the elements of the rth row are

$$(ka_{s1} + a_{r1} \quad ka_{s2} + a_{r2} \quad \cdots \quad ka_{sn} + a_{rn}).$$

The elements of the remaining rows of PA are identical with the corresponding rows of A. By theorem 9.2.4, the determinant of the matrix PA may be written as the sum of two determinants, one of which is the determinant of the matrix A. By theorem 9.2.6, the other determinant has the value zero. Thus $|PA| = |A|$. We state this result as

THEOREM 9.3.4   *If P is an elementary additive matrix, then $|PA| = |A|$.*

We have immediately, from theorem 9.3.4, the following

COROLLARY.   *If P is an elementary additive matrix, then*
$$|P| = |P \cdot I| = |I| = 1.$$
We now have

THEOREM 9.3.5   *If P is an elementary additive matrix, then*
$$|PA| = |P| \cdot |A|.$$

The following corollary is of interest.

COROLLARY.   *If any linear combination of the rows of a matrix A is the 1 $\times$ n zero matrix, then the determinant of A has the value zero.*

We may summarize the results of this section by stating that, if P is any elementary matrix and A is any square matrix, then $|PA| = |P| \cdot |A|$. Furthermore, since every nonsingular matrix P can be expressed as a product of elementary matrices, we have

THEOREM 9.3.6   *If A is any square matrix and P is a nonsingular matrix, then $|PA| = |P| \cdot |A|$.*

Also, it follows that the determinant of the nonsingular matrix P is the product of the determinants of the elementary matrices. Since the determinant of each elementary matrix is different from zero, we have

COROLLARY.   *The determinant of a nonsingular matrix is not zero.*

If A is an $n \times n$ matrix of rank $r < n$, we have seen that there exists a nonsingular matrix P such that PA has zero for the last $(n - r)$ rows. Hence $|PA| = 0$.   But, by theorem 9.3.6, $|PA| = |P| \cdot |A|$.   Since $|P| \neq 0$, then $|A| = 0$.   We state this result in the following

COROLLARY.   *The determinant of a singular matrix is zero.*

If the matrix P is singular, then the matrix PA is singular, and, since the determinant of each of these, $|P|$ and $|PA|$, is zero, we have
$$|PA| = |P| \cdot |A|.$$
Thus we have

THEOREM 9.3.7   *If P and A are n $\times$ n matrices, then $|PA| = |P| \cdot |A|$.*

Let A be an $m \times m$ matrix whereas B is of order n.   It is sometimes desirable to obtain a determinant having the value $|A| \cdot |B|$; however, AB is not defined.   Such a product determinant can be obtained in a very simple manner, for, suppose $m < n$ and write the $n \times n$ matrix $C = \begin{pmatrix} A & 0 \\ 0 & I \end{pmatrix}$

and form the product $|C| \cdot |B|$. It should now be clear that such products may be obtained in many different ways.

EXERCISES

1. Evaluate the determinants of each of the matrices A, B, AB, and BA, where

(a)
$$A = \begin{pmatrix} 2 & 7 \\ 1 & 3 \end{pmatrix}, \quad B = \begin{pmatrix} 0 & 1 \\ 2 & 2 \end{pmatrix}.$$

(b)
$$A = \begin{pmatrix} 2 & 1 & 3 \\ 5 & -1 & 3 \\ 7 & 0 & 5 \end{pmatrix}, \quad B = \begin{pmatrix} -1 & 0 & 1 \\ 2 & -3 & 2 \\ 1 & -3 & 5 \end{pmatrix},$$

and observe that $|AB| = |BA| = |A| \cdot |B|$.

2. Evaluate the following determinants.

(a)
$$\begin{vmatrix} 1 & 0 & 0 \\ 0 & 0 & 1 \\ 0 & 1 & 0 \end{vmatrix} \cdot$$

(b)
$$\begin{vmatrix} 1 & t & 0 \\ 0 & 1 & 0 \\ 0 & 0 & 1 \end{vmatrix} \cdot$$

(c)
$$\begin{vmatrix} 1 & 0 & 0 \\ 0 & 3 & 0 \\ 0 & 0 & 1 \end{vmatrix} \cdot$$

(d)
$$\begin{vmatrix} 0 & 1 & 0 \\ 1 & 0 & 5 \\ 0 & 0 & 3 \end{vmatrix} \cdot$$

3. Expand the general third order determinant $|a_{ij}|$ and expand the determinant of the product matrix

$$\begin{pmatrix} 0 & 0 & 1 \\ 0 & 1 & 0 \\ 1 & 0 & 0 \end{pmatrix} \begin{pmatrix} a_{11} & a_{12} & a_{13} \\ a_{21} & a_{22} & a_{23} \\ a_{31} & a_{32} & a_{33} \end{pmatrix},$$

and show that the second expansion is the negative of the first expansion.

4. Without expanding the following determinants, show that each has the value zero.

(a)
$$\begin{vmatrix} 15 & 16 & 17 \\ 18 & 19 & 20 \\ 21 & 22 & 23 \end{vmatrix},$$

(b)
$$\begin{vmatrix} 1 & 1 & 1 \\ a & b & c \\ b+c & a+c & a+b \end{vmatrix},$$

(c)
$$\begin{vmatrix} x-y & y-z & z-x \\ y-z & z-x & x-y \\ z-x & x-y & y-z \end{vmatrix},$$

(d)
$$\begin{vmatrix} 1 & 2 & 3 \\ 4 & 5 & 6 \\ 7 & 8 & 9 \end{vmatrix},$$

(e) $\begin{vmatrix} 0 & x & y \\ -x & 0 & -z \\ -y & z & 0 \end{vmatrix}$,

(f) $\begin{vmatrix} 1 & \omega & \omega^2 \\ \omega & \omega^2 & 1 \\ \omega^2 & 1 & \omega \end{vmatrix}$, where $\omega^3 = 1$.

(g) $\begin{vmatrix} (a-a)^3 & (a-b)^3 & (a-c)^3 \\ (b-a)^3 & (b-b)^3 & (b-c)^3 \\ (c-a)^3 & (c-b)^3 & (c-c)^3 \end{vmatrix}$,

(h) $\begin{vmatrix} 0 & 1 & 2^2 & 3^2 \\ 1 & 2^2 & 3^2 & 4^2 \\ 2^2 & 3^2 & 4^2 & 5^2 \\ 3^2 & 4^2 & 5^2 & 6^2 \end{vmatrix}$.

5. Without expanding the determinants, prove the following identities.

(a) $\begin{vmatrix} a+b & b+c & c+a \\ p+q & q+r & r+p \\ l+m & m+n & n+l \end{vmatrix} = 2 \begin{vmatrix} a & b & c \\ p & q & r \\ l & m & n \end{vmatrix}$;

(b) $\begin{vmatrix} a^2 & bc & a^2 \\ b^2 & ac & b^2 \\ ab & c^2 & c^2 \end{vmatrix} = \begin{vmatrix} ac & bc & ab \\ bc & ab & ac \\ ab & ac & bc \end{vmatrix}$,

thus $(ab + bc + ca)$ is a factor of each;

(c) $\begin{vmatrix} a+b & c & c \\ a & b+c & a \\ b & b & c+a \end{vmatrix} = 2 \begin{vmatrix} 0 & b & a \\ b & 0 & c \\ a & c & 0 \end{vmatrix}$.

6. Apply only permutative and additive row transformations to each of the following matrices to obtain an equivalent triangular matrix and evaluate the determinant of each matrix.

(a) $\begin{pmatrix} 8 & 7 & -3 \\ 1 & 1 & 2 \\ 1 & 1 & 3 \end{pmatrix}$,

(b) $\begin{pmatrix} -4 & -6 & 7 \\ 8 & -2 & -5 \\ -1 & 1 & 1 \end{pmatrix}$,

(c) $\begin{pmatrix} 0 & -2 & 1 \\ 7 & 5 & 2 \\ 5 & -2 & 6 \end{pmatrix}$.

9.4 Minors and Cofactors. The determinant of a square submatrix of the square matrix A is called a *minor* of the determinant $|A|$. In particular, we have the following

DEFINITION. *In the $n \times n$ matrix $A = (a_{ij})$, the determinant of the complementary submatrix of the element a_{ij} is called the* minor *of the element a_{ij} and is usually indicated by M_{ij}. The cofactor of a_{ij} is defined to be $(-1)^{i+j}M_{ij}$ and is denoted by A_{ij}.*

It is recalled that the symbol A_{ij} is used to represent a block submatrix of the matrix A when A is partitioned. The dual role of this symbol should cause no confusion since the context will indicate which is intended.

DEFINITION. *The determinants of complementary submatrices are called* complementary minors.

DEFINITION. *If, in the matrix A, we let M be the determinant of the $m \times m$ submatrix in which the elements common to the $k_1, k_2, \ldots, k_m$ rows and to the $l_1, l_2, \ldots, l_m$ columns of A occur and if M_c is the complementary minor of M, then the algebraic complement of M is defined to be $(-1)^p M_c$ where $p = \sum_{i=1}^{m} k_i + \sum_{i=1}^{m} l_i$.*

The terms "two-row minor," "three-row minor," $\ldots$, "t-row minor" are frequently used. These are self-explanatory. For every t-row minor of an $n \times n$ determinant there exists an $(n - t)$-row complementary minor.

DEFINITION. *In the $n \times n$ matrix A, the determinant of a principal submatrix is called a principal minor of $|A|$.*

The complementary minor of a principal minor is also a principal minor.

The following theorem is an immediate consequence of the definition of the value of a determinant and the definition of a cofactor.

THEOREM 9.4.1 *In the determinant $|A|$, the cofactor of the element a_{sj} is given by*

$$A_{sj} = (-1)^{s+j} \sum_{p(i_t)} (-1)^i a_{1i_1} a_{2i_2} \ldots a_{s-1,i_{s-1}} a_{s+1,i_{s+1}} \ldots a_{ni_n},$$

where the exponent i, of $(-1)^i$, represents the number of inversions among the column subscripts $1, 2, \ldots, j - 1, j + 1, \ldots, n$.

We have seen in Exercise 5 of section 9.2 that a determinant of order three or four can be written as a linear form in the elements of some row or some column. It is sometimes convenient to expand a general determinant in this manner, and we shall now show that such an expansion is possible.

The general term in the determinantal polynomial of the nth order determinant $|a_{ij}|$ is

(9.4.1) $(-1)^p a_{1i_1} a_{2i_2} \ldots a_{si_s} \ldots a_{ni_n},$

where p is the number of inversions in this permutation of the column subscripts $i_1, i_2, \ldots, i_n$. We now fix our attention on the element in the tth column and the sth row, namely a_{st}. That is, we wish to consider those terms for which, in the notation of (9.4.1), $i_s = t$. It is clear from Exercise 2 of section 9.2 that there are $(n - 1)!$ such terms. In fact, each of the elements a_{sj} $(j = 1, 2, \ldots, n)$ occurs in exactly $(n - 1)!$ different terms. We may now write the term given in (9.4.1) as

(9.4.2) $(-1)^{s+t} a_{st} (-1)^q a_{1i_1} a_{2i_2} \ldots a_{s-1,i_{s-1}} a_{s+1,i_{s+1}} \ldots a_{ni_n},$

where q is the number of inversions in the column subscripts $i_1, i_2, \ldots, i_n$ not including the element $i_s = t$. There are $(n - 1)!$ permutations of these $n - 1$ column subscripts. Consequently, the $(n - 1)!$ terms of the determinantal polynomial, containing a_{st}, are given by

(9.4.3) $(-1)^{s+t} a_{st} \sum_{p(i_t)} (-1)^q a_{1i_1} a_{2i_2} \ldots a_{ni_n},$

which, by theorem 9.3.7, is

(9.4.4) $a_{st} A_{st}.$

Thus, in the expansion of the determinant $|a_{ij}|$, there are $(n - 1)!$ terms containing each of the elements in the sth row, and these are given by (9.4.4) for $t = 1, 2, \ldots, n$. Since the determinantal polynomial of the determinant $|a_{ij}|$ is the sum of all these terms, it may be written

(9.4.5) $\sum_{t=1}^{n} a_{st} A_{st}.$

Hence, since we may select s to be $1, 2, \ldots, n$, we have

THEOREM 9.4.2 $|A| = \sum_{t=1}^{n} a_{st} A_{st}$ $(s = 1, 2, \ldots, n).$

Thus, we see from theorem 9.4.2 that the value of an $n \times n$ determinant is given by the sum of the products of the elements of any row by their corresponding cofactors. That is, we select any sth row which has elements $a_{s1}, a_{s2}, \ldots, a_{sn}$. The corresponding cofactors of these elements are $A_{s1}, A_{s2}, \ldots, A_{sn}$. Then, forming the products

$$a_{s1} A_{s1}, a_{s2} A_{s2}, \ldots, a_{sn} A_{sn},$$

we get $|A| = a_{s1} A_{s1} + a_{s2} A_{s2} + \cdots + a_{sn} A_{sn}.$

Illustration: Theorem 9.4.2, for $s = 2$, $n = 3$.

$$\begin{vmatrix} a_{11} & a_{12} & a_{13} \\ a_{21} & a_{22} & a_{23} \\ a_{31} & a_{32} & a_{33} \end{vmatrix} = a_{21} A_{21} + a_{22} A_{22} + a_{23} A_{23}$$

$$-a_{21}\,a_{12}a_{33} + a_{21}\,a_{13}a_{32} + a_{22}\,a_{11}a_{33} - a_{22}\,a_{31}a_{13}$$

$$= (-1)^{2+1} a_{21} \begin{vmatrix} a_{12} & a_{13} \\ a_{32} & a_{33} \end{vmatrix} + (-1)^{2+2} a_{22} \begin{vmatrix} a_{11} & a_{13} \\ a_{31} & a_{33} \end{vmatrix}$$

$$+ (-1)^{2+3} a_{23} \begin{vmatrix} a_{11} & a_{12} \\ a_{31} & a_{32} \end{vmatrix}.$$

$$-a_{23}\,a_{11}a_{32} + a_{23}\,a_{31}a_{12}$$

Also:

$$\begin{vmatrix} 2 & 8 & 3 \\ -6 & 5 & 4 \\ -2 & 3 & 7 \end{vmatrix} = (-1)^{2+1}(-6) \begin{vmatrix} 8 & 3 \\ 3 & 7 \end{vmatrix} + (-1)^{2+2}(5) \begin{vmatrix} 2 & 3 \\ -2 & 7 \end{vmatrix}$$

$$+ (-1)^{2+3}(4) \begin{vmatrix} 2 & 8 \\ -2 & 3 \end{vmatrix}.$$

Suppose, however, that we pair the elements of the rth row with the corresponding cofactors of the elements of the sth row and form the products $a_{r1}A_{s1}, a_{r2}A_{s2}, \ldots, a_{rn}A_{sn}$. We may then inquire as to the sum of these products, namely $a_{r1}A_{s1} + a_{r2}A_{s2} + \cdots + a_{rn}A_{sn}$, or, written more compactly,

$$\sum_{j=1}^{n} a_{rj}A_{sj} \qquad (r, s = 1, 2, \ldots, n; r \neq s).$$

Clearly this sum is completely independent of the elements $a_{s1}, a_{s2}, \ldots, a_{sn}$, for it contains none of these elements. It is also obvious that changing the elements in the sth row of the determinant $|A|$ will have no effect upon the sum,

$$\sum_{j=1}^{n} a_{rj}A_{sj}.$$

We may note that, if the sth row and the rth row of $|A|$ are identical, then

$$(-1)^{r-s-1} \sum_{j=1}^{n} a_{rj}A_{sj}$$

is the value of the determinant. But, by theorem 9.2.6, the value of $|A|$ is zero. Hence, in this case,

$$\sum_{j=1}^{n} a_{rj}A_{sj} = 0 \quad \text{for } r, s = 1, 2, \ldots, n; r \neq s.$$

However, as we have already observed,

$$\sum_{j=1}^{n} a_{rj}A_{sj}$$

is independent of the elements $a_{s1}, a_{s2}, \ldots, a_{sn}$; thus, if

$$\sum_{j=1}^{n} a_{rj}A_{sj} = 0 \quad \text{for one set of values of } a_{sj} \qquad (j = 1, 2, \ldots, n),$$

then

$$\sum_{j=1}^{n} a_{rj}A_{sj} = 0 \quad \text{for all values of these } a_{sj} \qquad (j = 1, 2, \ldots, n).$$

Illustration: Using the same determinants as in the illustration above, we see by actual expansion that

$$a_{11}A_{21} + a_{12}A_{22} + a_{13}A_{23} = 0,$$

$$a_{11}A_{31} + a_{12}A_{32} + a_{13}A_{33} = 0,$$

$$a_{21}A_{11} + a_{22}A_{12} + a_{23}A_{13} = 0,$$

. . . .

Applying this to the numerical illustration above, we have

$$(-1)^2 2 \begin{vmatrix} 8 & 3 \\ 3 & 7 \end{vmatrix} + (-1)^3 8 \begin{vmatrix} 2 & 3 \\ -2 & 7 \end{vmatrix} + (-1)^4 3 \begin{vmatrix} 2 & 8 \\ -2 & 3 \end{vmatrix} = 0.$$

The following is a statement of this result.

THEOREM 9.4.3   *The sum of the products of the elements of one row of a determinant by the cofactors of the corresponding elements of a different row of the determinant is zero.*

EXERCISES

Given the determinant

$$\begin{vmatrix} 2 & 1 & 3 \\ 7 & 5 & -1 \\ 0 & -2 & 4 \end{vmatrix} :$$

1. Indicate the minor of each element of the first column.
2. Find the cofactor of each element of the second row.
3. Verify theorem 9.4.3 for elements of the third row and the cofactors of the elements of the second row.
4. Evaluate the determinant by using theorem 9.4.2 for (a) $s = 1$, (b) $s = 2$.
5. Expand the general 3×3 determinant $|a_{ij}|$ in terms of the elements of the first row and their cofactors. Expand each cofactor in terms of the elements of its first row and their cofactors. Thus obtain the determinantal polynomial of the determinant $|a_{ij}|$.
6. Show that the general 4×4 determinant $|a_{ij}|$ is equal to

$$\begin{vmatrix} a_{11} & a_{12} \\ a_{21} & a_{22} \end{vmatrix} \cdot \begin{vmatrix} a_{33} & a_{34} \\ a_{43} & a_{44} \end{vmatrix} - \begin{vmatrix} a_{11} & a_{13} \\ a_{21} & a_{23} \end{vmatrix} \cdot \begin{vmatrix} a_{32} & a_{34} \\ a_{42} & a_{44} \end{vmatrix}$$

$$+ \begin{vmatrix} a_{11} & a_{14} \\ a_{21} & a_{24} \end{vmatrix} \cdot \begin{vmatrix} a_{32} & a_{33} \\ a_{42} & a_{43} \end{vmatrix} + \begin{vmatrix} a_{12} & a_{13} \\ a_{22} & a_{23} \end{vmatrix} \cdot \begin{vmatrix} a_{31} & a_{34} \\ a_{41} & a_{44} \end{vmatrix}$$

$$- \begin{vmatrix} a_{12} & a_{14} \\ a_{22} & a_{24} \end{vmatrix} \cdot \begin{vmatrix} a_{31} & a_{33} \\ a_{41} & a_{43} \end{vmatrix} + \begin{vmatrix} a_{13} & a_{14} \\ a_{23} & a_{24} \end{vmatrix} \cdot \begin{vmatrix} a_{31} & a_{32} \\ a_{41} & a_{42} \end{vmatrix}.$$

7. Verify that the expansion of $|a_{ij}|$ in Exercise 6 may be written

$$\sum_{p(i)} (-1)^{1+2+i_1+i_2}\{(-1)^p a_{1i_1} a_{2i_2}\}\{(-1)^q a_{3i_3} a_{4i_4}\}$$

and state what the p and q indicate.

9.5   The Laplace Expansion of a Determinant.   In theorem 9.4.1, we found the coefficients of the elements of the sth row of the determinant $|a_{ij}|$ whenever the determinant is written as the determinantal polynomial. The Laplace expansion of a determinant is a generalization of this idea.

The expression $(-1)^i a_{1i_1} a_{2i_2} \ldots a_{ni_n}$ is the general term in the determinantal polynomial of the $n \times n$ determinant $|a_{ij}|$, where the number of inversions in the column subscripts $i_1, i_2, \ldots, i_n$ is of parity i.   Select any t rows, say the $k_1, k_2, \ldots, k_t$, and factor out these elements of these rows. We see from this that the general term in the determinantal polynomial may be written

$$(9.5.1)\quad (-1)^l\{(-1)^p a_{k_1 i_{k_1}} a_{k_2 i_{k_2}} \cdots a_{k_t i_{k_t}}\}\{(-1)^q a_{k_{t+1} i_{k_{t+1}}} a_{k_{t+2} i_{k_{t+2}}} \cdots a_{k_n i_{k_n}}\},$$

where the row subscripts $k_1, k_2, \ldots, k_t, k_{t+1}, \ldots, k_n$ are the integers $1, 2, \ldots, n$ in some order and where $k_1 < k_2 < \cdots < k_t$ and also $k_{t+1} < k_{t+2} < \cdots < k_n$.   The exponents p and q represent the number of inversions in the column subscripts of the elements with which they are associated and

$$l = \sum_{r=1}^{t} (k_r + i_{k_r}).$$

Thus the value of the determinantal polynomial may be written

$(9.5.2)$

$$\sum \left\{\sum_{p(i_{k_r})} (-1)^p a_{k_1 i_{k_1}} a_{k_2 i_{k_2}} \cdots a_{k_t i_{k_t}}\right\} \times$$
$$\left\{(-1)^l \sum_{p(i_{k_r})} (-1)^q a_{k_{t+1} i_{k_{t+1}}} a_{k_{t+2} i_{k_{t+2}}} \cdots a_{k_n i_{k_n}}\right\},$$

where the second and third summations indicate that the elements within the respective braces are to be summed over all possible permutations of the subscripts i_{k_r} within the corresponding braces and the product of these two sums is to be obtained.   The first summation symbol indicates that the product of these sums is to be made for each of the $\binom{n}{t}$ selections of column elements common to the preselected row. Thus, we account for the $n!$ terms of the expansion of the determinantal polynomial. We have established

THEOREM 9.5.1 *The value of an $n \times n$ determinant $|a_{ij}|$ is equal to the sum of the products obtained by multiplying each of the $\binom{n}{t}$ t-row minors that can be formed from any t rows of the determinant by the corresponding algebraic complement.*

We should call attention to the fact that obtaining the value of the determinant of A by using

$$\sum_{p(i_t)} (-1)^i a_{1i_1} a_{2i_2} \ldots a_{ni_n}$$

is called *expanding the determinant by rows*, and using the expansion given by using

$$\sum_{p(j_t)} (-1)^j a_{j_11} a_{j_22} \ldots a_{j_nn}$$

is called *expanding the determinant by columns*. That these two give the same value is evident from the corollary of theorem 9.1.4. From this we have

THEOREM 9.5.2 $\displaystyle\sum_{p(i_t)} (-1)^i a_{1i_1} \ldots a_{ni_n} = \sum_{p(j_t)} (-1)^j a_{j_11} a_{j_22} \ldots a_{j_nn}.$

COROLLARY. *The determinant of the matrix A is equal to the determinant of the transpose of A; i.e., $|A| = |A^T|$.*

Obviously, $|AB|$, $|BA|$, $|A| \cdot |B|$, $|A^T B|$, $|A^T| \cdot |B^T|$, $|A| \cdot |B^T|$, $|AB^T|$, $|A^T B^T|$ are all equal. It is also obvious that, in all previous theorems concerning determinants, we may replace the word row (or rows) with the word column (or columns). From theorem 9.5.2, we get

$$\sum_{j=1}^n a_{rj} A_{rj} = \sum_{i=1}^n a_{ir} A_{ir}. \quad \text{Thus,} \quad \sum_{i=1}^n a_{ir} A_{ir} = |A|.$$

This may also be shown by using $|A^T|$ and obtaining the sum of the product of the elements in the rth row by their cofactors. It is easy to establish the fact that

$$\sum_{j=1}^{n} a_{jr} A_{js} = 0.$$

We may indicate these results in the following manner:

$$(a_{s1} \quad a_{s2} \quad \ldots \quad a_{sn}) \begin{pmatrix} A_{s1} \\ A_{s2} \\ \ldots \\ \ldots \\ A_{sn} \end{pmatrix} = |A| \, ;$$

$$(a_{s1} \quad a_{s2} \quad \ldots \quad a_{sn}) \begin{pmatrix} A_{r1} \\ A_{r2} \\ \ldots \\ \ldots \\ A_{rn} \end{pmatrix} = 0, \quad r \neq s \, ;$$

$$(A_{1r} \quad A_{2r} \quad \ldots \quad A_{nr}) \begin{pmatrix} a_{1r} \\ a_{2r} \\ \ldots \\ \ldots \\ a_{nr} \end{pmatrix} = |A| \, ;$$

$$(A_{1r} \quad A_{2r} \quad \ldots \quad A_{nr}) \begin{pmatrix} a_{1s} \\ a_{2s} \\ \ldots \\ \ldots \\ a_{ns} \end{pmatrix} = 0, \quad r \neq s \, .$$

It will be noted, then, that the product of the $n \times n$ matrix (a_{ij}) by the $n \times n$ matrix (A_{ij}) having the elements which are the cofactors of the a_{ij} gives

$$\begin{pmatrix} a_{11} & a_{12} & \ldots & a_{1n} \\ a_{21} & a_{22} & \ldots & a_{2n} \\ \ldots & & & \\ a_{n1} & a_{n2} & \ldots & a_{nn} \end{pmatrix} \begin{pmatrix} A_{11} & A_{21} & \ldots & A_{n1} \\ A_{12} & A_{22} & \ldots & A_{n2} \\ \ldots & & & \\ A_{1n} & A_{2n} & \ldots & A_{nn} \end{pmatrix} = \begin{pmatrix} |A| & 0 & \ldots & 0 \\ 0 & |A| & \ldots & 0 \\ \ldots & & & \\ 0 & 0 & \ldots & |A| \end{pmatrix}.$$

Thus, for $|A| \neq 0$, we have

$$A^I = \begin{pmatrix} \dfrac{A_{11}}{|A|} & \dfrac{A_{21}}{|A|} & \cdots & \dfrac{A_{n1}}{|A|} \\[2mm] \dfrac{A_{12}}{|A|} & \dfrac{A_{22}}{|A|} & \cdots & \dfrac{A_{n2}}{|A|} \\[1mm] \cdots\cdots\cdots\cdots\cdots \\[1mm] \dfrac{A_{1n}}{|A|} & \dfrac{A_{2n}}{|A|} & \cdots & \dfrac{A_{nn}}{|A|} \end{pmatrix}.$$

This is a rather cumbersome and tedious manner in which to find A^I, but it does, nevertheless, give the unique inverse. In fact, one of the easiest ways to determine the cofactors of the a_{ij} of a nonzero determinant, $|A|$, is to obtain A^I and read the cofactors.

Another point of considerable interest here is what we shall refer to as *wholesale elimination* in solving a system of linear equations. We shall illustrate this by using a nonsingular system,

$$a_{11}x_1 + a_{12}x_2 + a_{13}x_3 = k_1,$$

$$a_{21}x_1 + a_{22}x_2 + a_{23}x_3 = k_2,$$

$$a_{31}x_1 + a_{32}x_2 + a_{33}x_3 = k_3.$$

Multiplying the first equation by A_{11}, the second by A_{21}, the third by A_{31}, and adding gives

$$|A|x_1 + 0x_2 + 0x_3 = k_1 A_{11} + k_2 A_{21} + k_3 A_{31}.$$

Selecting the multipliers A_{12}, A_{22}, A_{32} and then A_{13}, A_{23}, A_{33} and summing gives

$$|A|x_2 = \sum_{i=1}^{3} k_i A_{i2},$$

$$|A|x_3 = \sum_{i=1}^{3} k_i A_{i3}.$$

And, since $|A| \neq 0$, it is easy to verify, by substitution, that

$$x_r = \frac{\displaystyle\sum_{i=1}^{3} k_i A_{ir}}{|A|} \qquad (r = 1, 2, 3).$$

This is, of course, the well known *Cramer's Rule*. The generalization of Cramer's Rule to an $n \times n$ system of linear equations having $|A| \neq 0$ should follow without difficulty.

EXERCISES

1. Write the algebraic complement of the minor $\begin{vmatrix} a_{12} & a_{14} \\ a_{32} & a_{34} \end{vmatrix}$ in the general determinant $|a_{ij}|$ of order four; five. Note that the relative arrangement of the rows and columns must not be disturbed.

2. Expand the general 4×4 determinant $|a_{ij}|$ by the Laplace expansion, using the second and fourth rows.

3. From the sum given in Exercise 2, compute two terms of the expansion of the original determinant and verify that these are actually terms of the determinantal polynomial.

4. Show that the general term of the determinantal polynomial may be written as in (9.5.1).

5. Show that the sum of products used in proving theorem 9.5.1 is a sum of products of pairs of complementary minors of the determinant $|a_{ij}|$.

6. Let A_t be a particular, t-row square submatrix of the general $n \times n$ matrix $A = (a_{ij})$, and let A_{n-t} be the complementary submatrix of A_t in A. Let p be the sum of the column subscripts and row subscripts of the elements in A_t.

(a) Form the product of any term in the expansion of $|A_t|$ and any term in the expansion of $|A_{n-t}|$. Multiply this product by $(-1)^p$ and show that the result thus obtained is a term in the expansion of $|A|$.

(b) Find the number of terms in the product of the determinantal polynomials of $|A_t|$ and $|A_{n-t}|$.

(c) Take any other $t \times t$ submatrix, B_t, from the same t rows of A as used to form A_t and let B_{n-t} be the complementary submatrix of B_t in A. Show that no term in the product of the determinantal polynomials of $|B_t|$ and $|B_{n-t}|$ is a duplicate of a term in the product of the determinantal polynomials of $|A_t|$ and $|A_{n-t}|$.

(d) How many different selections A_t, B_t, . . . are possible from these t rows?

(e) Show that every term in the expansion of $|A|$ is found in some one of the products described in (a) and (c) by showing that the total number of terms in all such products of these expansions is equal to $n!$, the number of terms in the expansion of $|A|$.

7. Verify that $|A| = |A^T|$ for

$$A = \begin{pmatrix} 2 & 7 & 1 \\ 3 & 5 & -1 \\ 4 & 1 & 6 \end{pmatrix}.$$

8. For the matrices $A = \begin{pmatrix} 2 & 3 \\ 5 & 7 \end{pmatrix}$ and $B = \begin{pmatrix} 1 & 2 \\ 1 & 3 \end{pmatrix}$, verify that

$|A| \cdot |B|$, $|AB|$, $|A^T| \cdot |B|$, $|A| \cdot |B^T|$, $|A^T| \cdot |B^T|$, and $|A^T \cdot B^T|$ are all equal.

9. Find the inverse of the matrix A, using the cofactor method, where

$$A = \begin{pmatrix} 3 & 1 & 1 \\ 4 & 2 & -1 \\ 7 & 3 & 1 \end{pmatrix}.$$

10. Use the results of Exercise 9 to solve by "wholesale elimination" the system

$$3x_1 + x_2 + x_3 = 5,$$
$$4x_1 + 2x_2 - x_3 = 7,$$
$$7x_1 + 3x_2 + x_3 = -3.$$

Solve the system by using the matrix equation $A^I A X = A^I K$.

11. Prove Cramer's Rule.

12. Describe the procedure used in expanding an 8×8 determinant, by the Laplace development, in terms of the 4×4 minors of some four rows and state the number of determinant products envolved. How does this differ from the Laplace development using 3×3 minors?

SUMMARY EXERCISES

1. Show that

$$\begin{vmatrix} a_{11} & a_{12} & 0 & 0 \\ a_{21} & a_{22} & 0 & 0 \\ -1 & 0 & b_{11} & b_{12} \\ 0 & -1 & b_{21} & b_{22} \end{vmatrix} = \begin{vmatrix} a_{11} & a_{12} & a_{11}b_{11} + a_{12}b_{21} & a_{11}b_{12} + a_{12}b_{22} \\ a_{21} & a_{22} & a_{21}b_{11} + a_{22}b_{21} & a_{21}b_{12} + a_{22}b_{22} \\ -1 & 0 & 0 & 0 \\ 0 & -1 & 0 & 0 \end{vmatrix}$$

$$= \begin{vmatrix} a_{11}b_{11} + a_{12}b_{21} & a_{11}b_{12} + a_{12}b_{22} \\ a_{21}b_{11} + a_{22}b_{21} & a_{21}b_{12} + a_{22}b_{22} \end{vmatrix},$$

and that

$$\begin{vmatrix} a_{11} & a_{12} & 0 & 0 \\ a_{21} & a_{22} & 0 & 0 \\ -1 & 0 & b_{11} & b_{12} \\ 0 & -1 & b_{21} & b_{22} \end{vmatrix} = \begin{vmatrix} a_{11} & a_{12} \\ a_{21} & a_{22} \end{vmatrix} \cdot \begin{vmatrix} b_{11} & b_{12} \\ b_{21} & b_{22} \end{vmatrix},$$

and thus prove theorem 9.3.7 for 2×2 matrices.

2. Extend the result of Exercise 1, by the same method, to determinants of order n.

3. Verify that the determinant

$$
\begin{vmatrix}
0 & (a-b)^2 & (a-c)^2 \\
(b-a)^2 & 0 & (b-c)^2 \\
(c-a)^2 & (c-b)^2 & 0
\end{vmatrix}
$$

may be factored into the product

$$
\begin{vmatrix}
a^2 & -2a & 1 \\
b^2 & -2b & 1 \\
c^2 & -2c & 1
\end{vmatrix}
\cdot
\begin{vmatrix}
1 & 1 & 1 \\
a & b & c \\
a^2 & b^2 & c^2
\end{vmatrix}.
$$

From this result, find factors of the determinant

$$
\begin{vmatrix}
0 & (a-b)^2 & (a-c)^2 & (a-d)^2 \\
(b-a)^2 & 0 & (b-c)^2 & (b-d)^2 \\
(c-a)^2 & (c-b)^2 & 0 & (c-d)^2 \\
(d-a)^2 & (d-b)^2 & (d-c)^2 & 0
\end{vmatrix}.
$$

Evaluate all determinants in each case and verify your results.

4. Find the product of the Vandermonde determinants

$$
\begin{vmatrix}
1 & 1 & 1 \\
a_1 & a_2 & a_3 \\
a_1^2 & a_2^2 & a_3^2
\end{vmatrix},
\qquad
\begin{vmatrix}
1 & a_1 & a_1^2 \\
1 & a_2 & a_2^2 \\
1 & a_3 & a_3^2
\end{vmatrix}.
$$

5. Using Exercise 4, find factors of the determinants

(a) $$
\begin{vmatrix}
1 & \sum a_i & \sum a^2 & \sum a_i^3 \\
\sum a_i & \sum a^2 & \sum a_i^3 & \sum a_i^4 \\
\sum a_i^2 & \sum a_i^3 & \sum a_i^4 & \sum a_i^5 \\
\sum a_i^3 & \sum a_i^4 & \sum a^5 & \sum a_i^6
\end{vmatrix},
$$

(b) $$
\begin{vmatrix}
\sum a_i & \sum a_i^3 & \sum a_i^5 & \sum a_i^7 \\
\sum a_i^3 & \sum a_i^5 & \sum a_i^7 & \sum a_i^9 \\
\sum a_i^5 & \sum a_i^7 & \sum a_i^9 & \sum a_i^{11} \\
\sum a_i^7 & \sum a_i^9 & \sum a_i^{11} & \sum a_i^{13}
\end{vmatrix},
$$

where the summation is made for $i = 1, 2, 3, 4$.

6. Find the product

$$
\begin{vmatrix}
1 & 0 & 0 \\
0 & 0 & 1 \\
0 & 1 & 0
\end{vmatrix}
\cdot
\begin{vmatrix}
1 & \alpha & \alpha^2 \\
\alpha^2 & 1 & \alpha \\
\alpha & \alpha^2 & 1
\end{vmatrix}
\cdot
\begin{vmatrix}
1 & -\alpha & 0 \\
0 & 1 & 0 \\
0 & 0 & 1
\end{vmatrix},
$$

and thus find the value of the *circulant*

$$
\begin{vmatrix}
1 & \alpha & \alpha^2 \\
\alpha^2 & 1 & \alpha \\
\alpha & \alpha^2 & 1
\end{vmatrix}.
$$

7. For the nonsingular 3×3 matrix A show that

$$
\begin{pmatrix} a_{11} & a_{12} & a_{13} \\ a_{21} & a_{22} & a_{23} \\ a_{31} & a_{32} & a_{33} \end{pmatrix}
\begin{pmatrix} \dfrac{A_{11}}{|A|} & \dfrac{A_{21}}{|A|} & \dfrac{A_{31}}{|A|} \\[2mm] \dfrac{A_{12}}{|A|} & \dfrac{A_{22}}{|A|} & \dfrac{A_{32}}{|A|} \\[2mm] \dfrac{A_{13}}{|A|} & \dfrac{A_{23}}{|A|} & \dfrac{A_{33}}{|A|} \end{pmatrix} = I.
$$

8. Extend the result of Exercise 7 to $n \times n$ nonsingular matrices.

9. Find the inverse of each of the following matrices by the use of determinants and cofactors as in Exercise 7.

(a) $\begin{pmatrix} 1 & 3 & -1 \\ 2 & 7 & 3 \\ 3 & 10 & 3 \end{pmatrix}.$ (b) $\begin{pmatrix} 2 & -1 & 1 \\ 3 & -1 & 0 \\ 1 & 0 & 0 \end{pmatrix}.$ (c) $\begin{pmatrix} 7 & 3 & 1 \\ 4 & 2 & -3 \\ 3 & 1 & 5 \end{pmatrix}.$

10. Find three different determinants which will have for their values the products of the determinants

$$
\begin{vmatrix} 1 & 2 \\ 3 & 5 \end{vmatrix} \cdot \begin{vmatrix} 3 & 2 & 1 \\ 1 & 2 & 3 \\ 5 & -7 & 0 \end{vmatrix}.
$$

11. Find the value of the 4×4 determinant $|A|$, where

$$
|A| = \begin{vmatrix} \dfrac{1}{1!} & \dfrac{1}{0!} & 0 & 0 \\[2mm] \dfrac{1}{2!} & \dfrac{1}{1!} & \dfrac{1}{0!} & 0 \\[2mm] \dfrac{1}{3!} & \dfrac{1}{2!} & \dfrac{1}{1!} & \dfrac{1}{0!} \\[2mm] \dfrac{1}{4!} & \dfrac{1}{3!} & \dfrac{1}{2!} & \dfrac{1}{1!} \end{vmatrix}.
$$

Note that the value can be ascertained by forming the product $|A| \cdot |B|$, where $|B|$ is defined by $|B| = |b_{ij}|$,

$$
b_{ij} = \frac{(-1)^{i+j}(j-1)!}{(i-1)!}
$$

for $i \leq j$ and $b_{ij} = 0$ for $i > j$. Extend this result to an $n \times n$ determinant having the same type skeleton as $|A|$.

12. Evaluate the determinant

$$\begin{vmatrix} 3! & \binom{3}{1} & \binom{3}{2} & \binom{3}{3} \\ 2! & \binom{2}{0} & \binom{2}{1} & \binom{2}{2} \\ 1! & 0 & \binom{1}{0} & \binom{1}{1} \\ 0! & 0 & 0 & \binom{0}{0} \end{vmatrix}.$$

Show that this determinant can be evaluated by multiplying it by the triangular determinant defined by

$$|A| = |a_{ij}|, \quad a_{1j} = (-1)^{j+1}\binom{3}{j-1}$$

for $j = 1, 2, 3, 4$; $a_{ij} = 1$ for $i = j$; all other $a_{ij} = 0$. Extend this result to the $(n+1) \times (n+1)$ determinant

$$\begin{vmatrix} n! & \binom{n}{1} & \binom{n}{2} & \cdots & \binom{n}{n} \\ (n-1)! & \binom{n-1}{0} & \binom{n-1}{1} & \cdots & \binom{n-1}{n-1} \\ (n-2)! & 0 & \binom{n-2}{0} & \cdots & \binom{n-2}{n-2} \\ \cdots\cdots\cdots\cdots\cdots\cdots\cdots\cdots\cdots\cdots \\ 0! & 0 & 0 & \cdots & \binom{0}{0} \end{vmatrix}.$$

13. Given the determinant $|A|$, defined by

$$|A| = \begin{vmatrix} 1 & -1 & 1 & -1 & 1 \\ 1 & 1 & 0 & 1 & 0 \\ 0 & 1 & 1 & 0 & 1 \\ 0 & 0 & 1 & 1 & 0 \\ 0 & 0 & 0 & 1 & 1 \end{vmatrix}.$$

ind a determinant which will multiply the determinant $|A|$ and give the deterinant $|B|$, where

$$|B| = \begin{vmatrix} 1 & -1 & 0 & 0 & 0 \\ 1 & 1 & -1 & 0 & 0 \\ 0 & 1 & 1 & -1 & 0 \\ 0 & 0 & 1 & 1 & -1 \\ 0 & 0 & 0 & 1 & 1 \end{vmatrix}.$$

ind a determinant which will multiply $|B|$ and reduce it to the triangular keleton. Thus evaluate $|A|$.

14. Evaluate the determinant $|A|$ defined by

$$|A| = \begin{vmatrix} \dfrac{1}{1!} & -1 & 0 & 0 & 0 \\[2mm] \dfrac{2^2}{2!} & \dfrac{1}{1!} & -2 & 0 & 0 \\[2mm] \dfrac{3^3}{3!} & \dfrac{2^2}{2!} & \dfrac{1}{1!} & -3 & 0 \\[2mm] \dfrac{4^4}{4!} & \dfrac{3^3}{3!} & \dfrac{2^2}{2!} & \dfrac{1}{1!} & -4 \\[2mm] \dfrac{5^5}{5!} & \dfrac{4^4}{4!} & \dfrac{3^3}{3!} & \dfrac{2^2}{2!} & \dfrac{1}{1!} \end{vmatrix}.$$

ind the product $|A| \cdot |B|$ and thus evaluate $|A|$, where

$$|B| = \begin{vmatrix} 1 & \dfrac{1^0 \cdot 1!}{2^0 \cdot 1!} & \dfrac{1^0 \cdot 2!}{3^1 \cdot 1!} & \dfrac{1^0 \cdot 3!}{4^2 \cdot 1!} & \dfrac{1^0 \cdot 4!}{5^3 \cdot 1!} \\[2mm] 0 & 1 & \dfrac{2^1 \cdot 2!}{3^1 \cdot 2!} & \dfrac{2^1 \cdot 3!}{4^2 \cdot 2!} & \dfrac{2^1 \cdot 4!}{5^3 \cdot 2!} \\[2mm] 0 & 0 & 1 & \dfrac{3^2 \cdot 3!}{4^2 \cdot 3!} & \dfrac{3^2 \cdot 4!}{5^3 \cdot 3!} \\[2mm] 0 & 0 & 0 & 1 & \dfrac{4^3 \cdot 4!}{5^3 \cdot 4!} \\[2mm] 0 & 0 & 0 & 0 & 1 \end{vmatrix}.$$

Explain what effect the column transformation of A by B has on the columns of A.

15. Show that

$$
\begin{vmatrix}
\binom{3}{2} & \binom{4}{2} & \binom{5}{2} & \binom{6}{2} & \binom{7}{2} \\
\binom{3}{3} & \binom{4}{3} & \binom{5}{3} & \binom{6}{3} & \binom{7}{3} \\
0 & \binom{4}{4} & \binom{5}{4} & \binom{6}{4} & \binom{7}{4} \\
0 & 0 & \binom{5}{5} & \binom{6}{5} & \binom{7}{5} \\
0 & 0 & 0 & \binom{6}{6} & \binom{7}{6}
\end{vmatrix} = \binom{7}{2}.
$$

Generalize this result to an $n \times n$ determinant.

16. Evaluate the determinant

$$
\begin{vmatrix}
1 & \frac{1}{2} & \frac{1}{3} \\
\frac{1}{2} & \frac{1}{3} & \frac{1}{4} \\
\frac{1}{3} & \frac{1}{4} & \frac{1}{5}
\end{vmatrix}
$$

by multiplying it by a determinant, of value 1, which transforms it into a triangular skeleton.

CHAPTER 10

MATRICES AND POLYNOMIALS

10.1 Matrices with Polynomial Elements. An expression of the form

$$(10.1.1) \qquad f(x) = a_0x^s + a_1x^{s-1} + \cdots + a_{s-1}x + a_s,$$

where s is a positive integer and the a_i belong to a field $\mathcal{F}$, is called a polynomial in x over $\mathcal{F}$. If each a_i is zero, the polynomial is the *zero polynomial* and is denoted by the symbol 0. The symbol x is an indeterminate over the field and is commutative with itself and with elements of the field. If $f(x)$ and $g(x)$ are polynomials in x over $\mathcal{F}$ and $g(x)$ is not the zero polynomial, the function

$$(10.1.2) \qquad R(x) = \frac{f(x)}{g(x)}$$

is called a rational function in x over $\mathcal{F}$.

The set of all rational functions in x over $\mathcal{F}$ is a field, denoted by $\mathcal{F}\{x\}$. We may treat matrices with elements in this field in much the same way that we have treated those with elements in a number field.

In studying matrices with elements in the field of real numbers, we could have considered the special case when those elements were ordinary integers. These matrices would then have been transformed into matrices having integers as elements if in the elementary additive transformation we had required the multiplier to be an integer, and if in the elementary multiplicative transformation we had required the multiplier to be $+1$ or -1. In the field $\mathcal{F}\{x\}$ the polynomials in x play much the same role as do ordinary integers in the field of real numbers.

We denote by $\mathcal{F}[x]$ the set of all polynomials in x over the field $\mathcal{F}$. In this chapter we study matrices with elements in $\mathcal{F}[x]$. Such matrices may also be considered as polynomials in x having as coefficients matrices with elements in $\mathcal{F}$. Thus, for example,

$$\begin{pmatrix} x^2 + x - 1 & x + 2 \\ x - 1 & x^2 + x \end{pmatrix} = \begin{pmatrix} 1 & 0 \\ 0 & 1 \end{pmatrix} x^2 + \begin{pmatrix} 1 & 1 \\ 1 & 1 \end{pmatrix} x + \begin{pmatrix} -1 & 2 \\ -1 & 0 \end{pmatrix},$$

where x is an indeterminate and may be commuted with its coefficients. In particular, the matrix $f(x)I$, where I is the identity matrix of order n,

147

may be written as a polynomial in x having coefficients which are scalar matrices of order n. Thus, for $f(x) = 2x^2 + x - 3$ and $n = 2$, we have

$$
f(x)I = \begin{pmatrix} 2x^2 + x - 3 & 0 \\ 0 & 2x^2 + x - 3 \end{pmatrix}
$$

$$
= \begin{pmatrix} 2 & 0 \\ 0 & 2 \end{pmatrix} x^2 + \begin{pmatrix} 1 & 0 \\ 0 & 1 \end{pmatrix} x + \begin{pmatrix} -3 & 0 \\ 0 & -3 \end{pmatrix}.
$$

The polynomials $f(x)I$ are called *scalar matric polynomials*. The set of all scalar matric polynomials in x (of a particular order) over $\mathcal{F}$ is isomorphic with $\mathcal{F}[x]$, where the isomorphism is defined by $f(x)I \leftrightarrow f(x)$.

We define three types of elementary transformations for matrices with elements in $\mathcal{F}[x]$. If A is any matrix with elements in $\mathcal{F}[x]$, then a matrix obtained from A by interchanging two rows (columns) is said to be obtained from A by an *elementary permutative transformation*. Any matrix obtained from A by adding to a row (column) the product of any other row (column) by an element of $\mathcal{F}[x]$ is said to be obtained from A by an *elementary additive transformation*. Any matrix obtained from A by multiplying a row (column) by a nonzero element of $\mathcal{F}$ (i.e., an element of $\mathcal{F}[x]$ having an inverse in $\mathcal{F}[x]$) is said to be obtained from A by an *elementary multiplicative transformation*. It is noted that in each case the resulting matrix has its elements in $\mathcal{F}[x]$.

If A and B are two matrices with elements in $\mathcal{F}[x]$, then B is said to be equivalent to A in $\mathcal{F}[x]$, if it is possible to obtain B from A by a finite number of elementary transformations of the types defined above. It may be readily shown that, if B is equivalent to A in $\mathcal{F}[x]$, then A is also equivalent to B in $\mathcal{F}[x]$, and we indicate this by writing $A \overset{\mathcal{F}[x]}{=} B$.

A matrix obtained from I by an elementary transformation in $\mathcal{F}[x]$ will be called an *elementary transformation matrix*. Such matrices are nonsingular, and their inverses have elements in $\mathcal{F}[x]$.

It is clear that, if B is equivalent to A in $\mathcal{F}[x]$, then B is also equivalent to A in the field $\mathcal{F}\{x\}$ in accordance with the definition of equivalence in a field. Thus, it is necessary that A and B have the same rank in order that they be equivalent in $\mathcal{F}[x]$. We shall see, however, that this condition is not sufficient for equivalence in $\mathcal{F}[x]$.

10.2 A Canonical Form for Matrices Having Elements in $\mathcal{F}[x]$. It is desirable to separate the $m \times n$ matrices with elements in $\mathcal{F}[x]$ into classes such that all matrices of each class are equivalent in $\mathcal{F}[x]$ and also such that no matrix of any class is equivalent to any matrix of another class in $\mathcal{F}[x]$. And, furthermore, it is desirable to select some particular matrix of each class as a representative of the class. To this end we recall certain definitions and theorems from the theory of polynomials over a field $\mathcal{F}$.

A polynomial with coefficients in $\mathcal{F}$ is said to be *monic* if the leading coefficient is the element 1 of $\mathcal{F}$. Two polynomials $f(x)$ and $g(x)$ with coefficients in $\mathcal{F}$ are said to be associates if $f(x) = cg(x)$, where c is a nonzero element of $\mathcal{F}$. Among all the associates of a nonzero polynomial $f(x)$ there is one and only one monic polynomial. In any set of nonzero polynomials there is one or more polynomials of lowest degree. The nonzero elements of $\mathcal{F}$ are polynomials of degree zero, and the zero element of $\mathcal{F}$ is the zero polynomial which has no degree. The greatest common divisor of a set of polynomials is the monic polynomial which is a common divisor of the polynomials of the set and which contains as a divisor every common divisor of the polynomials of the set.

If A is a nonzero matrix with elements in $\mathcal{F}[x]$, there is a polynomial $f_1(x)$ which is of the lowest possible degree among all the elements of all matrices equivalent to A in $\mathcal{F}[x]$. There is an equivalent matrix A_1 which has this element $f_1(x)$ in the upper left-hand corner. This element $f_1(x)$ is a factor of every element in the first row of A_1 and also a factor of every element in the first column of A_1. For, if $f(x)$ is any element in the first row or first column of A_1, then $f(x) = q(x)f_1(x) + r(x)$, where $r(x)$ is zero or is a polynomial of lower degree than $f_1(x)$. Hence, by applying an elementary additive transformation to A_1, we may obtain an equivalent matrix with the element $r(x)$. Since such an element cannot be of lower degree than $f_1(x)$, it follows that $r(x)$ is the zero polynomial. By applying a sequence of elementary additive transformations to A_1 we obtain an equivalent matrix

$$(10.2.1) \qquad \begin{pmatrix} f_1(x) & 0 \\ 0 & A_2 \end{pmatrix}.$$

If $A_2 \neq 0$, then it is equivalent to

$$\begin{pmatrix} f_2(x) & 0 \\ 0 & A_3 \end{pmatrix},$$

where $f_2(x)$ is of the lowest possible degree for any polynomials in any matrix equivalent to A_2. If in (10.2.1) we apply elementary transformations to the rows and columns of A_2 only, the first row and first column are not disturbed and hence A is equivalent to

$$\begin{pmatrix} f_1(x) & 0 & 0 \\ 0 & f_2(x) & 0 \\ 0 & 0 & A_3 \end{pmatrix}.$$

If $A_3 \neq 0$, this process may be continued. Thus, the matrix A is equivalent to a matrix of one of the following types:

$$(10.2.2) \qquad D, \qquad \begin{pmatrix} D & 0 \\ 0 & 0 \end{pmatrix}, \qquad \begin{pmatrix} D \\ 0 \end{pmatrix}, \qquad (D \quad 0),$$

where

$$(10.2.3) \qquad D = \text{diag.} \{f_1(x), f_2(x), \ldots, f_r(x)\}$$

and r is the rank of A in $\mathcal{F}\{x\}$. If in (10.2.3) the polynomial $f_i(x)$ is replaced by any one of its associates, the resulting matrix is equivalent to D. Hence, each $f_i(x)$ in D will be taken to be monic.

In this chain, we have

$$A_i \overset{\mathcal{F}[x]}{=} \begin{pmatrix} f_i(x) & 0 & 0 \\ 0 & f_{i+1}(x) & 0 \\ 0 & 0 & A_{i+2} \end{pmatrix} \overset{\mathcal{F}[x]}{=} \begin{pmatrix} f_i(x) & 0 & 0 \\ f_i(x) & f_{i+1}(x) & 0 \\ 0 & 0 & A_{i+2} \end{pmatrix},$$

where $f_i(x)$ is a polynomial of the lowest possible degree in any matrix equivalent to A_i. It follows that $f_i(x)$ is a factor of $f_{i+1}(x)$. These results may be stated as

THEOREM 10.2.1   *Every nonzero matrix A with elements in $\mathcal{F}[x]$ is equivalent in $\mathcal{F}[x]$ to a matrix of one of the types given by (10.2.2) where $f_i(x)$ is a monic polynomial which is a factor of $f_{i+1}(x)$.*

Since each elementary transformation on A may be accomplished by multiplying A on the left or on the right by an elementary transformation matrix, then any matrix equivalent to A in $\mathcal{F}[x]$ may be written as PAQ, where P and Q are products of elementary transformation matrices. Each elementary transformation matrix has an inverse which is an elementary transformation matrix with elements in $\mathcal{F}[x]$, and hence P and Q have inverses with elements in $\mathcal{F}[x]$.

Suppose now that A is a nonsingular matrix with elements in $\mathcal{F}[x]$ and that A^I also has all of its elements in $\mathcal{F}[x]$. There exist matrices P and Q with elements in $\mathcal{F}[x]$ and having inverses with elements in $\mathcal{F}[x]$ such that $PAQ = \text{diag.}\{f_1(x), f_2(x), \ldots, f_n(x)\}$, where the $f_i(x)$, $i = 1, 2, \ldots, n$, are monic polynomials. The matrix $(PAQ)^I$ has elements in $\mathcal{F}[x]$. But, PAQ has a unique inverse with elements in the field $\mathcal{F}\{x\}$ and hence

$$(PAQ)^I = \text{diag.}\left\{\frac{1}{f_1(x)}, \frac{1}{f_2(x)}, \ldots, \frac{1}{f_n(x)}\right\}.$$

Consequently, since $1/[f_i(x)]$ is a polynomial and $f_i(x)$ is a monic polynomial, it follows that $f_1(x) = f_2(x) = \cdots = f_n(x) = 1$. That is, $PAQ = I$.

Then, $A = P^I Q^I$, and thus A is a product of elementary transformation matrices.

DEFINITION. *A nonsingular matrix with elements in $\mathcal{F}[x]$ is defined to be* elementary *if its inverse has elements in $\mathcal{F}[x]$.*

We have established

THEOREM 10.2.2 *Any nonsingular matrix A with elements in $\mathcal{F}[x]$ is elementary if and only if A is a product of elementary transformation matrices.*

In particular, the matrices P and Q above are elementary and we have

THEOREM 10.2.3 *Two matrices A and B with elements in $\mathcal{F}[x]$ are equivalent in $\mathcal{F}[x]$ if and only if there exist elementary matrices P and Q such that $PAQ = B$.*

Let D be the matrix defined in (10.2.3), where each $f_i(x)$ is monic, and let M be the corresponding matrix in (10.2.2). Then every matrix equivalent to M in $\mathcal{F}[x]$ is given by PMQ, where P and Q are elementary matrices. But it follows from theorem 10.2.1 that every element of PMQ is divisible by $f_1(x)$, and hence that $f_1(x)$ is the greatest common divisor of all the elements of all matrices equivalent to A in $\mathcal{F}[x]$. That is, the lowest degree monic polynomial in any matrix equivalent to M in $\mathcal{F}[x]$ is unique. Also, since $f_i(x)$ is a divisor of $f_{i+1}(x)$, every t-row determinant in PMQ is divisible by $d_t(x) = f_1(x)f_2(x) \ldots f_t(x)$.* But $d_t(x)$ is a t-row determinant of M, and hence $f_1(x)f_2(x) \ldots f_t(x)$ is the greatest common divisor of all t-row determinants from all matrices equivalent to M in $\mathcal{F}[x]$. It may also be shown that $d_t(x)$ is the greatest common divisor of all t-row determinants in any one matrix equivalent to M.

Let $PMQ = N$, where N is of type (10.2.2) with

$$D = \text{diag. } \{g_1(x), g_2(x), \ldots, g_r(x)\}$$

and where $g_i(x)$ is monic and is a divisor of $g_{i+1}(x)$. Then it follows that $d_t(x) = g_1(x)g_2(x) \ldots g_t(x)$. Hence, we have $f_1(x)f_2(x) \ldots f_t(x) = g_1(x)g_2(x) \ldots g_t(x)$, $t \leq r$. Since each of these is a factor of the other in $\mathcal{F}[x]$, and since they are monic, they must be equal. It follows that $f_i(x) = g_i(x)$ $(i = 1, 2, \ldots, r)$.

We have shown that the polynomials $f_1(x), f_2(x), \ldots, f_r(x)$ are determined uniquely for the matrix A. The polynomials $f_i(x)$ are called the *invariant factors* of A. We have established

THEOREM 10.2.4 *Two $m \times n$ matrices with elements in $\mathcal{F}[x]$ are equivalent in $\mathcal{F}[x]$ if and only if they have the same invariant factors.*

* L. E. Dickson, *Modern Algebraic Theories*, pp. 49–51. Consider PMQ as either $(PM)Q$ or $P(MQ)$.

The unique matrix (10.2.2) equivalent to A is referred to as the *Smith normal* form for matrices equivalent to A in $\mathcal{F}[x]$.

EXERCISES

1. Write the following matrices as polynomials in x with matrices as coefficients.

(a) $\begin{pmatrix} x^2 + x - 1 & x^2 + 1 \\ x + 2 & 2x^2 - x - 3 \end{pmatrix}$,

(b) $\begin{pmatrix} x^2 + x & x \\ x^2 & x^2 - x \end{pmatrix}$,

(c) $\begin{pmatrix} x^3 + 1 & 2x^3 - 1 & x^3 + 2 \\ x + 1 & x - 2 & x^3 + x \end{pmatrix}$.

2. Write $(x^2 + x + 2)I_3$ as a matrix with elements in $\mathcal{F}[x]$ and as a polynomial with scalar matrices as coefficients.

3. Reduce the following matrices to equivalent matrices as described in theorem 10.2.1.

(a) $\begin{pmatrix} x - 1 & 0 & 0 \\ 0 & x + 1 & 0 \\ 0 & 0 & x - 1 \end{pmatrix}$,

(b) $\begin{pmatrix} x & 1 & 0 \\ 0 & x & 1 \\ 2 & 3 & x - 1 \end{pmatrix}$,

(c) $\begin{pmatrix} x + 1 & x - 1 \\ x & 0 \end{pmatrix}$.

10.3 Matric Polynomials. Let A be an $m \times n$ nonzero matrix with elements in $\mathcal{F}[x]$, and let s be the degree of the polynomial of greatest degree in A. We may then write

(10.3.1) $\qquad A = A_0 x^s + A_1 x^{s-1} + \cdots + A_{s-1}x + A_s,$

where each A_i is an $m \times n$ matrix with elements in $\mathcal{F}$ and $A_0 \neq 0$. Whenever we wish to emphasize the fact that we are considering A as a polynomial in x with matric coefficients, we shall write $A = A(x)$ and we shall call $A(x)$ a *matric polynomial*. The matrix A_0 is called the *leading coefficient* of $A(x)$, and s is called the *degree* of $A(x)$.

If A is the zero matrix, then $A(x)$ is called the zero matric polynomial. The zero matric polynomial has no degree. Nonzero matrices having all elements in $\mathcal{F}$ may be considered matric polynomials of degree zero.

If A and B are $m \times n$ matrices with elements in $\mathcal{F}[x]$, then $A + B$ is an $m \times n$ matrix with elements in $\mathcal{F}[x]$. If we write $C = A + B$, then C may be written as a matric polynomial, $C(x)$. In this case the sum of two matric polynomials is defined by the relation $C(x) = A(x) + B(x)$. The following theorem is evident.

THEOREM 10.3.1 *If $A(x)$ and $B(x)$ are matric polynomials, then the degree of $A(x) + B(x)$ is not greater than the greater of the degrees of $A(x)$ and $B(x)$.*

We have seen that both $A + B$ and AB are defined for two matrices A and B if and only if A and B are square and of the same order. *In what is to follow, we shall restrict our attention to square matrices having elements in $\mathcal{F}[x]$.* The corresponding matric polynomials will have as coefficients square matrices with elements in $\mathcal{F}$. We define the *product of two matric polynomials* to be the matric polynomial corresponding to the product of the two matrices. Thus, if $C = AB$, then $A(x)B(x) = C(x)$. Matric polynomials may be multiplied in the same way as polynomials over a field, except that *care must be taken in forming the products of coefficients to keep them in proper order since, in general, $AB \neq BA$.* For example:

$$(A_0 x + A_1)(B_0 x + B_1) = A_0 B_0 x^2 + (A_0 B_1 + A_1 B_0)x + A_1 B_1.$$

The following theorem is evident from this definition.

THEOREM 10.3.2 *If $A(x)$ is a matric polynomial of degree s with leading coefficient A_0 and $B(x)$ is a matric polynomial of degree t with leading coefficient B_0, then $A(x)B(x)$ is a matric polynomial which is zero or of degree not greater than $s + t$. The degree of $A(x)B(x)$ is $s + t$ if and only if $A_0 B_0 \neq 0$, and in this case $A_0 B_0$ is the leading coefficient of $A(x)B(x)$.*

From the definition of equal matrices, it follows that two matric polynomials are equal if and only if their corresponding coefficients are equal. Let

$$A = A_0 x^s + A_1 x^{s-1} + \cdots + A_s \quad \text{and} \quad B = B_0 x^t + B_1 x^{t-1} + \cdots + B_t$$

be two matric polynomials such that A_0 is not zero, B_0 is nonsingular, and $s > t$. Then

(10.3.2)
$$A(x) - A_0 B_0^I x^{s-t} B(x) = R_1(x) \quad \text{and}$$
$$A(x) - B(x) B_0^I A_0 x^{s-t} = L_1(x),$$

where $R_1(x)$ and $L_1(x)$ are matric polynomials each of which is zero or is of degree less than s. These are the first steps of what is called *right division* and *left division*, respectively, of $A(x)$ by $B(x)$. The matric polynomials $R_1(x)$ and $L_1(x)$ are the first *right remainder* and the first *left remainder*, respectively. If at any stage a remainder is of greater degree than $B(x)$, it may be divided by $B(x)$ to obtain another remainder of lower degree than itself. If each right remainder is divided on the right by $B(x)$ and each left remainder is divided on the left by $B(x)$, we ultimately obtain

$$(10.3.3) \quad A(x) = P(x)B(x) + R(x) \quad \text{and} \quad A(x) = B(x)Q(x) + L(x),$$

where $P(x)$ and $Q(x)$ are matric polynomials each of degree $s - t$ and $R(x)$ and $L(x)$ are matric polynomials each of which is either zero or is of degree less than t.

In case $s < t$, (10.3.3) is true where $P(x) = Q(x) = 0$ and $R(x) = L(x) = A(x)$. Hence, (10.3.3) hold for all matric polynomials $A(x)$ and $B(x)$ such that the leading coefficient of $B(x)$ is nonsingular. Furthermore, $P(x)$, $Q(x)$, $R(x)$, and $L(x)$ are defined uniquely by (10.3.3). For, if $P(x)B(x) + R(x) = P_0(x)B(x) + R_0(x)$, where $R(x)$ and $R_0(x)$ satisfy the conditions as described for (10.3.3), then

$$(10.3.4) \qquad [P(x) - P_0(x)]B(x) = R_0(x) - R(x).$$

If $R_0(x) - R(x)$ is not the zero polynomial, then, by theorem 10.3.1, its degree is less than t. If $P(x) - P_0(x)$ is not the zero polynomial, then, by theorem 10.3.2, the degree of $[P(x) - P_0(x)]B(x)$ is t or greater since the leading coefficient of $B(x)$ is nonsingular. Hence, (10.3.4) cannot hold in this case. Consequently, $R_0(x) = R(x)$ and $P_0(x) = P(x)$. A similar argument shows that the quotient and remainder are unique in the left division of $A(x)$ by $B(x)$. We have thus established the following theorem.

THEOREM 10.3.3 *Let $A(x)$ and $B(x)$ be matric polynomials of respective degrees s and t, and let the leading coefficient of $B(x)$ be nonsingular. Then there exist unique matric polynomials $P(x)$, $Q(x)$, $R(x)$, and $L(x)$ such that $A(x) = P(x)B(x) + R(x) = B(x)Q(x) + L(x)$, where each of the matric polynomials $R(x)$ and $L(x)$ is either the zero polynomial or is of degree less than t.*

If $R(x) = 0$ in (10.3.3), then $B(x)$ is said to be a *right divisor* of $A(x)$. If $L(x) = 0$, $B(x)$ is said to be a *left divisor* of $A(x)$. If $R(x) = L(x) = 0$, then $B(x)$ is said to be a *divisor* of $A(x)$.

EXERCISES

1. For the matrices

$$A = \begin{pmatrix} x^2 + 2x - 1 & x^2 - 1 \\ x + 3 & x - 7 \end{pmatrix}, \qquad B = \begin{pmatrix} x^2 + 3x - 2 & 2x + 1 \\ 3 - x^2 & x - 5 \end{pmatrix}$$

write $A(x)$, $B(x)$; compute $C = AB$; write $C(x)$; compute $A(x)B(x)$.

2. For the matrix A of Exercise 1 find A^2, $A^2(x)$, and $[A(x)]^2$.

3. Given the matrices

$$B = \begin{pmatrix} x^2 + 2 & 2x - 1 \\ x + 4 & 3x^2 - 5x + 2 \end{pmatrix}, \qquad P = \begin{pmatrix} x + 3 & 2 \\ x - 5 & x - 1 \end{pmatrix},$$

compute $A(x) = P(x)B(x)$, and find $Q(x)$ and $L(x)$ such that $A(x) = B(x)Q(x) + L(x)$, where $L(x)$ is of degree at most one.

10.4　Characteristic Matrix. Let C be a square matrix of n rows with elements in a field $\mathcal{F}$. Then $Ix - C$ is a matric polynomial of degree one which may also be considered a matrix with elements in $\mathcal{F}[x]$. This matrix, $Ix - C$, is called the *characteristic matrix* of C. Every matrix polynomial $A(x)$ may be divided by $Ix - C$. In this case the remainders $R(x)$ and $L(x)$ are independent of x and thus are matrices with elements in $\mathcal{F}$. For a given matric polynomial, $A(x)$, these remainders are clearly determined by the matrix C.

If in the relations $A(x) = P(x)(Ix - C) + R = (Ix - C)Q(x) + L$ we replace x by the matrix C, we obtain $A(C) = R$ and $A(C) = L$. However, R and L are not usually equal, and also the quantity $A(C)$ is not well defined in the usual sense. For example, if $A(x) = A_0 x^2$, then, since x is commutative with A_0, we may equally well write $A(x) = x^2 A_0 = x A_0 x$, and hence $A(C)$ may denote either $A_0 C^2$, $C^2 A_0$, or $CA_0 C$ and, in general, no two of these are equal. Each of these is obtained from $A(x)$ by replacing x by C in some representation of $A(x)$. We may, however, define certain matrices obtained from $A(x)$ by replacing x by C, and this we shall do.

Let $A(x) = A_0 x^s + A_1 x^{s-1} + \cdots + A_{s-1} x + A_s$, where the coefficients are square matrices of n rows with elements in $\mathcal{F}$. Let C be a square matrix of n rows with elements in $\mathcal{F}$. We now define $A_R(C)$ (read: "A of C on the right") and $A_L(C)$ (read: "A of C on the left") by

$$(10.4.1) \qquad A_R(C) = A_0 C^s + A_1 C^{s-1} + \cdots + A_{s-1} C + A_s$$

and

$$(10.4.2) \qquad A_L(C) = C^s A_0 + C^{s-1} A_1 + \cdots + CA_{s-1} + A_s.$$

We now establish

THEOREM 10.4.1 *The right remainder and the left remainder on division of $A(x)$ by $Ix - C$ are $A_R(C)$ and $A_L(C)$, respectively.*

Since the argument is essentially the same for both, we shall establish the theorem for the right remainder only. We have: $A(x) = P(x)(Ix - C) + R$. Write $P(x) = P_0 x^{s-1} + P_1 x^{s-2} + \cdots + P_{s-1}$. Then

$$A(x) = (P_0 x^s + P_1 x^{s-1} + \cdots + P_{s-1} x)$$
$$- (P_0 C x^{s-1} + P_1 C x^{s-2} + \cdots + P_{s-1} C) + R.$$

By definition, $A_R(C)$ is obtained from $A(x)$ by replacing x by C in each term, with x written to the right of its coefficient. Hence, we may write

$$A_R(C) = (P_0 C^s + P_1 C^{s-1} + \cdots + P_{s-1} C)$$
$$- (P_0 C^s + P_1 C^{s-1} + \cdots + P_{s-1} C) + R,$$

from which $A_R(C) = R$.

From the definition of divisor of $A(x)$ we have

THEOREM 10.4.2   *The matric polynomial $A(x)$ has the right divisor $Ix - C$ if and only if $A_R(C) = 0$; and it has the left divisor $Ix - C$ if and only if $A_L(C) = 0$.*

Necessary and sufficient conditions have been established for two matrices with elements in $\mathcal{F}[x]$ to be equivalent in $\mathcal{F}[x]$. These conditions apply to all matrices with elements in $\mathcal{F}[x]$. The characteristic matrix of C is completely determined by C. Consequently, the condition for the equivalence of $Ix - C$ and $Ix - D$ may be expressed as a relation between C and D. Two n-row square matrices C and D with elements in $\mathcal{F}$ are similar in $\mathcal{F}$ if there exists a nonsingular matrix P with elements in $\mathcal{F}$ such that $PCP^I = D$. This relation is set forth in

THEOREM 10.4.3   *Two matrices C and D, with elements in $\mathcal{F}$, are similar in $\mathcal{F}$ if and only if their characteristic matrices are equivalent in $\mathcal{F}[x]$.*

First, we suppose that C and D are similar in $\mathcal{F}$, that is, $PCP^I = D$. Then $P(Ix - C)P^I = Ix - D$. But, since P has elements in $\mathcal{F}$, the elements of P^I are in $\mathcal{F}$ and, consequently, P is an elementary matrix in $\mathcal{F}[x]$. Hence, $Ix - C \overset{\mathcal{F}[x]}{=} Ix - D$.

Conversely, if $Ix - C \overset{\mathcal{F}[x]}{=} Ix - D$, then

(10.4.3) $P(x)(Ix - C)Q(x) = Ix - D$

for some elementary matric polynomials $P(x)$ and $Q(x)$, and, hence,

(10.4.4) $P(x)(Ix - C) = (Ix - D)Q^I(x).$

Dividing $P(x)$ on the left by $Ix - D$ gives

(10.4.5) $P(x) = (Ix - D)P_0(x) + P_1.$

Then, substituting for $P(x)$ in (10.4.4) gives

(10.4.6) $[(Ix - D)P_0(x) + P_1](Ix - C) = (Ix - D)Q^I(x),$

and, consequently, $Ix - D$ is a left divisor of $P_1(Ix - C)$. It follows that $P_1(Ix - C) = (Ix - D)P_1$, and thus $P_1 C = DP_1$. It remains to be shown that P_1 is nonsingular. Replacing $P_1(Ix - C)$ by $(Ix - D)P_1$ in (10.4.6), we have $(Ix - D)[P_0(x)(Ix - C) + P_1] = (Ix - D)Q^I(x)$. From the uniqueness of the quotient it follows that

(10.4.7) $Q^I(x) = P_0(x)(Ix - C) + P_1.$

Also from (10.4.3), we have $(Ix - C)Q(x) = P^I(x)(Ix - D)$. Divide $Q(x)$ on the right by $Ix - D$ to obtain

(10.4.8) $Q(x) = Q_0(x)(Ix - D) + Q_1.$

Then

$$(Ix - C)[Q_0(x)(Ix - D) + Q_1] = P^I(x)(Ix - D),$$

and hence

(10.4.9) $(Ix - C)Q_1 = Q_1(Ix - D).$

Consequently,

(10.4.10) $P^I(x) = (Ix - C)Q_0(x) + Q_1.$

We now have, from (10.4.5) and (10.4.10),

$$P(x)P^I(x) = (Ix - D)P_0(x)(Ix - C)Q_0(x)$$
$$+ (Ix - D)P_0(x)Q_1 + P_1(Ix - C)Q_0(x) + P_1Q_1 = I.$$

Replacing $P_1(Ix - C)$ by $(Ix - D)P_1$ gives $I = (Ix - D)K(x) + P_1Q_1$, where $K(x) = P_0(x)(Ix - C)Q_0(x) + P_0(x)Q_1 + P_1Q_0(x)$. Consequently, the quotient $K(x)$ is zero and the remainder P_1Q_1 is I, from which it follows that P_1 is nonsingular. Since $P_1C = DP_1$, then $P_1CP_1^I = D$. We have thus established that D is similar to C in $\mathcal{F}$, and this completes the proof of the theorem. In particular, it should be noted that two n-row square matrices with elements in $\mathcal{F}$ are similar in $\mathcal{F}$ if and only if their characteristic matrices have the same invariant factors.

EXERCISES

1. Given the matrix

$$C = \begin{pmatrix} 1 & 2 & -1 \\ 2 & -3 & 2 \\ 5 & 7 & 0 \end{pmatrix}$$

and the matric polynomial

$$A(x) = \begin{pmatrix} 2 & 0 & 1 \\ -3 & 1 & 0 \\ 0 & 1 & 1 \end{pmatrix} x^2 + \begin{pmatrix} 1 & 0 & 1 \\ 2 & 1 & 0 \\ 0 & 0 & -1 \end{pmatrix} x + \begin{pmatrix} 1 & -1 & 3 \\ 7 & 2 & 1 \\ -1 & 0 & 1 \end{pmatrix},$$

find $P(x)$, $Q(x)$, R, and L such that

$$A(x) = P(x)(Ix - C) + R = (Ix - C)Q(x) + L,$$

where R and L are independent of x.

2. In Exercise 1, verify that $R = A_R(C)$ and $L = A_L(C)$.

3. If $f(x) = x^2 + 2x + 3$ and $A(x) = f(x)I_3$, find $P(x)$, $Q(x)$, R, and L such that $A(x) = P(x)(Ix - C) + R = (Ix - C)Q(x) + L$, where R and L

are independent of x. In this case, $P(x) = Q(x)$ and $R = L$. Prove this to be true in general when $A(x) = f(x)I$ and C is a square matrix.

4. Given the matrices

$$C = \begin{pmatrix} 2 & 1 \\ 5 & 3 \end{pmatrix}, \qquad D = \begin{pmatrix} 1 & 3 \\ 1 & 4 \end{pmatrix},$$

find elementary matric polynomials $P(x)$ and $Q(x)$ such that

$$P(x)(Ix - C)Q(x) = (Ix - D).$$

From these, determine P such that $PCP^I = D$.

10.5 Scalar Matric Polynomials. Let $f(x)$ be a polynomial over the field $\mathcal{F}$. The scalar matrix $f(x)I$ has elements in $\mathcal{F}[x]$. The coefficients of the corresponding matric polynomial are scalar matrices with elements in $\mathcal{F}$. Such a matric polynomial is called a *scalar matric polynomial*. If the polynomial $f(x)$ is monic, the corresponding matric polynomial is called monic. That is, the leading coefficient is I. Since the coefficients in scalar matric polynomials are commutative, the polynomials may be multiplied and divided just as are ordinary polynomials over a field.

If $f(x) = a_0 x^s + a_1 x^{s-1} + \cdots + a_s$ and $A = f(x)I_n$, then $A(x) = a_0 I x^s + a_1 I x^{s-1} + \cdots + a_s I$. If C is any n-row matrix with elements in $\mathcal{F}$, then $A_L(C) = A_R(C)$ and, in fact, $A(C)$ is well defined. Thus,

$$(10.5.1) \qquad A(C) = a_0 C^s + a_1 C^{s-1} + \cdots + a_{s-1} C + a_s I.$$

The matrix C is called a *root* of the scalar matric polynomial $A(x)$ if $A(C) = 0$. From theorem 10.4.1, it follows that C is a root of $A(x)$ if and only if the characteristic matrix of C is a divisor of $A(x)$. In this case, the left quotient and the right quotient are equal and the quotient is a scalar matric polynomial if and only if C is a scalar matrix.

The determinant of the characteristic matrix $Ix - C$ is a monic polynomial, $f(x)$, of degree n. This determinant is called the *characteristic determinant* of the matrix C. The equation $f(x) = 0$ is called the *characteristic equation* of C, and the roots of this equation are called the *characteristic roots* of the matrix C. If α is a characteristic root of C, there exists a one-column matrix $\xi \neq 0$ such that $(I\alpha - C)\xi = 0$; conversely, such a matrix ξ exists only if α is a characteristic root of C. The matrix ξ is called a *characteristic vector* of C corresponding to the characteristic root α.

EXERCISES

1. Given the polynomial $f(x) = x^3 + 2x^2 - x + 3$ and the matrix

$$C = \begin{pmatrix} 2 & -3 \\ -1 & 1 \end{pmatrix},$$

write the scalar matric polynomial $A(x) = f(x)I$ and determine the matrix $A(C)$.

2. Solve Exercise 1 with $f(x)$ replaced by the polynomial $x^3 - x^2 - 7x - 2$.

3. Given the matrix

$$C = \begin{pmatrix} 2 & -1 & 0 \\ -1 & 2 & 0 \\ 0 & 0 & 2 \end{pmatrix},$$

write the characteristic matrix, the characteristic determinant, find the characteristic roots, and determine a characteristic vector corresponding to each characteristic root.

4. In the relation $C\xi = \alpha\xi$, where

$$C = \begin{pmatrix} 0 & 1 & 0 \\ 0 & 0 & 1 \\ 2 & 3 & -4 \end{pmatrix} \quad \text{and} \quad \xi = \begin{pmatrix} x_1 \\ x_2 \\ x_3 \end{pmatrix},$$

assume $\xi \neq 0$ and eliminate x_1, x_2, and x_3. Thus obtain the condition that α be a characteristic root of the matrix C. Determine the characteristic vector ξ corresponding to the characteristic root α.

5. Given the matrix

$$C = \begin{pmatrix} 0 & 1 & 0 \\ 0 & 0 & 1 \\ a & b & c \end{pmatrix},$$

show that, if α is a characteristic root of C, then a characteristic vector of C corresponding to α is

$$\begin{pmatrix} 1 \\ \alpha \\ \alpha^2 \end{pmatrix}.$$

10.6 Rational Canonical Form of a Matrix. We now consider a special type of matrix denoted by

(10.6.1) $$C = \begin{pmatrix} 0 & 1 & 0 & \cdots & 0 \\ 0 & 0 & 1 & \cdots & 0 \\ \cdots\cdots\cdots\cdots\cdots\cdots \\ 0 & 0 & 0 & \cdots & 1 \\ a_1 & a_2 & a_3 & \cdots & a_n \end{pmatrix},$$

where a_i $(i = 1, 2, \ldots, n)$ are elements of $\mathcal{F}$. If $\xi = (x_i)$ $(i = 1, 2, \ldots, n)$ is a one-column matrix, then $C\xi$ is a one-column matrix having as its ith $(i < n)$ row the element x_{i+1} and having as its nth row the element

$$\sum_{i=1}^{n} a_i x_i.$$

If $C\xi = \alpha\xi$, then $x_{i+1} = x_i\alpha = x_1\alpha^i$ $(i < n)$ and

$$\sum_{i=1}^{n} a_i x_i = x_1 \alpha^n.$$

Hence,

$$x_1\left(\alpha^n - \sum_{i=1}^{n} a_i\alpha^{i-1}\right) = 0.$$

If $\xi \neq 0$, then $x_1 \neq 0$ and

$$\alpha^n - \sum_{i=1}^{n} a_i\alpha^{i-1} = 0.$$

That is, if α is a characteristic root of C, then α is a root of

(10.6.2) $f(x) = x^n - (a_1 + a_2 x + a_3 x^2 + \cdots + a_n x^{n-1}) = 0.$

Let

$$Q(x) = \begin{pmatrix} 1 & 0 & 0 & \ldots & 0 \\ x & 1 & 0 & \ldots & 0 \\ x^2 & x & 1 & \ldots & 0 \\ \cdots\cdots\cdots\cdots\cdots\cdots\cdots \\ x^{n-1} & x^{n-2} & x^{n-3} & \ldots & 1 \end{pmatrix},$$

then

$$(Ix - C)Q(x) = \begin{pmatrix} 0 & -I_{n-1} \\ f(x) & v \end{pmatrix},$$

where v is a $1 \times (n-1)$ matrix with elements in $\mathcal{F}[x]$. Let

$$P(x) = \begin{pmatrix} I_{n-1} & 0 \\ v & 1 \end{pmatrix} \quad \text{and} \quad R(x) = \begin{pmatrix} 0 & 1 \\ -I_{n-1} & 0 \end{pmatrix},$$

then

$$P(x)(Ix - C)Q(x)R(x) = \begin{pmatrix} I_{n-1} & 0 \\ 0 & f(x) \end{pmatrix}.$$

Hence,

$$Ix - C \overset{\mathcal{F}[x]}{=} \text{diag. } \{1, 1, \ldots, 1, f(x)\}.$$

The invariant factor 1 is called *trivial*, and the other invariant factors are called *nontrivial*. We may now state

THEOREM 10.6.1   *An n-row square matrix D with elements in the field $\mathcal{F}$ is similar in $\mathcal{F}$ to C given by (10.6.1) if and only if the only nontrivial invariant factor of $Ix - D$ is $f(x)$ given by (10.6.2).*

Since $P(x)$, $Q(x)$, and $R(x)$ are all of determinant one, the characteristic function of C is the $f(x)$ given in (10.6.2).

DEFINITION. *The matrix C in (10.6.1) is called the* companion matrix *of the monic polynomial $f(x)$ in (10.6.2).*

Illustration: If

$$f(x) = x^4 + 2x^3 - 3x^2 - 5x + 2 = x^4 - (-2 + 5x + 3x^2 - 2x^3),$$

the companion matrix of $f(x)$ is

$$C = \begin{pmatrix} 0 & 1 & 0 & 0 \\ 0 & 0 & 1 & 0 \\ 0 & 0 & 0 & 1 \\ -2 & 5 & 3 & -2 \end{pmatrix}.$$

If $f_1(x), f_2(x), \ldots, f_k(x)$, where $f_{i+1}(x)$ is a factor of $f_i(x)$, are the nontrivial invariant factors of $Ix - A$ and n_i is the degree of $f_i(x)$, then, since

$$\sum_{i=1}^{k} n_i = n,$$

it follows that

$$Ix - A \overset{\mathfrak{F}[x]}{=} \text{diag. } \{I_{n_1-1}, f_1(x), I_{n_2-1}, f_2(x), \ldots, I_{n_k-1}, f_k(x)\}$$
$$\overset{\mathfrak{F}[x]}{=} \text{diag. } \{I_{n_1}x - C_1, I_{n_2}x - C_2, \ldots, I_{n_k}x - C_k\},$$

where C_i is the companion matrix of $f_i(x)$. Hence, we have

(10.6.3) $A \overset{\text{S}}{=} \text{diag. } \{C_1, C_2, \ldots, C_k\}.$

This establishes

THEOREM 10.6.2 *A square matrix, A, with elements in $\mathfrak{F}$, is similar in $\mathfrak{F}$ to a diagonal block matrix where each diagonal block is the companion matrix of one of the nontrivial invariant factors of $Ix - A$.*

DEFINITION. *The diagonal block matrix in (10.6.3) is called the* rational canonical form *for the set of matrices similar to A.*

If $A = (a_1 \ a_2 \ \ldots \ a_n)$ is a $1 \times n$ matrix with elements in $\mathfrak{F}$, we may associate with A the polynomial $a_1 + a_2x + \cdots + a_nx^{n-1}$ of virtual degree $n - 1$, and we shall denote this polynomial by $a(x)$. The polynomials $1, x, \ldots, x^{n-1}$ are said to constitute a basis for all polynomials of degree $n - 1$ over $\mathfrak{F}$ and are associated with $1 \times n$ matrices which are denoted by $E_1, E_2, \ldots, E_n$, respectively. The one-row matrix A may be written

$$A = \sum_{i=1}^{n} a_i E_i.$$

If any n-row matrix P is multiplied on the left by E_i, the resulting matrix is the ith row of the matrix P. The successive rows of the matrix C in (10.6.1) are $E_2, E_3, \ldots, E_n, A$. It follows that $E_iC = E_{i+1}$ $(i = 1, 2, \ldots, n - 1)$, and that $E_nC = A$. If we define $C^0 = I$, it follows that $E_i = E_1C^{i-1}$ $(i = 1, 2, \ldots, n)$.

We may now write

$$I = \begin{pmatrix} E_1 \\ E_2 \\ \vdots \\ E_n \end{pmatrix} = \begin{pmatrix} E_1 \\ E_1C \\ \vdots \\ E_1C^{n-1} \end{pmatrix}.$$

Since $C^{i-1} = IC^{i-1}$ and $E_1C^{i-1} = E_i$ $(i = 1, 2, \ldots, n)$, we have

$$(10.6.4) \qquad C^{i-1} = \begin{pmatrix} E_i \\ E_iC \\ \vdots \\ E_iC^{n-1} \end{pmatrix} \qquad (i = 1, 2, \ldots, n),$$

and, since $E_nC = A$, we have

$$C^n = \begin{pmatrix} A \\ AC \\ \vdots \\ AC^{n-1} \end{pmatrix}.$$

If $b(x)$ is a polynomial, $b_1 + b_2x + \cdots + b_nx^{n-1}$, of virtual degree $n - 1$, then

$$(10.6.5) \quad b(C) = \sum_{i=1}^{n} b_iC^{i-1} = \begin{pmatrix} \sum_{i=1}^{n} b_iE_i \\ \sum_{i=1}^{n} b_iE_iC \\ \vdots \\ \sum_{i=1}^{n} b_iE_iC^{n-1} \end{pmatrix} = \begin{pmatrix} B \\ BC \\ \vdots \\ BC^{n-1} \end{pmatrix}$$

We say that (10.6.5) is a scalar polynomial in C over $\mathfrak{F}$ of *virtual degree* $n - 1$ if $b \neq 0$. It is of degree $n - 1$ if $b_n \neq 0$.

THEOREM 10.6.3   *A scalar polynomial in C over $\mathfrak{F}$ of virtual degree $n - 1$ is a matrix with successive rows $B, BC, \ldots, BC^{n-1}$, where B is the matrix whose elements are the coefficients of the polynomial in ascending order.*

Illustration:

$$C = \begin{pmatrix} 0 & 1 & 0 & 0 \\ 0 & 0 & 1 & 0 \\ 0 & 0 & 0 & 1 \\ 2 & 1 & -3 & 4 \end{pmatrix},$$

then

$$2I + 3C - 2C^3 = \begin{pmatrix} 2 & 3 & 0 & -2 \\ -4 & 0 & 9 & -8 \\ -16 & -12 & 24 & -23 \\ -46 & -39 & 57 & -68 \end{pmatrix}.$$

The first row is the set of coefficients in order of ascending powers of C. The second row is obtained from the first by multiplying on the right by C. Thus, $(2, 3, 0, -2)C = (-4, 0, 9, -8)$. Each succeeding row is obtained from the one that precedes it in this same manner.

We note that the matrix $b(C)$ is zero if and only if $B = 0$. Hence, no polynomial in C of degree less than n is zero. We also note that the matrix C^n is identical with the matrix $a(C)$. We may now write $f(x)$ in (10.6.2) as $f(x) = x^n - a(x)$, and we note that $f(C) = 0$.

DEFINITION. *The lowest degree monic scalar polynomial in any matrix over $\mathcal{F}$ which is equal to the zero matrix is called the* minimum function *of the matrix.*

We may now state

THEOREM 10.6.4   *The minimum function of C is identical with its characteristic function and is given by (10.6.2).*

DEFINITION. *A matrix is called nonderogatory if its minimum function is identical with its characteristic function.*

If $g(x)$ is any polynomial over $\mathcal{F}$ and A is any matrix similar to C in $\mathcal{F}$, then $A = PCP^I$ for some nonsingular matrix P and $g(A) = g(PCP^I) = Pg(C) P^I$. Hence $g(A) = 0$ if and only if $g(C) = 0$. This is true without regard to the particular form of C. Also, $|Ix - A| = |Ix - PCP^I| = |P(Ix - C)P^I| = |Ix - C|$, so that A and C have the same characteristic functions, and we state

THEOREM 10.6.5   *If two matrices are similar in $\mathcal{F}$, then their minimum functions are identical and their characteristic functions are indentical.*

If $f(x)$ is the minimum function of a matrix A and $g(x)$ is any polynomial, we may write $g(x) = q(x)f(x) + r(x)$, where $r(x)$ is zero or is of lower degree than $f(x)$. If $r(x) \neq 0$ and $g(A)$ is zero, then, since $f(A) = 0$, it is necessary that $r(A) = 0$. If $s(x)$ is the monic polynomial obtained by multiplying $r(x)$ by an element k of $\mathcal{F}$, then $s(A) = 0$. Since $s(x)$ is monic and of lower degree than $f(x)$, this is not possible. Hence, if $g(A) = 0$, then $r(x)$ must be the zero polynomial, and thus $f(x)$ is a factor of $g(x)$. This establishes

THEOREM 10.6.6 *If A is any square matrix and $g(x)$ is any polynomial, then $g(A) = 0$ if and only if the minimum function of A is a factor of $g(x)$.*

It has been seen that any matrix A is similar to a diagonal block matrix whose diagonal blocks are the companion matrices of the nontrivial invariant factors of $Ix - A$. Hence, there exists a nonsingular matrix P such that

$$(10.6.6) \qquad PAP^I = \text{diag. } \{C_1, C_2, \ldots, C_k\}.$$

Then

$$g(PAP^I) = Pg(A)P^I = \text{diag. } \{g(C_1), g(C_2), \ldots, g(C_k)\},$$

and hence $g(A) = 0$ if and only if $g(x)$ is divisible by each of the polynomials $f_1(x), f_2(x), \ldots, f_k(x)$. But $f_i(x)$ is a factor of $f_1(x)$ $(i = 2, 3, \ldots, k)$, consequently $g(A) = 0$ if and only if $f_1(x)$ is a factor of $g(x)$. Also,

$$(10.6.7) \qquad |Ix - A| = |P(Ix - A)P^I| = |Ix - PAP^I|$$
$$= |Ix - C_1||Ix - C_2| \cdots |Ix - C_k|$$
$$= f_1(x)f_2(x) \cdots f_k(x).$$

Thus, we have

THEOREM 10.6.7 *The minimum function of a matrix A is the highest degree invariant factor of $Ix - A$, and the characteristic function of A is the product of the invariant factors of $Ix - A$.*

The preceding discussion establishes

THEOREM 10.6.8 (Hamilton-Cayley) *If A is any square matrix and $f(x)$ is the characteristic function of A, then $f(A) = 0$.*

We now justify the term *rational canonical form* as used here. Let A and B be two n-row square matrices with elements in $\mathcal{F}$. Consider the equation

$$(10.6.8) \qquad AX = XB,$$

where X is to be determined. If we equate corresponding elements of the two products AX and XB, we obtain a system of n^2 linear homogeneous equations in the n^2 unknown elements of X. Such a system has solutions in $\mathcal{F}$ which are obtained by rational operations. If A and B are similar, there is a solution $X = P$ which is nonsingular. Such a solution need not contain elements outside the smallest field containing all elements of A and B. It follows that, *if A and B are similar in $\mathcal{F}$, they are similar in the smallest field which contains all elements of both.*

The invariant factors of $Ix - A$ are determined by elementary transformations which involve only rational operations on the elements of the matrix. These uniquely determine the rational canonical form described. If B is the rational canonical form of A, then any nonsingular matrix P which satisfies (10.6.8) is such that $P^I A P$ is in rational canonical form. We shall discuss the reduction of A to rational canonical form more fully later.

EXERCISES

1. Write the companion matrices of the following:

(a) $x^3 + x^2 - 2x - 3$,
(b) $x^3 + x - 1$,
(c) $x^3 + x^2 - x$.

Write the matrix $a_1 I + a_2 C + a_3 C^2$, where C denotes the companion matrix in each case.

2. Write the companion matrices of the following:

(a) $(x - 2)^3$,
(b) $(x - 2)^2(x + 2)$,
(c) $(x - 2)(x + 2)(x - 3)$.

Determine the characteristic vectors associated with each characteristic root.

3. Write the rational canonical matrix for matrices similar to one whose characteristic matrix has the nontrivial invariant factors $(x - 1)^2(x - 2)^2$ and $(x - 1)(x - 2)$. Determine the characteristic vectors associated with each characteristic root.

4. If α is a characteristic root of A and ξ is a characteristic vector associated with α, then α is also a characteristic root of PAP^I. What is the corresponding characteristic vector?

5. Give an example of two matrices A and B which have the same minimum function and the same characteristic function but are not similar.

6. If α is a characteristic root of A and ξ is a characteristic vector associated with α, prove that $g(\alpha)$ is a characteristic root of $g(A)$ and ξ is the corresponding characteristic vector for every polynomial $g(x)$.

7. If A is nonsingular and α is a characteristic root of A, prove that $1/\alpha$ is a characteristic root of A^I.

10.7　Matrices and Polynomials.　Let $f(x)$ be a monic polynomial of degree n and let C be the companion matrix of $f(x)$. Let $b(x) = b_1 +$

$b_2x + \cdots + b_nx^{n-1}$ be a polynomial of virtual degree $n - 1$. As shown in (10.6.5), the rows of the matrix $b(C)$ are $B, BC, \ldots, BC^{n-1}$. If $d = (d_1, d_2, \ldots, d_n)$ and $d(x)$ is the associated polynomial, the first row of the matrix $b(C)d(C)$ is $Db(C)$ and the first row of the matrix $d(C)b(C)$ is $Bd(C)$. But $b(C)d(C) = d(C)b(C)$, and hence we have

THEOREM 10.7.1 *If B and D are two $1 \times n$ matrices and $b(x)$ and $d(x)$ are the respective associated polynomials and if C is the companion matrix of any monic polynomial of degree n, then $Bd(C)$ and $Db(C)$ are identical $1 \times n$ matrices.*

The successive rows of the matrix $b(C)d(C)$ are $Db(C)$, $Db(C)C$, $\ldots$, $Db(C)C^{n-1}$. Hence, $Db(C) = 0$ if and only if $b(C)d(C) = 0$. If $b(C)$ is of rank r $(r < n)$, the first r rows of $b(C)$ are linearly independent and the row $r + 1$ is a linear combination of these r rows. That is,

(10.7.1) $BC^r = k_1B + k_2BC + \cdots + k_rBC^{r-1}.$

If $k(x) = x^r - (k_1 + k_2x + \cdots + k_rx^{r-1})$ and k is the associated $1 \times n$ matrix, then from (10.7.1) it follows that $Bk(C) = 0$. Hence, $b(C)k(C) = 0$, which implies that $f(x)$ is a factor of $b(x)k(x)$, since $f(x)$ is the minimum function of C. Furthermore, $k(x)$ is the lowest degree polynomial for which this is true. Thus, $k(x)b(x)$ is the lowest common multiple of $f(x)$ and $b(x)$. If $g(x)$ is the greatest common divisor of $f(x)$ and $b(x)$, then $g(x)k(x) = f(x)$.

DEFINITION. *We call $k(x)$ the* minimum function *of C relative to B if $k(x)$ is the lowest degree polynomial such that $Bk(C) = 0$.*

We have established

THEOREM 10.7.2 *If $f(x)$ is a monic polynomial of degree n and C is its companion matrix and if $b(x)$ is a polynomial of virtual degree $n - 1$, then the degree of the greatest common divisor, $g(x)$, of $f(x)$ and $b(x)$ is the nullity of $b(C)$ and $g(x) = f(x)/k(x)$, where $k(x)$ is the minimum function of C relative to B.*

If $b(C)$ is nonsingular, then $k(x) = f(x)$ and $g(x) = 1$. If $h(x)$ is any polynomial of degree greater than $n - 1$, we may write

$$h(x) = q(x)f(x) + r(x),$$

where $r(x)$ is zero or is of virtual degree $n - 1$. If $r(x) = 0$, then $f(x)$ is the greatest common divisor of $f(x)$ and $h(x)$ and $h(C) = 0$. If $r(x) \neq 0$, then the greatest common divisor of $f(x)$ and $h(x)$ is the same as the greatest common divisor of $f(x)$ and $r(x)$. Also, $h(C) = r(C)$, so we may replace $h(x)$ by $r(x)$ and apply theorem 10.7.2 to get the greatest common divisor of $f(x)$ and $h(x)$.

Illustration: Suppose that $f(x) = x^4 - 2x^3 + x^2 + 4x - 6$ and that $b(x) = x^3 - x^2 + x + 3$, then $B = (3\ 1\ -1\ 1)$ and the companion matrix of $f(x)$ is

$$C = \begin{pmatrix} 0 & 1 & 0 & 0 \\ 0 & 0 & 1 & 0 \\ 0 & 0 & 0 & 1 \\ 6 & -4 & -1 & 2 \end{pmatrix}.$$

From theorem 10.6.3, we have

$$b(C) = \begin{pmatrix} 3 & 1 & -1 & 1 \\ 6 & -1 & 0 & 1 \\ 6 & 2 & -2 & 2 \\ 12 & -2 & 0 & 2 \end{pmatrix}.$$

The matrix $b(C)$ is of rank two, and the third row is twice the first row. Hence, $(-2\ 0\ 1\ 0)b(C) = 0$ and $k(x) = x^2 - 2$ is the minimum function of C relative to B. The greatest common divisor of $f(x)$ and $b(x)$ is $f(x)/k(x) = x^2 - 2x + 3$.

10.8 The Matrix Equation $AX = XB$. If A is an $n \times n$ matrix and B is an $m \times m$ matrix, the equation $AX = XB$ is equivalent to mn linear homogeneous equations in the mn elements of X. In particular, suppose that $A = \text{diag. } \{C_1, C_2, \ldots, C_k\}$, where C_i is $n_i \times n_i$ and is the companion matrix of $f_i(x)$ and where $f_{i+1}(x)$ is a factor of $f_i(x)$. The polynomials $f_i(x)$ are then the invariant factors of $Ix - A$. Partition the matrix X into row blocks $X_1, X_2, \ldots, X_k$, where X_i has n_i rows. The equation $AX = XB$ is then equivalent to the k equations

(10.8.1) $C_i X_i = X_i B$ $(i = 1, 2, \ldots, k)$.

If the successive rows of X_i are the $1 \times m$ matrices $X_{i1}, X_{i2}, \ldots, X_{in_i}$, then from (10.8.1) it follows that $X_{ij} = X_{ij-1}B = X_{i1}B^{j-1}$ $(j = 2, 3, \ldots, n_i)$, and that

$$\sum_{j=1}^{n_i} c_{ij} X_{ij} = X_{in_i} B,$$

where $(c_{i1}\ c_{i2}\ \ldots\ c_{in_i})$ is the last row of C_i. Substituting $X_{i1}B^{j-1}$ for X_{ij}, we have

$$X_{i1} \sum_{j=1}^{n_i} c_{ij} B^{j-1} = X_{i1} B^{n_i}.$$

Hence, the matrix X_{i1} must be such that $X_{i1} f_i(B) = 0$, and the successive rows of X_i are $X_{i1}, X_{i1}B, \ldots, X_{i1}B^{n_i-1}$. This enables us to write all matrices X satisfying the equation $AX = XB$. In particular, when $m = n$ and B is similar to A, there exists a nonsingular matrix P such that $A = PBP^I$, from which $AP = PB$. Hence, if PBP^I is to be in rational canonical form, the matrix P must have the structure described for X above. The problem is then to determine an X which is nonsingular. The first row, X_{11}, of X must be such that the product $X_{11}f_1(B)$ is zero. Since $f_1(B) = 0$, it may seem that X_{11} could be chosen arbitrarily. But this is not the case. For, if $X_{11}g(B) = 0$, where $g(x)$ is of lower degree than $f_1(x)$, then the rows $X_{11} X_{12} \ldots X_{1n_1}$ are linearly dependent and X is singular. Similar statements hold for each of the blocks of X.

10.9   Elementary Divisors. Let A be any matrix with elements in $\mathcal{C}[x]$, where $\mathcal{C}$ is the field of complex numbers. Each invariant factor of A may be factored uniquely into a product of powers of distinct linear factors. Since each invariant factor is a divisor of each of those that precede it, we may write the ith invariant factor as

$$(10.9.1) \quad f_i(x) = (x - \alpha_1)^{e_{i1}}(k - \alpha_2)^{e_{i2}} \ldots (x - \alpha_s)^{e_{is}} \quad (i = 1, 2, \ldots, r),$$

where $\alpha_1, \alpha_2, \ldots, \alpha_s$ are the distinct roots of $f_1(x)$ and where $0 \leq e_{i+1,j} \leq e_{ij}$ $(j = 1, 2, \ldots, s)$. The rs functions $(x - \alpha_j)^{e_{ij}}$ are called the elementary divisors of A. Those for which $e_{ij} \neq 0$ are called *nontrivial* elementary divisors, and those for which $e_{ij} = 0$ are called *trivial*. The elementary divisors completely determine the invariant factors, and the invariant factors completely determine the elementary divisors.

Illustration: If the nontrivial elementary divisors of A are x, x, x^2, $(x + 1)$, $(x + 1)^2$, $(x - 1)$, and $(x - 1)^3$ and if $r = 5$, then $f_1(x) = x^2(x + 1)^2(x - 1)^3$, $f_2(x) = x(x + 1)(x - 1)$, $f_3(x) = x$, and $f_4(x) = f_5(x) = 1$.

We state without proof

THEOREM 10.9.1   *Two $m \times n$ matrices with elements in $\mathcal{C}[x]$ are equivalent in $\mathcal{C}[x]$ if and only if they have the same rank and the same nontrivial elementary divisors.*

Two additional theorems will be established to obtain what is called the *classical canonical form* for the set of matrices similar to C in the field of complex numbers. Let C be the n-row square matrix given by

$$(10.9.2) \qquad C = \begin{pmatrix} \alpha & 1 & 0 & \ldots & 0 & 0 \\ 0 & \alpha & 1 & \ldots & 0 & 0 \\ 0 & 0 & \alpha & \ldots & 0 & 0 \\ \multicolumn{6}{c}{\dotfill} \\ 0 & 0 & 0 & \ldots & \alpha & 1 \\ 0 & 0 & 0 & \ldots & 0 & \alpha \end{pmatrix},$$

where each element of the principal diagonal is a complex number α, each element of the first superdiagonal is 1, and each remaining element is zero.

THEOREM 10.9.2 *If C is the n-row square matrix given in* (10.9.2), *then the only nontrivial invariant factor of the characteristic matrix of C is* $(x - \alpha)^n$.

We note that $C - \alpha I$ is the companion matrix of x^n and hence the minimum function of the matrix $C - \alpha I$ is x^n, and, consequently, the minimum function of C is $(x - \alpha)^n$. Since $(x - \alpha)^n$ is also the characteristic function of C, the theorem is proved. We now establish

THEOREM 10.9.3 *If $g_1(x), g_2(x), \ldots, g_k(x)$ are the minimum functions of $A_1, A_2, \ldots, A_k$, respectively, and if $g(x)$ is the minimum function of A = diag. $\{A_1, A_2, \ldots, A_k\}$, then $g(x)$ is the lowest common multiple of $g_1(x), g_2(x), \ldots, g_k(x)$.*

Since $g(A)$ = diag. $\{g(A_1), g(A_2), \ldots, g(A_k)\}$ = 0, it follows from theorem 10.6.5 that $g_i(x)$ is a factor of $g(x)$, $i = 1, 2, \ldots, k$. And, since $g(x)$ is the minimum function of A, it is the lowest common multiple of $g_1(x), g_2(x), \ldots, g_k(x)$. In particular, if $g_1(x), g_2(x), \ldots, g_k(x)$ are relatively prime in pairs, then $g(x) = g_1(x)g_2(x) \cdots g_k(x)$.

It now follows that the companion matrix of $f_i(x)$ in (10.9.1) is similar to diag. $\{C_{i1}, C_{i2}, \cdots, C_{is}\}$, where

$$(10.9.3) \qquad C_{ij} = \begin{pmatrix} \alpha_j & 1 & 0 & \ldots & 0 & 0 \\ 0 & \alpha_j & 1 & \ldots & 0 & 0 \\ 0 & 0 & \alpha_j & \ldots & 0 & 0 \\ \multicolumn{6}{c}{\dots\dots\dots\dots\dots\dots} \\ 0 & 0 & 0 & \ldots & \alpha_j & 1 \\ 0 & 0 & 0 & \ldots & 0 & \alpha_j \end{pmatrix}.$$

Whenever $e_{ij} = 0$, there is of course no corresponding C_{ij} in the diagonal form.

We have established

THEOREM 10.9.4 *Every square matrix A is similar to a diagonal block matrix where each diagonal block is of the form given in* (10.9.3).

These blocks may be so arranged that all blocks containing a particular characteristic root appear successively. This particular form is called the *classical canonical form* for matrices similar to A. This form cannot generally be obtained by rational operations since it involves determination of the characteristic roots of A.

Illustration: If $f_1(x) = (x - 1)^3(x - 2)^2$ and $f_2(x) = (x - 1)^2$, the companion matrices of $f_1(x)$ and $f_2(x)$ are similar to

$$\left(\begin{array}{ccc|cc} 1 & 1 & 0 & 0 & 0 \\ 0 & 1 & 1 & 0 & 0 \\ 0 & 0 & 1 & 0 & 0 \\ \hline 0 & 0 & 0 & 2 & 1 \\ 0 & 0 & 0 & 0 & 2 \end{array}\right) \quad \text{and} \quad \begin{pmatrix} 1 & 1 \\ 0 & 1 \end{pmatrix},$$

respectively. If A is any matrix such that $Ix - A$ has the nontrivial invariant factors $f_1(x)$ and $f_2(x)$ only, then A is similar to

$$(10.9.4) \qquad C = \left(\begin{array}{ccc|cc|cc} 1 & 1 & 0 & 0 & 0 & 0 & 0 \\ 0 & 1 & 1 & 0 & 0 & 0 & 0 \\ 0 & 0 & 1 & 0 & 0 & 0 & 0 \\ \hline 0 & 0 & 0 & 1 & 1 & 0 & 0 \\ 0 & 0 & 0 & 0 & 1 & 0 & 0 \\ \hline 0 & 0 & 0 & 0 & 0 & 2 & 1 \\ 0 & 0 & 0 & 0 & 0 & 0 & 2 \end{array}\right)$$

since, in a diagonal block matrix, the diagonal blocks may be permuted in any desired order by similarity transformations.

EXERCISES

1. Determine a matrix P so that

$$PCP^I = \begin{pmatrix} C_1 & 0 \\ 0 & C_2 \end{pmatrix},$$

where C is the matrix in (10.9.4) and C_1 and C_2 are the companion matrices of $f_1(x)$ and $f_2(x)$ in the illustration above.

2. If the nontrivial elementary divisors of $Ix - A$ are x, x, x^3, $(x - 1)^2$, $x - 1$, and $x + 1$, write the nontrivial invariant factors.

3. If the nontrivial invariant factors of $Ix - A$ are $f_1 = (x - 1)^2(x + 1)^2$ and $f_2 = (x - 1)(x + 1)^2$, write the nontrivial elementary divisors. Write the rational canonical matrix, A_1, and the classical canonical matrix, A_2, which are similar to matrix A.

4. Determine a nonsingular matrix P such that $PA_2P^I = A_1$, where A_1 and A_2 are the matrices determined in Exercise 3.

5. If C is the companion matrix of $x^4 + 2x^3 - 3x + 1$, determine all matrices X such that $CX = XC$.

6. If C_1 is the companion matrix of $x^3 + 2x^2 - 3$ and C_2 is the companion matrix of $x^3 - 3x + 2$, determine all matrices X such that $C_1X = XC_2$.

7. If $C = $ diag. (C_1, C_2), where C_1 and C_2 are as given in Exercise 6, determine all matrices X such that $CX = XC$.

8. If C_1 and C_2 are the matrices given in Exercise 6 and if $b(x) = x^2 + x + 1$, $d(x) = x^2 - 1$, write $b(C_1)$, $b(C_2)$, $d(C_1)$, and $d(C_2)$ and verify theorem 10.7.1 in each case.

9. Use theorem 10.7.2 to determine the greatest common divisor of the polynomials
   (a) $x^4 - 2x^3 + 4x^2 - 2x + 3$ and $3x^3 - 4x^2 + 5x + 6$;
   (b) $x^4 + x^3 - 2x^2 - 3x - 3$ and $2x^3 + 5x^2 + 5x + 3$.

10.10 Matrices Equivalent to $Ix - A$ in $\mathcal{F}[x]$. If $b(x) = b_1 + b_2x + \cdots + b_nx^{n-1}$, we have associated with $b(x)$ the $1 \times n$ matrix $B = (b_1\ b_2\ \ldots\ b_n)$. Some of the elements in this matrix may be zero. For example, if $b(x) = 2 - x^2$ and $n = 5$, then $B = (2\ 0\ -1\ 0)$. We could equally well associate $b(x)$ with an $m \times n$ matrix having B as one of its rows.

DEFINITION. *If $b(x) = b_1 + b_2x + \cdots + b_nx^{n-1}$ is of virtual degree $n - 1$ and B is an $m \times n$ matrix having $(b_1\ b_2\ \ldots\ b_n)$ as its last row and zeros for all other elements, we say that B is an associate $m \times n$ matrix of $b(x)$.*

Let $N = (a_{ij})$ be an $n \times n$ matrix with elements in $\mathcal{F}$. Choose any $1 \times n$ matrix P_1 and determine P_1N^k, $k = 1, 2, \ldots, (t_1 - 1)$, as linearly independent rows of a matrix P. The number t_1 cannot exceed the degree of the minimum function of N relative to P_1. Now choose another row, P_2, for P independent of the preceding rows and determine P_2N^k, $k = 1, 2, \ldots, (t_2 - 1)$, as additional rows of P so that the first $t_1 + t_2$ are linearly independent. Continue this process until n successive rows have been obtained. The resulting matrix P will be nonsingular. Since $PP^I = I$, the product of the ith row of P by P^I is E_i. Thus we have $P_1P^I = E_1$, $P_1N^kP^I = E_{k+1}$ for $k = 1, 2, \ldots, (t_1 - 1)$; $P_2P^I = E_{t_1+1}$, $P_2N^kP^I = E_{t_1+k+1}$ for $k = 1, 2, \ldots, (t_2 - 1)$, etc. The rows of the matrix PN are $P_1N, P_1N^2, \ldots, P_1N^{t_1}, P_2N, P_2N^2, \ldots, P_2N^{t_2}$, etc. Consequently, the rows of PNP^I are $E_2, E_3, \ldots, E_{t_1}, B_1, E_{t_1+2}, \ldots, E_{t_1+t_2}, B_2, E_{t_1+t_2+2}$, etc., where B_i is the $1 \times n$ matrix $P_iN^{t_i}P^I$. This gives

(10.10.1)
$$PNP^I = \begin{pmatrix} C_1 & A_{12} & \ldots & A_{1t} \\ A_{21} & C_2 & \ldots & A_{2t} \\ \cdots\cdots\cdots\cdots\cdots \\ A_{t1} & A_{t2} & \ldots & C_t \end{pmatrix},$$

where C_i is the companion matrix of some polynomial $g_i(x)$ of degree t_i and A_{ij} is a $t_i \times t_j$ matrix associate of a polynomial $a_{ij}(x)$ of virtual degree $t_j - 1$.

In particular, if the rows of P are developed so that $P_i N^{t_i}$ is a linear combination of the preceding rows of P for each t_i, then the row $P_i N^{t_i} P^I$ is a linear combination of the first $t_1 + t_2 + \cdots + t_i$ rows of I and in the matrix (10.10.1) $A_{ij} = 0$ for $j > i$. In this case, (10.10.1) becomes a triangular block matrix with zeros above the diagonal.

Illustration: Let

$$(10.10.2) \qquad N = \begin{pmatrix} 1 & -1 & 1 & 2 \\ -2 & 0 & 1 & -1 \\ 1 & 1 & 0 & -1 \\ -1 & 1 & -2 & 1 \end{pmatrix}.$$

Choose $P_1 = (1\ 0\ 0\ 0)$ and $P_2 = (0\ 0\ 1\ 0)$, then determine $P_1 N$ and $P_2 N$ to get

$$P = \begin{pmatrix} P_1 \\ P_1 N \\ P_2 \\ P_2 N \end{pmatrix} = \begin{pmatrix} 1 & 0 & 0 & 0 \\ 1 & -1 & 1 & 2 \\ 0 & 0 & 1 & 0 \\ 1 & 1 & 0 & -1 \end{pmatrix}.$$

Since $P_1 N^2 = (2, 2, -4, 4) = -12P_1 + 6P_1 N - 10P_2 + 8P_2 N$, and $P_1 P^I = E_1$, $P_1 N P^I = E_2$, $P_2 P^I = E_3$, and $P_2 N P^I = E_4$, we get $P_1 N^2 P^I = (-12, 6, -10, 8)$. Similarly, $P_2 N^2 = 6P_1 - 2P_1 N + 6P_2 - 4P_2 N$, and hence $P_2 N^2 P^I = (6, -2, 6, -4)$. If follows that

$$(10.10.3) \qquad PNP^I = \left(\begin{array}{cc|cc} 0 & 1 & 0 & 0 \\ -12 & 6 & -10 & 8 \\ \hline 0 & 0 & 0 & 1 \\ 6 & -2 & 6 & -4 \end{array} \right).$$

In this case P_1, $P_1 N$, $P_1 N^2$, and $P_1 N^3$ are linearly independent and $P_1 N^4 = 12P_1 - 16P_1 N + 2P_1 N^2 + 2P_1 N^3$. If we now choose for P the matrix given by

$$P = \begin{pmatrix} P_1 \\ P_1 N \\ P_1 N^2 \\ P_1 N^3 \end{pmatrix} = \begin{pmatrix} 1 & 0 & 0 & 0 \\ 1 & -1 & 1 & 2 \\ 2 & 2 & -4 & 4 \\ -10 & -2 & -4 & 10 \end{pmatrix},$$

then

$$PNP^I = \begin{pmatrix} 0 & 1 & 0 & 0 \\ 0 & 0 & 1 & 0 \\ 0 & 0 & 0 & 1 \\ 12 & -16 & 2 & 2 \end{pmatrix},$$

and this is the companion matrix of

(10.10.4) $f(x) = x^4 - (12 - 16x + 2x^2 + 2x^3).$

The matrix N is nonderogatory, and $f(x)$ is the only nontrivial invariant factor of $Ix - N$.

Consider now an $n \times n$ matrix M, as given in (10.10.1), which can be partitioned into a $t \times t$ block matrix in such a way that the ith diagonal block, C_i, is the companion matrix of $f_i(x)$ and the block in the ith row and jth column, A_{ij} $(i \neq j)$ is an associate of the polynomial $a_{ij}(x)$, where $f_i(x)$ is of degree t_i and $a_{ij}(x)$ is of virtual degree $t_j - 1$. Let $M(x)$ denote the matrix in which the ith diagonal element is $f_i(x)$ and the ijth element is $-a_{ij}(x)$. We now establish

THEOREM 10.10.1   *The matrix $Ix - M$ is equivalent in $\mathcal{F}[x]$ to the matrix*

$$\begin{pmatrix} I_{n-t} & 0 \\ 0 & M(x) \end{pmatrix}.$$

Define a matrix $T = \text{diag. } \{T_1, T_2, \ldots, T_t\}$, where

(10.10.5) $$T_j = \begin{pmatrix} 1 & 0 & \cdots & 0 \\ x & 1 & \cdots & 0 \\ x^2 & x & \cdots & 0 \\ \cdots\cdots\cdots\cdots\cdots\cdots \\ x^{t_j-1} & x^{t_j-2} & \cdots & 1 \end{pmatrix}.$$

Then

$$(Ix - C_j)T_j = \begin{pmatrix} 0 & -I_{t_j-1} \\ f_j(x) & U_j \end{pmatrix} \quad \text{and} \quad A_{ij}T_j = \begin{pmatrix} 0 & 0 \\ a_{ij}(x) & V_{ij} \end{pmatrix},$$

where U_j and V_{ij} are $1 \times (t_j - 1)$ matrices with elements in $\mathcal{F}[x]$. In the block matrix $(Ix - M)T$, permute the rows and columns so that the third becomes the second, the fifth becomes the third, and, in general, the $2k - 1$th becomes the kth, leaving the remaining rows and columns in normal order. The resulting matrix will be

$$\begin{pmatrix} 0 & -I_{n-t} \\ M(x) & K \end{pmatrix},$$

where K is a matrix with elements in $\mathcal{F}[x]$. Then we have

$$\begin{pmatrix} I_{n-t} & 0 \\ K & I_t \end{pmatrix}\begin{pmatrix} 0 & -I_{n-t} \\ M(x) & K \end{pmatrix}\begin{pmatrix} 0 & I_t \\ -I_{n-t} & 0 \end{pmatrix} = \begin{pmatrix} I_{n-t} & 0 \\ 0 & M(x) \end{pmatrix}.$$

This completes the proof of the theorem.

The elements of a matrix may be considered companion matrices of polynomials of degree one or associates of polynomials of degree zero. Thus the matrix $M = (a_{ij})$ may be considered a special case of the preceding, where a_{ii} is the companion of $x - a_{ii}$ and a_{ij} $(i \neq j)$ is the associate of itself. In this case, $M(x)$ and $Ix - M$ are identical.

Illustration: The matrix (10.10.3) is similar to N in (10.10.2), and hence their characteristic matrices are equivalent in $\mathcal{F}[x]$. Thus the matrix $Ix - N$ is equivalent in $\mathcal{F}[x]$ to

$$\begin{pmatrix} I_2 & 0 \\ 0 & M(x) \end{pmatrix}, \quad \text{where} \quad M(x) = \begin{pmatrix} x^2 - 6x + 12 & -8x + 10 \\ 2x - 6 & x^2 + 4x - 6 \end{pmatrix}.$$

It is readily verified that the determinant of $M(x)$ is $f(x)$ given in (10.10.4).

Denoting the companion matrix of a polynomial $f(x)$ by $C(f)$ and denoting an associate matrix of a polynomial $h(x)$ by $A(h)$, we state several corollaries which follow from theorem 10.10.1.

COROLLARY. *If $f(x)$ and $g(x)$ are monic polynomials and $h(x)$ is a polynomial of lower degree than $f(x)$, and if $d(x)$ is the greatest common divisor of $f(x)$, $g(x)$, and $h(x)$, then the matrix*

$$\begin{pmatrix} C(f) & 0 \\ A(h) & C(g) \end{pmatrix}$$

is similar in $\mathcal{F}$ to $C(fg)$ for $d(x) = 1$ and is similar in $\mathcal{F}$ to

$$\begin{pmatrix} C(d) & 0 \\ 0 & C(fg/d) \end{pmatrix}$$

for $d(x) \neq 1$.

This follows immediately from the fact that the lowest degree invariant factor of the matrix

$$\begin{pmatrix} f(x) & 0 \\ h(x) & g(x) \end{pmatrix}$$

is $d(x)$ and that the product of the invariant factors is $f(x)g(x)$.

Let M be a $t \times t$ block matrix given by

(10.10.6) $M = \begin{pmatrix} C(f) & A(1) & 0 & \ldots & 0 \\ 0 & C(f) & A(1) & \ldots & 0 \\ \ldots\ldots\ldots\ldots\ldots\ldots\ldots \\ 0 & 0 & 0 & \ldots & C(f) \end{pmatrix},$

where $A(1)$ is a square matrix associated with the polynomial 1. The characteristic matrix of (10.10.6) has the same nontrivial invariant factors as

$M(x) = \begin{pmatrix} f(x) & 1 & 0 & \ldots & 0 \\ 0 & f(x) & 1 & \ldots & 0 \\ \ldots\ldots\ldots\ldots\ldots\ldots \\ 0 & 0 & 0 & \ldots & f(x) \end{pmatrix}.$

But the only nontrivial invariant factor of $M(x)$ is $[f(x)]^t$. Hence, we have

COROLLARY.   *The matrix M in* (10.10.6) *is similar in $\mathcal{F}$ to* $C(f^t)$.

It follows that any square matrix is similar to a diagonal block matrix where each diagonal block is of the type in (10.10.6). The polynomials determining the blocks may be the irreducible (in $\mathcal{F}$) factors of the invariant factors of the characteristic matrix. The classical canonical form is the special case of this when $\mathcal{F}$ is the field of complex numbers.

Since a matrix $M(x)$ is equivalent in $\mathcal{F}[x]$ to its transpose, we have the following

COROLLARY.   *The matrix given in* (10.10.1) *is similar to the one obtained by transposing it as a block matrix.*

By examining the matrix $M(x)$ it is sometimes quite easy to tell whether or not the original matrix is nonderogatory and also to determine the invariant factors of its characteristic matrix.

Illustrations: Given

$M = \begin{pmatrix} 0 & 1 & 0 & 0 \\ -1 & 2 & 1 & -1 \\ 0 & 0 & 0 & 1 \\ -1 & -1 & -1 & 2 \end{pmatrix}.$

Then

$M(x) = \begin{pmatrix} x^2 - 2x + 1 & x - 1 \\ x + 1 & x^2 - 2x + 1 \end{pmatrix}.$

Since the greatest common divisor of the elements of $M(x)$ is 1, it has only one nontrivial invariant factor. Hence M and all matrices similar to it are nonderogatory. If

$$P = \begin{pmatrix} 0 & 0 & 1 & 0 \\ 0 & 0 & 0 & 1 \\ -1 & -1 & -1 & 2 \\ -1 & -5 & -3 & 4 \end{pmatrix},$$

then

$$PMP^I = \begin{pmatrix} 0 & 1 & 0 & 0 \\ 0 & 0 & 1 & 0 \\ 0 & 0 & 0 & 1 \\ -2 & 4 & -5 & 4 \end{pmatrix}.$$

As a second illustration, suppose

$$M = \begin{pmatrix} 0 & 1 & 0 & 0 \\ 2 & -1 & 2 & -2 \\ 0 & 0 & 0 & 1 \\ -2 & 2 & -2 & 3 \end{pmatrix},$$

then

$$M(x) = \begin{pmatrix} x^2 + x - 2 & 2x - 2 \\ -2x + 2 & x^2 - 3x + 2 \end{pmatrix}.$$

The greatest common divisor of the elements of $M(x)$ is $x - 1$, and hence one invariant factor is $x - 1$ and the other is $x^3 - x^2$. Take P to be the matrix given by

$$P = \begin{pmatrix} P_1 \\ P_1 M \\ P_1 M^2 \\ P_2 \end{pmatrix} = \begin{pmatrix} 1 & 0 & 0 & 0 \\ 0 & 1 & 0 & 0 \\ 2 & -1 & 2 & -2 \\ 0 & 0 & 1 & 0 \end{pmatrix}.$$

Since $P_1 M^3 = (2\ -1\ 2\ -2) = P_1 M^2$ and $P_2 M = (0\ 0\ 0\ 1) = P_1 - \frac{1}{2}P_1 M - \frac{1}{2}P_1 M^2 + P_2$, it follows that

$$PMP^I = \begin{pmatrix} 0 & 1 & 0 & 0 \\ 0 & 0 & 1 & 0 \\ 0 & 0 & 1 & 0 \\ 1 & -\frac{1}{2} & -\frac{1}{2} & 1 \end{pmatrix}.$$

In this case

$$M(x) = \begin{pmatrix} x^3 - x^2 & 0 \\ -\frac{1}{2}x^2 - \frac{1}{2}x + 1 & x - 1 \end{pmatrix}.$$

Now, since

$$P_2(M - I) = P_1(-\tfrac{1}{2}M^2 - \tfrac{1}{2}M + I) = P_1(M - I)(-\tfrac{1}{2}M - I)$$

and

$$P_1(M^3 - M^2) = P_1 M^2(M - 1) = 0,$$

we know that $P_2 M^2(M - I) = 0$. Hence, if we replace P_2 in P above by $P_2 M^2 = (0\ 0\ 0\ 1)M = (-2\ 2\ -2\ 3) = Q_2$, then $Q_2 M = Q_2$. Hence, if Q is the matrix obtained by replacing P_2 by Q_2 in P, we have

$$QMQ^I = \begin{pmatrix} 0 & 1 & 0 & 0 \\ 0 & 0 & 1 & 0 \\ 0 & 0 & 1 & 0 \\ 0 & 0 & 0 & 1 \end{pmatrix}.$$

EXERCISES

1. Let

$$N = \begin{pmatrix} 1 & 0 & 2 & -1 \\ 0 & 1 & -1 & 0 \\ 2 & 0 & 1 & 1 \\ 1 & 2 & 0 & -1 \end{pmatrix}.$$

Construct matrix P having E_2 as first row and such that PNP^I is a companion matrix. Write out $f(x)$, the minimum function of N. Determine the characteristic roots of N and find a characteristic vector associated with each characteristic root.

2. Using the matrix N in Exercise 1, determine the matrix P whose rows are E_2, E_2N, E_3, E_3N. Write PNP^I in the form given in (10.10.1). Write $M(x)$ and show that the determinant of $M(x)$ is $f(x)$ as found in Exercise 1.

3. Using the matrix N in Exercise 1, determine a matrix P so that $PNP^I = N^T$.

4. Given the matrices

$$N_1 = \begin{pmatrix} 0 & 1 & 0 & 0 \\ 2 & 3 & 1 & 2 \\ 0 & 0 & 0 & 1 \\ 3 & -2 & -1 & 1 \end{pmatrix}, \quad N_2 = \begin{pmatrix} 0 & 1 & 0 & 0 \\ 2 & 3 & 3 & -2 \\ 0 & 0 & 0 & 1 \\ 1 & 2 & -1 & 1 \end{pmatrix},$$

$$N_3 = \begin{pmatrix} 0 & 1 & 0 & 0 \\ -1 & 1 & 1 & 2 \\ 0 & 0 & 0 & 1 \\ 3 & -2 & 2 & 3 \end{pmatrix}, \quad \text{and} \quad N_4 = \begin{pmatrix} 0 & 1 & 0 & 0 \\ -1 & 1 & 3 & -2 \\ 0 & 0 & 0 & 1 \\ 1 & 2 & 2 & 3 \end{pmatrix},$$

verify that N_1, N_2, N_3, and N_4 are similar.

5. Show that, if a companion matrix is regularly partitioned in any way, the resulting block matrix is of the type given in (10.10.1).

6. Determine the rational canonical form for matrices similar to

$$M = \begin{pmatrix} 0 & 1 & 0 & 0 \\ -2 & 3 & 1 & -1 \\ 0 & 0 & 0 & 1 \\ -2 & 2 & 1 & 0 \end{pmatrix}.$$

Determine a nonsingular matrix P such that PMP^I is in rational canonical form.

7. If

$$M(x) = \begin{pmatrix} x^2 + x - 2 & 0 \\ x - 1 & x^2 - 3x + 2 \end{pmatrix},$$

write the corresponding matrix M in the form given in (10.10.1). Use the fact that $IMI^I = M$ and determine a row P_1 so that, if P has the rows E_1, E_2, P_1, P_1M, then PMP^I will be a diagonal block matrix having diagonal blocks which are the companion matrices of the diagonal blocks of $M(x)$.

CHAPTER 11

SPECIAL MATRICES

11.1 Normal Matrices. In this chapter we consider matrices whose elements are in the field of complex numbers. If $A = (a_{ij})$ is an $m \times n$ matrix, the matrix obtained from A by replacing each element by its complex conjugate is called the *conjugate* of A and is denoted by A^C. The transpose of the conjugate of A is also the conjugate of the transpose of A and will be denoted by A^{CT}. We shall be interested primarily in square matrices.

DEFINITION. *The matrix A is called* normal *if $AA^{CT} = A^{CT}A$.*

DEFINITION. *The matrix A is called* Hermitian *if $A^{CT} = A$.*

DEFINITION. *The matrix A is called* unitary *if $AA^{CT} = I$, that is, if $A^{CT} = A^I$.*

Hermitian matrices and unitary matrices are special types of normal matrices.

If A and B are $n \times n$ unitary matrices, then $(AB)^{CT} = B^{CT}A^{CT} = B^I A^I = (AB)^I$, and we have

THEOREM 11.1.1 *The product of two unitary matrices is a unitary matrix.*

If A is any square matrix, the matrices

$$G = \frac{1}{2}(A + A^{CT}) \quad \text{and} \quad H = \frac{1}{2i}(A - A^{CT})$$

are both Hermitian and $A = G + iH$. If $A = R + iS$, where R and S are Hermitian, then $A^{CT} = R - iS$, and it follows that $R = G$ and $S = H$. This establishes

THEOREM 11.1.2 *Every square matrix A can be written uniquely as $G + iH$, where G and H are Hermitian matrices.*

Illustration:

$$\begin{pmatrix} 1+i & 2+4i & 2i \\ 4-2i & 2-i & 4 \\ 4 & 2i & 1 \end{pmatrix}$$

$$= \begin{pmatrix} 1 & 3+3i & 2+i \\ 3-3i & 2 & 2-i \\ 2-i & 2+i & 1 \end{pmatrix} + i \begin{pmatrix} 1 & 1+i & 1+2i \\ 1-i & -1 & 1-2i \\ 1-2i & 1+2i & 0 \end{pmatrix}.$$

If A is normal, then A may be written as $G + iH$, and it follows that $(G+iH)(G-iH) = (G-iH)(G+iH)$. This gives $G^2 + i(HG - GH) + H^2 = G^2 - i(HG - GH) + H^2$, and, hence, $HG - GH = 0$. Conversely, if $HG = GH$, then $AA^{CT} = A^{CT}A$. This establishes

THEOREM 11.1.3 *The matrix A is normal if and only if the Hermitian matrices G and H in theorem 11.1.2 are commutative.*

If $A_i = (a_{i1}\ a_{i2}\ \ldots\ a_{in})$ for $i = 1, 2, \ldots, k;\ k < n$, it is always possible to find $X = (x_1, x_2, \ldots, x_n) \neq 0$ such that $A_i X^{CT} = 0$ for $i = 1, 2, \ldots, k$. Since $X \neq 0$, XX^{CT} is a real positive number, ν^2, called the squared norm of X. If $Y = (1/\nu)X$, then Y is such that $YY^{CT} = 1$ and $A_i Y^{CT} = 0$. We may then begin with A_1, such that $A_1 A_1^{CT} = 1$, as the first row of a square matrix, A, and determine the successive rows $A_2, A_3, \ldots, A_n$ so that $A_i A_j^{CT} = 0$ for $i \neq j$ and $A_i A_i^{CT} = 1$. The element in the ith row and jth column of AA^{CT} is $A_i A_j^{CT}$, and, hence, $AA^{CT} = I$ and A is unitary. We now establish

THEOREM 11.1.4 *If A is any $n \times n$ $(n > 1)$ matrix and $\alpha_1, \alpha_2, \ldots, \alpha_n$ are the characteristic roots of A in any prescribed order, there exists a unitary matrix U such that $U^{CT}AU$ is triangular with the diagonal elements $\alpha_1, \alpha_2, \ldots, \alpha_n$ in that order and zeros below the diagonal.*

Since α_1 is a characteristic root of A, there exists a column vector ξ_1 such that $\xi_1^{CT}\xi_1 = 1$ and $A\xi_1 = \alpha_1\xi_1$. We now construct a unitary matrix U^{CT} having ξ_1^{CT} as first row and write $U = (\xi_1, \xi_2, \ldots, \xi_n)$. The element in the ith row and jth column of $U^{CT}AU$ is $\xi_i^{CT}A\xi_j$. Since $A\xi_1 = \alpha_1\xi_1$, we have $\xi_i^{CT}A\xi_1 = \alpha_1\xi_i^{CT}\xi_1$ for $i = 1, 2, \ldots, n$. But $\xi_i^{CT}\xi_1 = 0$ if $i \neq 1$ and $\xi_1^{CT}\xi_1 = 1$, and, hence,

$$(11.1.1) \qquad U^{CT}AU = \begin{pmatrix} \alpha_1 & V_1 \\ 0 & A_1 \end{pmatrix},$$

where V_1 is a $1 \times (n-1)$ matrix and A_1 is an $(n-1) \times (n-1)$ matrix. Since $U^{CT} = U^I$, the characteristic functions of A and $U^{CT}AU$ are identical and the characteristic roots of A_1 are $\alpha_2, \alpha_3, \ldots, \alpha_n$. If $n = 2$, the proof is complete. Since the theorem is now known to be true for $n = 2$, we assume it to be true for matrices of order $n - 1$. That is, there exists a unitary matrix U_1 such that $U_1^{CT} A_1 U_1$ is in the desired triangular form. We now write

$$V = \begin{pmatrix} 1 & 0 \\ 0 & U_1 \end{pmatrix}.$$

Then

$$V^{CT} = \begin{pmatrix} 1 & 0 \\ 0 & U_1^{CT} \end{pmatrix} \quad \text{and} \quad VV^{CT} = \begin{pmatrix} 1 & 0 \\ 0 & U_1 U_1^{CT} \end{pmatrix} = I$$

and hence V is unitary. Now write $W = UV$, and we have, from (11.1.1),

$$W^{CT} A W = \begin{pmatrix} 1 & 0 \\ 0 & U_1^{CT} \end{pmatrix} \begin{pmatrix} \alpha_1 & V_1 \\ 0 & A_1 \end{pmatrix} \begin{pmatrix} 1 & 0 \\ 0 & U_1 \end{pmatrix} = \begin{pmatrix} \alpha_1 & V_1 U_1 \\ 0 & U_1^{CT} A_1 U_1 \end{pmatrix}.$$

This completes the proof, since W is a unitary matrix and by assumption $U_1^{CT} A_1 U_1$ is triangular with $\alpha_2, \alpha_3, \ldots, \alpha_n$ as diagonal elements in that order and zeros below the diagonal.

Illustration: Let

$$A = \begin{pmatrix} -2 & 1 & 3 \\ -1 & 0 & 3 \\ -5 & 1 & 6 \end{pmatrix}.$$

The characteristic function of A is $x^3 - 4x^2 + x + 6$ and the characteristic roots are $-1, 2, 3$. Let $(x_1 \ x_2 \ x_3)^T$ be a characteristic vector of A associated with the characteristic root -1. Then

$$\begin{pmatrix} -2 & 1 & 3 \\ -1 & 0 & 3 \\ -5 & 1 & 6 \end{pmatrix} \begin{pmatrix} x_1 \\ x_2 \\ x_3 \end{pmatrix} = -1 \begin{pmatrix} x_1 \\ x_2 \\ x_3 \end{pmatrix},$$

and hence

$$-2x_1 + x_2 + 3x_3 = -x_1,$$
$$-x_1 \qquad + 3x_3 = -x_2,$$
$$-5x_1 + x_2 + 6x_3 = -x_3,$$

or

$$-x_1 + x_2 + 3x_3 = 0,$$
$$-x_1 + x_2 + 3x_3 = 0,$$
$$-5x_1 + x_2 + 7x_3 = 0.$$

A solution is $(x_1 \; x_2 \; x_3) = (1 \; -2 \; 1)$. The first row of U^{CT} may then be $(1/\sqrt{6} \; -2/\sqrt{6} \; 1/\sqrt{6})$, and we determine other rows to get

$$
U^{CT} = \begin{pmatrix} \dfrac{1}{\sqrt{6}} & \dfrac{-2}{\sqrt{6}} & \dfrac{1}{\sqrt{6}} \\ \dfrac{1}{\sqrt{3}} & \dfrac{1}{\sqrt{3}} & \dfrac{1}{\sqrt{3}} \\ \dfrac{1}{\sqrt{2}} & 0 & \dfrac{-1}{\sqrt{2}} \end{pmatrix},
$$

$$
U^{CT}AU = \begin{pmatrix} \dfrac{1}{\sqrt{6}} & \dfrac{-2}{\sqrt{6}} & \dfrac{1}{\sqrt{6}} \\ \dfrac{1}{\sqrt{3}} & \dfrac{1}{\sqrt{3}} & \dfrac{1}{\sqrt{3}} \\ \dfrac{1}{\sqrt{2}} & 0 & \dfrac{-1}{\sqrt{2}} \end{pmatrix} \begin{pmatrix} -2 & 1 & 3 \\ -1 & 0 & 3 \\ -5 & 1 & 6 \end{pmatrix} \begin{pmatrix} \dfrac{1}{\sqrt{6}} & \dfrac{1}{\sqrt{3}} & \dfrac{1}{\sqrt{2}} \\ \dfrac{-2}{\sqrt{6}} & \dfrac{1}{\sqrt{3}} & 0 \\ \dfrac{1}{\sqrt{6}} & \dfrac{1}{\sqrt{3}} & \dfrac{-1}{\sqrt{2}} \end{pmatrix}
$$

$$
= \begin{pmatrix} -1 & 0 & \dfrac{-4}{3} \\ 0 & 2 & \dfrac{-20}{6} \\ 0 & 0 & 3 \end{pmatrix}.
$$

We note here that the triangular form is obtained in one step. This is not usually the case.

If A is a normal matrix, then the matrix $U^{CT}AU$ of theorem 11.1.4 is of a very special form. This special case is considered after we establish

THEOREM 11.1.5 *If A is a normal matrix and U is a unitary matrix, then $U^{CT}AU$ is a normal matrix.*

Since U is a unitary matrix, $UU^{CT} = I$, and hence

$$(U^{CT}AU)(U^{CT}AU)^{CT} = U^{CT}AUU^{CT}A^{CT}U = U^{CT}AA^{CT}U$$

and

$$(U^{CT}AU)^{CT}(U^{CT}AU) = U^{CT}A^{CT}UU^{CT}AU = U^{CT}A^{CT}AU.$$

But, since A is normal, $AA^{CT} = A^{CT}A$, and the theorem is established. We now return to the special case of theorem 11.1.4.

THEOREM 11.1.6 *A matrix A is normal if and only if there exists a unitary matrix U such that $U^{CT}AU$ is a diagonal matrix.*

It is sufficient to show that for a triangular matrix to be normal it must be diagonal.   Suppose

$$T = \begin{pmatrix} \alpha_1 & T_1 \\ 0 & T_2 \end{pmatrix},$$

where α_1 is a complex number and T_1 is a $1 \times (n-1)$ matrix and T_2 is a triangular matrix of order $n-1$.   Then

$$TT^{CT} = \begin{pmatrix} \alpha_1 & T_1 \\ 0 & T_2 \end{pmatrix} \begin{pmatrix} \bar{\alpha}_1 & 0 \\ T_1^{CT} & T_2^{CT} \end{pmatrix} = \begin{pmatrix} \alpha_1 \bar{\alpha}_1 + T_1 T_1^{CT} & T_1 T_2^{CT} \\ T_2 T_1^{CT} & T_2 T_2^{CT} \end{pmatrix},$$

where $\bar{\alpha}_1$ is the conjugate of α_1.   Similarly,

$$T^{CT}T = \begin{pmatrix} \alpha_1 \bar{\alpha}_1 & \bar{\alpha}_1 T_1 \\ \alpha_1 T_1^{CT} & T_1^{CT} T_1 + T_2^{CT} T_2 \end{pmatrix}.$$

If T is normal, it follows that $T_1 T_1^{CT} = 0$, and consequently $T_1 = 0$.   If $n = 2$, the theorem is true.   We now assume it true for matrices of order $n-1$.   Since $T_1 = 0$ and T is normal, it follows that T_2 is normal and must be a diagonal matrix.   The converse follows immediately since any two diagonal matrices are commutative.

Suppose now that A is normal and that $U^{CT}AU = D$, where D is a diagonal matrix, with the first k diagonal elements $\alpha_1, \alpha_2, \ldots, \alpha_k$ $(k \le n)$ distinct, and suppose that each of the remaining diagonal elements is equal to some one of the first k.   Let $g(x)$ be the polynomial of degree $k-1$ such that $g(\alpha_i) = \bar{\alpha}_i$ for $i = 1, 2, \ldots, k$.   Then $D^{CT} = D^C = g(D)$, and consequently

$$A^{CT} = UD^{CT}U^{CT} = Ug(D)U^{CT} = g(UDU^{CT}) = g(A).$$

Also, every scalar polynomial in a matrix commutes with the matrix and hence we have

Theorem 11.1.7   *The matrix A is normal if and only if A^{CT} is a scalar polynomial in A.*

EXERCISES

1. Construct a unitary matrix with first row

(a) $\left(\dfrac{2}{5} \quad \dfrac{1+2i}{5} \quad \dfrac{4}{5} \right)$,

(b) $\left(\dfrac{1}{2} \quad \dfrac{i}{2} \quad \dfrac{1-i}{2} \right)$,

(c) $\left(\dfrac{1}{2} \quad \dfrac{i}{2} \quad \dfrac{-1}{2} \quad \dfrac{-i}{2} \right)$.

2. Prove that

$$A = \begin{pmatrix} 1 + 3i & 4i \\ 4i & 1 - 3i \end{pmatrix}$$

is a normal matrix. Determine the characteristic roots of A, and find a unitary matrix U such that $U^{CT}AU$ is a diagonal matrix.

3. If A is the matrix in Exercise 2, write A^{CT} as a scalar polynomial in A.

4. Prove that the matrix

$$\begin{pmatrix} a + ib & ic \\ ic & a - ib \end{pmatrix}$$

is normal if a, b, and c are real numbers.

5. If

$$A = \begin{pmatrix} 1 + i & 2 & 1 - i \\ -i & 1 & 2 + i \end{pmatrix},$$

compute AA^{CT} and $A^{CT}A$.

6. If A and B are $n \times n$ Hermitian matrices, is the matrix AB Hermitian? Is the matrix $A + B$ Hermitian?

7. Is the sum of two unitary matrices a unitary matrix?

8. Prove that $B^{CT} = -B$, where U is a unitary matrix and $U + I$ is nonsingular and $B = (U - I)(U + I)^I$.

9. Show that every unitary matrix U such that $U + I$ is nonsingular may be written $U = (I - B)^I(I + B)$, where $B^{CT} = -B$.

11.2 Field of Values of a Matrix. If A is a square matrix and ξ is a column vector, then $\xi^{CT}A\xi$ is a complex number.

DEFINITION. *The set of complex numbers $\xi^{CT}A\xi$ such that $\xi^{CT}\xi = 1$ is called the field of values of A.*

If η is a nonzero column vector and $\alpha = \eta^{CT}A\eta/\eta^{CT}\eta$, then α is in the field of values of A and every element in the field of values may be written in this form for some η.

If α is a characteristic root of the matrix A, then there is a nonzero column vector ξ such that $A\xi = \alpha\xi$. Multiplying each member on the left by ξ^{CT}, we have $\xi^{CT}A\xi = \alpha\xi^{CT}\xi$, from which we get

THEOREM 11.2.1 *Every characteristic root of A is in the field of values of A.*

Let $\alpha = \xi^{CT}A\xi/\xi^{CT}\xi$ be any number in the field of values of A, and let U be any unitary matrix. Write $\eta = U^{CT}\xi$, then $\xi = U\eta$ and $\xi^{CT}\xi = \eta^{CT}U^{CT}U\eta = \eta^{CT}\eta$, and it follows that

$$\alpha = \frac{\eta^{CT}U^{CT}AU\eta}{\eta^{CT}\eta}.$$

Hence α is in the field of values of $U^{CT}AU$. Similarly, any element in the field of values of $U^{CT}AU$ is in the field of values of A, and we have

THEOREM 11.2.2　*The field of values of $U^{CT}AU$ is identical with the field of values of A for every unitary matrix U.*

Since $E_iAE_i^T = a_{ii}$ and $E_iE_i^T = 1$, every diagonal element of A is in the field of values of A. Also, if $\alpha = \xi^{CT}A\xi$, $\xi^{CT}\xi = 1$, then α is in the field of values of A. If U is a unitary matrix whose first column is ξ, then α is the first diagonal element of $U^{CT}AU$. Hence we have

THEOREM 11.2.3　*The field of values of A is identical with the set of all diagonal elements of all matrices $U^{CT}AU$, where U is a unitary matrix.*

11.3　Hermitian Matrices. If A is an Hermitian matrix and α is a characteristic root of A, then there is a column vector ξ such that $\xi^{CT}\xi = 1$ and such that $A\xi = \alpha\xi$. It follows that $\xi^{CT}A\xi = \alpha\xi^{CT}\xi = \alpha$, and hence $\xi^{CT}A^{CT}\xi = \bar{\alpha}$. Since $A^{CT} = A$, it follows that $\bar{\alpha} = \alpha$ and we have

THEOREM 11.3.1　*The characteristic roots of an Hermitian matrix are all real; also, every element in the field of values of an Hermitian matrix is real.*

Since the Hermitian matrix A is normal, there exists a unitary matrix U such that $U^{CT}AU = D = \text{diag.}\ \{\alpha_1, \alpha_2, \ldots, \alpha_n\}$, where $\alpha_1 \leq \alpha_2 \leq \cdots \leq \alpha_n$ are the (real) characteristic roots of A. Since the field of values of A is identical with the field of values of D, every element α in the field of values is of the form

$$\alpha = \sum_{i=1}^{n} \alpha_i x_i \bar{x}_i, \quad \text{where} \quad \sum_{i=1}^{n} x_i \bar{x}_i = 1.$$

Hence we have

$$\alpha_1 = \alpha_1 \sum_{i=1}^{n} x_i \bar{x}_i \leq \sum_{i=1}^{n} \alpha_i x_i \bar{x}_i \leq \alpha_n \sum_{i=1}^{n} x_i \bar{x}_i = \alpha_n,$$

and thus $\alpha_1 \leq \alpha \leq \alpha_n$. If $\alpha_1 = \alpha_n$, then $\alpha = \alpha_1 = \alpha_n$. If $\alpha_1 < \alpha_n$ and if α is any number between α_1 and α_n, then we may determine numbers x_1 and x_n such that $\alpha_1 x_1 \bar{x}_1 + \alpha_n x_n \bar{x}_n = \alpha$ and $x_1 \bar{x}_1 + x_n \bar{x}_n = 1$. Substitute $x_n \bar{x}_n = 1 - x_1 \bar{x}_1$ to get $\alpha_1 x_1 \bar{x}_1 + \alpha_n - \alpha_n x_1 \bar{x}_1 = \alpha$, from which $x_1 \bar{x}_1 = (\alpha_n - \alpha)/(\alpha_n - \alpha_1)$ and consequently $x_n \bar{x}_n = (\alpha - \alpha_1)/(\alpha_n - \alpha_1)$. It is sufficient to take x_1 and x_n as any two numbers satisfying these conditions. We have established

THEOREM 11.3.2　*The field of values of an Hermitian matrix is the set of real numbers from the least to the greatest characteristic root of the matrix.*

We may also state the

COROLLARY. *If A is an Hermitian matrix and α_1 is the least and α_n the greatest of its characteristic roots, then $\alpha_1 \leq a_{ii} \leq \alpha_n$.*

If A is an $m \times n$ matrix, then, since $(A^{CT}A)^{CT} = A^{CT}A$, it follows that $A^{CT}A$ is an Hermitian matrix. Also $\xi^{CT}A^{CT}A\xi$ is the squared norm of the vector $\xi^{CT}A^{CT}$ and hence is zero or positive.

THEOREM 11.3.3   *The matrix $A^{CT}A$ is Hermitian, and its characteristic roots are real and nonnegative.*

If A is a square matrix with the characteristic root α and if $A\xi = \alpha\xi$, then $\xi^{CT}A^{CT} = \bar{\alpha}\xi^{CT}$ and hence $\xi^{CT}A^{CT}A\xi = \alpha\bar{\alpha}\xi^{CT}\xi$. Consequently, $\alpha\bar{\alpha}$ is in the field of values of $A^{CT}A$, and we have

THEOREM 11.3.4   *If α is a characteristic root of the matrix A, then $0 \leq m \leq \alpha\bar{\alpha} \leq g$, where m is the least and g is the greatest of the characteristic roots of the matrix $A^{CT}A$.*

EXERCISES

1. Write the characteristic function of the matrix

$$A = \begin{pmatrix} 0 & 1 & 0 \\ 0 & 0 & 1 \\ -2 & 1 & 2 \end{pmatrix}.$$

Find the characteristic roots and determine a unitary matrix U so that $U^{CT}AU$ is triangular.

2. If $A = G + iH$, where G and H are Hermitian, prove that A is normal if and only if there exists a unitary matrix U such that both $U^{CT}GU$ and $U^{CT}HU$ are diagonal.

3. If the matrix A has characteristic roots $\alpha_1, \alpha_2, \ldots, \alpha_n$, prove that A is normal if and only if $A + A^{CT}$ has the characteristic roots $\alpha_i + \bar{\alpha}_i$ for $i = 1, 2, \ldots, n$. Show also that $A - A^{CT}$ has characteristic roots $\alpha_i - \bar{\alpha}_i$ in this case.

4. If the matrix A has the characteristic roots $\alpha_1, \alpha_2, \ldots, \alpha_n$, prove that A is normal if and only if the characteristic roots of $A^{CT}A$ are $\alpha_i\bar{\alpha}_i$, $i = 1, 2, \ldots, n$.

5. If A is an Hermitian matrix having its characteristic roots as its diagonal elements, prove that A is diagonal.

6. If A is a normal matrix having its characteristic roots as its diagonal elements, prove that A is diagonal.

7. If A is a normal matrix which can be partitioned regularly in such a way that its characteristic function is the product of the characteristic function of its diagonal blocks A_{ii}, prove that $A = \text{diag.} \{A_{11}, A_{22}, \ldots, A_{kk}\}$. (*Hint:* Prove first for A Hermitian.)

8. If α is a characteristic root of the unitary matrix U, prove that $\alpha\bar{\alpha} = 1$.

9. If the matrix A has two of the three properties (a) real, (b) symmetric, (c) Hermitian, prove that it also has the third property.

10. If the matrix A has any two of the three properties (a) real, (b) orthogonal, (c) unitary, prove that it also has the third property.

11. Prove that the field of values of every principal submatrix of A is in the field of values of A.

12. If A is a real symmetric matrix, prove that there exists a real orthogonal matrix P such that $P^T A P$ is diagonal.

13. If U is a unitary matrix, prove that $U^k = I$ for some positive integer k if and only if each characteristic root of U is a kth root of unity.

14. If A is a square matrix, prove that $A^{CT}A$ and AA^{CT} have the same field of values.

15. If $A^{CT}A = B^{CT}B$, prove that there exists a unitary matrix U such that $B = UA$.

16. If A is any square matrix, prove that there exists a unitary matrix U such that AU is Hermitian.

BIBLIOGRAPHY

The references listed here are only a few of the many available to the student who may desire to refer to additional topics on the theory and applications of matrices. For current literature on the subject the student is referred to the many mathematical journals and to those technical journals in his own field of interest. Especially should he avail himself of the use of *Mathematical Reviews*, which carries reviews of all known worth-while publications in the field of mathematics.

AITKEN, A. C. *Determinants and Matrices.* 8th ed. New York: Interscience Publishers, Inc., 1954.

ALBERT, A. A. *Fundamental Concepts of Higher Algebra.* Chicago: University of Chicago Press, 1956.

———. *Introduction to Algebraic Theories.* Chicago: University of Chicago Press, 1941.

ALLEN, R. G. D. *Mathematical Analysis for Economists.* London: Macmillan & Co., Ltd., 1953.

ANDREE, R. V. *Modern Abstract Algebra.* New York: Henry Holt & Co., Inc., 1958.

BARNARD, S., and J. M. CHILD. *Advanced Algebra.* London: Macmillan & Co., Ltd., 1939.

———. *Higher Algebra.* London: Macmillan & Co., Ltd., 1947.

BEAUMONT, R. A., and R. W. BALL. *Introduction to Modern Algebra and Matrix Theory.* New York: Rinehart & Co., Inc., 1954.

BECKENBACH, E. F. *Modern Mathematics for the Engineer.* New York, McGraw-Hill Book Co., Inc., 1956.

BIRKHOFF, G., and S. MACLANE. *A Survey of Modern Algebra.* Rev. ed. New York: The Macmillan Co., 1953.

BLACKWELL, D., and M. A. GIRSHICK. *Theory of Games and Statistical Decisions.* New York: John Wiley & Sons, Inc., 1954.

BÔCHER, M. *Introduction to Higher Algebra.* New York: The Macmillan Co., 1907.

BODEWIG, E. *Matrix Calculus.* New York: Interscience Publishers, Inc., 1956.

BOOTH, A. D. *Numerical Methods.* London: Butterworth & Co., Ltd., 1955.

BROWNE, E. T. *Theory of Determinants and Matrices.* Chapel Hill: University of North Carolina Press, 1958.

BUCK, R. C. *Advanced Calculus.* New York: McGraw-Hill Book Co., Inc., 1956.

CHURCHMAN, C. W., R. L. ACKOFF, and E. L. ARNOFF. *Operations Research.* New York: John Wiley & Sons, Inc., 1957.

COOKE, R. G. *Infinite Matrices and Sequence Spaces.* London: Macmillan & Co., Ltd., 1950.

CRAMÉR, H. *Mathematical Methods of Statistics.* Princeton, N. J.: Princeton University Press, 1946.

DICKSON, L. E. *Modern Algebraic Theories.* New York: Benj. H. Sanborn & Co., 1926.

FELLER, W. *Probability Theory and Its Applications.* 2d ed. New York: John Wiley & Sons, Inc., 1957.

FERRAR, W. L. *Algebra: A Text-book of Determinants, Matrices, and Algebraic Forms.* London: Clarendon Press, 1941.

———. *Finite Matrices.* London: Clarendon Press, 1951.

FRAZER, R. A., W. J. DUNCAN, and A. R. COLLAR. *Elementary Matrices and Some Applications to Dynamics and Differential Equations.* London: Cambridge University Press, 1950.

GANTMACHER, F. R. *The Theory of Matrices.* New York: Chelsea Publishing Co., 1959.

GASKELL, R. E. *Engineering Mathematics.* New York: The Dryden Press, Inc., 1958.

GOLDBERG, S. *Difference Equations.* New York: John Wiley & Sons, Inc., 1958.

HALL, H. S., and S. R. KNIGHT. *Higher Algebra.* London: Macmillan & Co., Ltd., 1946.

HALMOS, P. R. *Finite-Dimensional Vector Spaces.* 2d ed., Princeton, N. J.: D. Van Nostrand Co., Inc., 1958.

HANCOCK, H. *Minkowski Geometry of Numbers.* New York: The Macmillan Co., 1939.

HASSE, H. *Higher Algebra and Exercises to Higher Algebra.* New York: Frederick Ungar Publishing Co., 1954.

HASTINGS, C., JR. *Approximations for Digital Computers.* Princeton, N. J.: Princeton University Press, 1955.

HILDEBRAND, F. B. *Introduction to Numerical Analysis.* New York: McGraw-Hill Book Co., Inc., 1956.

HOUSEHOLDER, A. S. *Principles of Numerical Analysis.* New York: McGraw-Hill Book Co., Inc., 1953.

JACOBSON, N. *Lectures in Abstract Algebra.* Princeton, N. J.: D. Van Nostrand Co., Inc. Vol. I, *Basic Concepts,* 1951. Vol. II, *Linear Algebra,* 1953.

JOHNSON, R. E. *First Course in Abstract Algebra.* Englewood Cliffs, N. J.: Prentice-Hall, Inc., 1953.

KEMENY, J. G., J. L. SNELL, and G. L. THOMPSON. *Finite Mathematics.* Englewood Cliffs, N. J.: Prentice-Hall, Inc., 1957.

KEMPTHORNE, O. *Genetic Statistics.* New York: John Wiley & Sons., Inc., 1957.

KUNZ, K. S. *Numerical Analysis.* New York: McGraw-Hill Book Co., Inc., 1957.

LANCZOS, C. *Applied Analysis.* Englewood Cliffs, N. J.: Prentice-Hall, Inc., 1956.

LITTLEWOOD, D. E. *The Theory of Group Characters and Matrix Representations of Groups.* London: Clarendon Press, 1950.

LUCE, R. D., and H. RAIFFA. *Games and Decisions.* New York: John Wiley & Sons, Inc., 1957.

McCRACKEN, D. D. *Digital Computer Programming.* New York: John Wiley & Sons, Inc., 1957.

MacDUFFEE, C. C. *An Introduction to Abstract Algebra.* New York: John Wiley & Sons, Inc., 1940.

———. *The Theory of Matrices.* 2d ed. New York: Chelsea Publishing Co., 1946.

———. *Vectors and Matrices.* Carus Mathematical Monograph No. 7. Menasha, Wis.: The Mathematical Association of America, 1943.

McKINSEY, J. C. C. *Introduction to the Theory of Games.* New York: McGraw-Hill Book Co., Inc., 1952.

MICHAL, A. D. *Matrix and Tensor Calculus.* New York: John Wiley & Sons, Inc., 1947.

MILNE, W. E. *Numerical Calculus.* Princeton, N. J.: Princeton University Press, 1949.

———. *Numerical Solution of Differential Equations.* New York: John Wiley & Sons, Inc., 1953.

MUIR, T. *Contributions to the History of Determinants.* London: Blackie & Son, Ltd., 1930.

———. *The Theory of Determinants.* 4 vols. London: Macmillan & Co., Ltd., 1890–1923.

MURDOCH, D. C. *Linear Algebra for Undergraduates.* New York: John Wiley & Sons, Inc., 1957.

MURNAGHAN, F. D. *Introduction to Applied Mathematics.* New York: McGraw-Hill Book Co., Inc., 1957.

———. *The Theory of Group Representation.* Baltimore: Johns Hopkins University Press, 1938.

PERLIS, S. *Theory of Matrices.* Reading, Mass.: Addison-Wesley Publishing Co., Inc., 1952.

PIPES, L. A. *Applied Mathematics for Engineers and Physicists.* 2d ed. New York: McGraw-Hill Book Co., Inc., 1958.

REED, M. B., and G. B. REED. *Mathematical Methods in Electrical Engineering.* New York: Harper & Bros., 1951.

REINFELD, N. V., and W. R. VOGEL. *Mathematical Programming.* Englewood Cliffs, N. J.: Prentice-Hall, Inc., 1958.

SCHREIER, O., and E. SPERNER. *An Introduction to Modern Algebra and Matrix Theory.* New York: Chelsea Publishing Co., 1952.

SCOTT, E. J. *Transform Calculus.* New York: Harper & Bros., 1955.

SCOTT, R. F., and G. B. MATHEWS. *The Theory of Determinants and Their Applications.* London: Cambridge University Press, 1904.

SPEISER, A. *Die Theorie der Gruppen von endlicher Ordnung.* 4th ed.   Basel: Birkhäuser Verlag, 1956.

STOLL, R. R. *Linear Algebra and Matrix Theory.* New York: McGraw-Hill Book Co., Inc., 1952.

THRALL, R. M., and L. TORNHEIM. *Vector Spaces and Matrices.* New York: John Wiley & Sons., Inc., 1957.

TURNBULL, H. W. *Theory of Determinants, Matrices, and Invariants.* London: Blackie & Son, Ltd., 1928.

————, and A. C. AITKEN. *An Introduction to the Theory of Canonical Matrices.* London: Blackie & Son, Ltd., 1932.

VAJDA, S. *The Theory of Games and Linear Programming.* New York: John Wiley & Sons, Inc., 1956.

VAN DER WAERDEN, B. L. *Gruppen von linearen Transformationen.* Berlin: Springer-Verlag, 1935.

WEDDERBURN, J. H. M. *Lectures on Matrices.* Providence, R. I.: American Mathematical Society, 1934.

WILKES, M. V., D. J. WHEELER, and S. GILL. *The Preparation of Programs for an Electronic Digital Computer.* Cambridge, Mass.: Addison-Wesley Publishing Co., Inc., 1951.

INDEX